Lecture Notes
in Business Information Processing 168

Series Editors

Wil van der Aalst
Eindhoven Technical University, The Netherlands
John Mylopoulos
University of Trento, Italy
Michael Rosemann
Queensland University of Technology, Brisbane, Qld, Australia
Michael J. Shaw
University of Illinois, Urbana-Champaign, IL, USA
Clemens Szyperski
Microsoft Research, Redmond, WA, USA

Henrik Leopold

Natural Language in Business Process Models

Theoretical Foundations, Techniques, and Applications

 Springer

Author

Henrik Leopold
Humboldt University Berlin
Institute of Information Systems
Berlin, Germany
E-mail: henrik.leopold@wiwi.hu-berlin.de

ISSN 1865-1348   e-ISSN 1865-1356
ISBN 978-3-319-04174-2   e-ISBN 978-3-319-04175-9
DOI 10.1007/978-3-319-04175-9
Springer Cham Heidelberg New York Dordrecht London

Library of Congress Control Number: 2013956237

Typesetting: Camera-ready by author, data conversion by Scientific Publishing Services, Chennai, India

Printed on acid-free paper

Springer is part of Springer Science+Business Media (www.springer.com)

To Franzi and to my family.

Preface

Natural language is one of the most important means of human communication. It enables us to express our will, to exchange thoughts, and to document our knowledge in written sources. Owing to its substantial role in many facets of human life, technology for automatically analyzing and processing natural language has recently become increasingly important. In fact, natural language processing tools have paved the way for entirely new business opportunities.

One of the most recent innovations is the natural language interface *Siri* produced by Apple. It combines speech and language processing technology to provide users with the possibility to interact with a system via oral natural language instructions. While Siri represents an important technological step, most organizations could benefit from natural language processing technology in a much simpler way: by automatically processing textual sources. The potential and business value of such endeavors is increasingly recognized. For instance, pharmaceutical companies employ natural language processing techniques for automatically analyzing discussions from Internet forums in order to learn about unknown side effects of their drugs. Moreover, internal sources such as reports, documentations, and e-mails are analyzed to effectively collect and extract knowledge about business operations.

While existing natural language processing techniques can be applied to standard texts in a rather straightforward fashion, they are not applicable to semi-formal representations such as business process models. Considering the huge uptake of business process modeling initatives with hundreds to thousands of models, the automated analysis of these models would be associated with many benefits. However, in order to automatically exploit, maintain, and improve such process model repositories, current natural language processing techniques need to be enriched with the ability to deal with the specifics of process models.

The goal of this book is to facilitate the automatic analysis of natural language in process models and to employ this analysis for assisting process model stakeholders. Therefore, we define a technique that automatically recognizes and annotates process model element labels. In addition, we leverage this technique for supporting organizations in effectively utilizing their process models in various ways. In particular, this book contains the following contributions:

- *Conceptualization of the Role of Natural Language in Process Models*: Although the main focus of prior research on process model quality was on formal process properties, some authors also investigated the quality of natural language in process models (e.g., [95, 105, 225]). The problem is, however, that there is currently no common understanding of the conceptual role of natural language in this context. While some authors consider natural language as a pragmatic aspect, other authors discuss it as a syntactical issue. In Chap. 1, we address this inconsistency by incorporating natural language into the modeling technique conceptualization from Karagiannis and Kühn [173]. We clarify that both, modeling language as well as natural language, consist of a syntactic and a semantic dimension. Thus, the overall semantics of a process model is the combination of the semantics of the modeling and the natural language.

- *Taxonomy of Process Model Element Styles*: Many modeling initiatives in practice include causal modelers that are not sufficiently trained [289]. As a consequence, process model elements are often labeled in a rather arbitrary fashion [225]. More specifically, many different labeling styles can be observed in process models from practice. In Chap. 3, we provide a taxonomy of existing labeling styles derived from a manual anaylsis of almost 30,000 labels. The taxonomy does not only reveal the current labeling practices but also represents an essential input for the automated analysis of process model elements.

- *Annotation of Process Model Element Labels*: The labels of process model elements capture valuable linguistic information. Nevertheless, the automated usage of this information is impeded by the shortness and ambiguity of many element labels. Because of these characteristics, it is complex to automatically detect the various labeling styles we face in process models from practice. In Chap. 3, we provide a solution to this problem by introducing a technique that automatically recognizes the labeling style and accordingly derives and annotates a label with its semantic components. The technique is based on the introduced labeling style taxonomy and can be effectively adapted to languages other than English.

- *Detection and Correction of Linguistic Guideline Violations*: Establishing guidelines represents an important strategy to assure the quality and consistency of process models. However, as modelers typically do not respect all aspects of such modeling guidelines, it is particularly useful to check the guideline compliance in an automated fashion. One important yet unaddressed aspect in this context is the automatic detection and correction of linguistic aspects in process models. Existing approaches address this issue, for instance, by enforcing certain labeling structures during the modeling process [92, 38]. Nevertheless, these approaches are neither applicable for checking labels after they were created nor for correcting detected violations. In Chap. 4, we address this issue by introducing a corpus-based approach for automatically detecting and correcting linguistic guideline violations in process models. As a result, process models can be automatically checked for compliance with linguistic guideline specifications.

- *Generation of Natural Language Texts from Process Models*: Although many companies use process models for various purposes, often only business analysists are capable of understanding them in detail. Typically, this is a serious problem as the feedback of domain experts is essential for creating a model that is appropriately reflecting the business operations. In Chap. 5, we address this problem by introducing a technique for automatically transforming BPMN process models into natural language texts. The technique builds on the linguistic analysis of process model text labels and the transformation of a process model into a tree structure. The results show that the text generation can reliably generate appropriate texts that fully explain the semantics of a process model.

- *Derivation of Service Candidates from Process Models*: Process models represent an important artifact for identifying service candidates in the context of a service-oriented architecture [139]. The problem is, however, that none of the existing approaches considers the potential of fully automating the steps from process model analysis to the identification of suitable service candidates. Hence, these approaches do not scale up to large companies with hundreds or thousands of process models. In Chap. 6, we address this problem by introducing an automatic approach for deriving a list of ranked service candidates from process models. The technique employs the linguistic analysis of process model activities to explicitly address the semantic label components, such as action and business object. As an overall result, the service identification using process models is reduced to selecting appropriate candidates from a ranked list.

This book is organized into seven chapters. It starts with an overview of business process management and linguistics. It then continues with the conceptual contributions on parsing and annotation process model elements, detection and correction of process model guideline violations, generation of natural language from process models, and derivation of service candidates from process models.

- *Chapter 1: Business Process Management.* This chapter presents the background of business process management. More specifically, we introduce the main concepts and definitions and clarify the role of natural language in business process management and in business process models.
- *Chapter 2: Linguistics.* In this chapter, we discuss the foundations from the field of linguistics. That includes central concepts from theoretical linguistics, such as syntax and morphology, as well as technological aspects related to natural language processing. Then, we investigate the intersection of natural language processing and conceptual modeling. The review illustrates that the automatic analysis of natural language in conceptual models is associated with considerable challenges that have not been addressed by prior research.
- *Chapter 3: Parsing and Annotating Process Model Elements.* This chapter introduces a technique for facilitating the automatic analysis of process model elements. As a basis, we conduct an extensive analysis of process model element

styles using three large process model collections from practice. Building on the insights on grammatical structures, we define an approach that can reliably deal with the shortness and ambiguity of process model element labels. We evaluate the technique using three large process model collections from practice including almost 30,000 labels.

- *Chapter 4: Detecting and Correcting Linguistic Guideline Violations.* This chapter presents a technique for automatically detecting and correcting linguistic guideline violations. The technique is motivated by the research gap of automatically checking guideline specifications that are concerned with natural language and hence complements techniques that focus on checking structural aspects of process models. In order to provide the user with the possibility to freely define the desired rules, we define a technique that builds on a corpus. As a result, we can reliably determine the parts of speech of a given label and determine its compliance with respect to a predefined linguistic pattern. In case a violation was detected, we further provide the possibility of automatically correcting labels. By rearranging the components of the label according to a desired labeling style, detected violations are automatically resolved. Both techniques are tested on three large process model collections from practice.
- *Chapter 5: Generation of Natural Language from Process Models.* In this chapter, we define an approach for automatically generating natural language text from process models. Building on the automatic label analysis and the transformation of a process model into a tree representation, we reliably generate natural language texts. An evaluation with a test sample including manually created texts illustrates the benefits of the defined technique. The generated texts are very stable with respect to characteristics such as complexity and full coverage of the model content and can be created and updated in a fully automated fashion.
- *Chapter 6: Service Derivation from Process Models.* This chapter presents a technique for the automatic derivation of service candidates from process models. A discussion of existing research reveals that many authors considered the derivation of service candidates from process models; however, none of them addresses the full automation of the service identification process. Furthermore, they do not make use of a sophisticated consideration of natural language. Hence, these approaches cannot scale up to large companies with hundreds or thousands of process models. We close this gap by presenting a fully automated service derivation technique. An evaluation with three industry process model collections illustrates that the technique can successfully identify useful service candidates.
- *Chapter 7: Conclusion.* In this chapter, we summarize the findings of this book and give an outlook on future research. Furthermore, we discuss the implications of the findings for the linguistic analysis in conceptual models, quality of business process models, matching of business process models, task of modeling business processes, range and impact of business process models, and alignment of business and IT.

Acknowledgments

The major share of this book stems from my doctoral thesis I submitted to Humboldt University Berlin in April 2013. Hence, I would like to express my sincere gratitude to all people who were indirectly involved in its creation. First and foremost, I would like to thank my supervisor Prof. Dr. Jan Mendling for his excellent support, his constant interest and feedback, and his unceasing trust. Furthermore, I want to thank him for his openness and for providing me with all the possible freedom to develop my ideas. Second, I would like to express my gratefulness to my second supervisor Prof. Dr. Hajo Reijers. I want to thank him for believing in and supporting my research, for his helpful feedback, and for providing me with the possibility to stay and research at the Technical University in Eindhoven.

I was happy to work and collaborate with many excellent people in different contexts. At this stage, I would like to particularly thank Sergey, Monika, and Fabian for the great work we conducted and the fruitful discussions. It was a big pleasure working with you. Further, I want to thank Leonardo Azevedo, Fernanda Baião, and Leonardo Aragão for enabling my research stay in Rio de Janeiro. I really enjoyed my stay in Brazil and I was happy to learn how to parse Portuguese process models (without actually speaking Portuguese). I enjoyed our joint work very much. Moreover, I want to thank my colleagues Hanna Krasnova, Till Winkler, and Benjamin Fabian for their support. It was a pleasure to work with you and to run our institute. My thanks also go to Norbert Ahrend, who relieved me from many obligations in order to give me time for my thesis. I particularly want to thank Thomas and Fabian for proofreading my thesis and for various discussions on my work.

Last, but most importantly, I would like to thank Franzi for her patience, encouragement, and incredible support in many regards. I am really grateful that you invested time and effort to read (and to correct) my thesis.

October 2013   Henrik Leopold

Contents

List of Figures

List of Tables

Acronyms

AC	Academic Collection
AN	Action-Noun Style
API	Application Interface
AQ	Adjective-Question Style
AS	Adjective Style
ATTR	Attributive Relation in a Deep-Syntactic Tree
BPM	Business Process Management
BPMN	Business Process Modeling and Notation
BS	Business Service
CE	Correction Effect
CEA	Corpus del Español
CFG	Context-Free Grammar
CG	Correction Gain
CH	Claims Handling Model Collection
CM	Conceptual Model
COORD	Conjoining Element Relation in a Deep-Syntactic Tree
CS	Categorization Style
DES	Descriptive Style
DSynT	Deep-Syntactic Tree
eEPC	Extended EPC
EN	English
EPC	Event-driven Process Chain
EQ	Equation-Question Style
ER	Entity-Relationship
GER	German
GoM	Guidelines of Modeling
HMM	Hidden Markov Model
HPSG	Head-driven Phrase Structure Grammar
IFQ	Infinitive-Question Style
IS	Information Systems
MS	Modal Style

NA	No-Action Style
NL	Natural Language
NLG	Natural Language Generation
NLP	Natural Language Processing
NP	Noun Phrase
OANC	Open American National Corpus
ORM	Object-Role Modeling
PCFG	Probabilistic Context Free Grammar
PM	Process Model
PQ	Participle-Question Style
PS	Participle Style
PT	Portuguese
RealPro	Surface Realization Component
RG	Relational Grammar
RPST	Refined Process Structure Tree
SAP	German Software Corporation, also used to refer to SAP Reference Model
SQL	Structured Query Language
SWS	Software Service
TC	Telecommunication Service Provider Collection
UML	Unified Modeling Language
VO	Verb-Object Style
VP	Verb Phrase
XML	Extensible Markup Language

Chapter 1
Business Process Management

Business process management (BPM) represents one of the core concepts enabling companies to flexibly react to the constantly changing business environment. The actual relevance of business process management is, for instance, illustrated by the size of the BPM software market. A recent study of Global Industry Analysts forecasts that the global market for BPM software will reach a volume of over 5 billion US dollars by the year 2017 [18]. The importance of BPM in academia is demonstrated by its constant presence among top-ranked information system conferences [32, 2, 1, 271]. In fact, this also highlights that BPM has become one of the core areas of information systems research. The range of addressed topics goes from general organizational aspects of BPM to specific technical issues concerning business process models. Due to the importance of business process models for documenting and redesigning the operations of companies, many researchers have focused on aspects of process model design and process model quality. Nevertheless, there are still many significant aspects that have not been addressed by prior research.

A particular problem in this regard is how to properly deal with natural language in process models. Prior research clearly demonstrates the importance of natural language in process models for the overall model understanding [225]. This is also acknowledged by many recommendations from research and practice asking for a particular syntactic format of the natural language text in process model activities [301, 224, 122, 304, 17]. However, up until now there is no approach that is capable of automatically analyzing these textual fragments.

This chapter gives an overview of business process management and business process modeling. Section 1.1 provides a short historical outline and introduces the discipline of business process management by building on the business process life cycle. Recognizing that business process models represent an important artifact in this context, Section 1.2 continues by discussing the activity of business process modeling. In particular, it investigates the notion of a model, modeling technique, and how process models are created. Subsequently, Section 1.3 analyzes the role of natural language in the business process management life cycle and proposes a refined conceptualization of a modeling technique. To provide the basis for a precise characterization of process models, Section 1.4 introduces a formal definition of process models. Finally, Section 1.5 gives a brief summary of the chapter.

1.1 Overview of Business Process Management

The steadily growing interest in business process management from practice as well as from academia clearly demonstrates the importance of this discipline in today's business environment. In short, business process management aims for the efficient coordination of business related activities within and between companies [223, p. 5].

Looking into the history of business process management, one of the most prominent innovators is Frederick Winslow Taylor who proposed a set of key ideas to improve the operations of businesses [316]. For instance, in his monograph *Principles of Scientific Management*, he argues for the systematic analysis of work in order to identify the best way of performing tasks [316, p. 69]. Later, in 1903, Henry Ford founded the Ford Motor Company and introduced a groundbreaking approach for manufacturing cars. By organizing work in the context of an *assembly line*, the production cycle times were significantly reduced [116, p. 60]. In 1934, Fritz Nordsieck was among the first academics who pointed out the general necessity of a process-oriented organizational design [244, p. 9]. However, the effective adoption of process-oriented design by organizations took place much later. In 1985, Porter presented the value chain model that introduced the notion of a chain of activities that deliver a product for the market [267]. In the nineties, Davenport presented his work on process innovation [83] and Hammer and Champy introduced the discipline of reengineering [141]. Building on these management concepts and the insights on the role of technology by Scheer [294], companies widely started to implement process orientation in the early 1990's [335, p. 4].

Today, business process management is a well-established practice and research area, combining various disciplines such as management, organizational theory, and computer science. The main focus and core concept of BPM is the *business process*. Since the beginning of process orientation, many different definitions for a business process have been proposed and different aspects have been emphasized. For example, Hammer and Champy characterize a business process as a collection of activities, transforming an input into an output that is valuable for the customer [141, p. 38]. By doing so, they implicitly abstract from the execution constraints between the activities. In this regard, Davenport and Short are more specific by defining a business process as a *set of logically-related tasks* which are performed to realize a desired business goal [84]. This is in line with the view of van der Aalst and van Hee who equally emphasize that the order of activities is determined by a set of conditions [13, p. 4]. Against the background of the multitude of definitions, it does not appear useful to introduce a refinement here. Hence, we adopt the definition provided by Weske as it comprehensively summarizes the aforementioned aspects.

Definition 1.1. A business process consists of a set of activities which are performed in an organizational and technical environment in a coordinated fashion. In this manner, they jointly achieve a desired business goal. Although each business process is performed by a single organization, it may also interact with business processes from other organizations [335, p. 5].

Building on this definition of a business process, the discipline of business process management can be generally defined as the set of all activities which are related to business processes [223, p. 5]. As suggested by many authors, these activities are typically arranged in the context of a life cycle [12, 239],[53, p.5],[335, p. 12][223, p. 5]. Since this book is particularly concerned with the artifact of a process model, we follow the life cycle proposed in [102, p. 21]. It clearly demonstrates how the different life cycle steps are related to process models and comprehensively summarizes the essential steps. Figure 1.1 illustrates the proposed life cycle including the outputs which are produced by each life cycle activity. In total, the life cycle comprises the following six phases:

- *Process Identification*: Based on a business goal or problem, the relevant processes and their inter-relations are identified. The results are reflected in a newly created or updated process architecture which gives an overview of the identified processes and their relationships.
- *Process Discovery*: In this phase, the selected processes are documented in their current state. The result is a set of as-is process models.
- *Process Analysis*: By analyzing the as-is process models, issues and potentials for improvement are identified and documented.
- *Process Redesign*: Based on the insights on weaknesses of the current process, a redesigned version of the process is developed. The results are documented in a set of to-be process models. Here it is important to note that process analysis and process redesign are tightly connected. Using process analysis techniques, the to-be process models can be equally anaylzed for weaknesses. Hence, there might be several iterations of process analysis and process redesign.
- *Process Implementation*: In this phase, the required changes for the transition from the as-is to the to-be process are put into practice. As a result, there might be several changes in the organizational as well as in the infrastructural environment.
- *Process Monitoring and Controlling*: In order to assess the performance of the redesigned process, it needs to be monitored and controlled. Accordingly, relevant data from the process execution is collected and anaylzed with respect to the pre-defined performance measures. Since new and unexpected issues might arise over time, it is important to continuously monitor and control the process. Once a process is not performing well according to the predefined measures, a new iteration of the life cycle is entered.

Considering the different outputs of the life cycle activities, it becomes clear that process modeling is an essential activity in the context of business process management. It is used for documenting as-is processes, the subsequent analyses, and

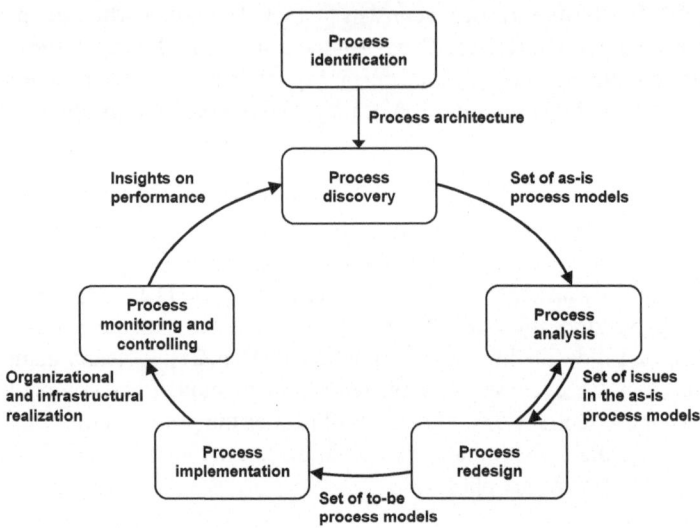

Fig. 1.1 Business Process Management Life Cycle, adapted from [102, p. 21]

for the design of to-be processes. Recognizing the importance of business process modeling, the next section elaborates on business process modeling and the related concepts.

1.2 Business Process Modeling

The business process model is the central artifact in the context of business process modeling. Hence, we first investigate the concept of a business process model and derive an according definition.

As indicated by the last word, a business process model is a specific type of a model. In order to properly define a business process model, we take a broader viewpoint and first investigate the meaning of a *model* in general. The term model is derived from the Latin word *modulus*, which means *measure* or *rule*. Examples for models from everyday life include maps, ground plans, and also architectural models. According to Stachowiak [310, pp. 131-132] a model has to meet three essential characteristics:

- *Mapping*: A model is a mapping from a real-world or artificial original which can be a model itself.
- *Simplification*: The model only contains a subset of the attributes of the original. Hence, it represents a simplification.
- *Pragmatism*: A model is created by a modeler at a certain point of time and with a particular purpose in mind.

Following the characterization from Stachowiak, we can define a model as a simplification of an original, which was created at specific point in time and with a particular intention or objective. In fact, this definition has been adapted by many authors in the domain of software engineering [212, 318, 117, 54, 43]. For instance Bézivin and Gerbé define a model as the simplification of a system which was created with an intended goal [43].

However, some authors also criticize that the characteristics from Stachowiak abstract from the subjective perception of the modeler [297, 223, 275]. For instance, Schuette and Rotthowe [297] argue that a model cannot be defined as a mapping from reality, as such a definition would require the reality to be independent from their observers and assumes an epistemic objectivity. Thus, the mapping-based definition from Stachowiak can only be supported if the subjective perception of all individuals congruently corresponds to reality. That this is not a very realistic assumption is, for instance, discussed by referring to the mental model construction of humans [111]. The key insight here is that the conceptualization of a real world phenomenon is the result of combining the individual perception and pre-existing knowledge. Using this knowledge, the perception can be organized into coherent structures [242, 245]. Following this line of argumentation, a model should not be defined as a formal mapping but rather as the result of the mental construction of a modeler [297]. Against this background and the definition proposed in [223], we can define a business process model as follows:

Definition 1.2. A business process model is the result of mapping a business process as perceived by a modeler. The business process can be a real-world process, or a process which has been conceptualized by the modeler.

As a result of the subjectivity and the varying perceptions of different modelers, the creation of a model is considered to be a complex task [285, 151]. Following van der Aalst et al., the term business process modeling can be defined as follows [12]:

Definition 1.3. Business process modeling describes the manual task of identification and specification of business processes.

While the task can be easily defined, it yet remains unclear which challenges are associated with it. In order to fully understand all facets of process modeling, it is useful to introduce the notion of a *modeling technique* as presented by Karagiannis and Kühn [173] (see Figure 1.2). According to their definition, a modeling technique consists of two parts: a *modeling language* and a *modeling procedure*.[1] Building on the work from Harel and Rumpe [143], they subdivide the *modeling language* into three parts: syntax, semantics, and a notation. The *syntax* defines a set of constructs and according rules for how these constructs can be combined.

---

[1] It is important to note that several authors use heterogeneous terminology to refer to the terms modeling language and modeling procedure. For example, in [328, 329, 59, 276] a modeling language is referred to as a *grammar* and a procedure is called a *method*. In [223], the terms *notation* and *method* are used.

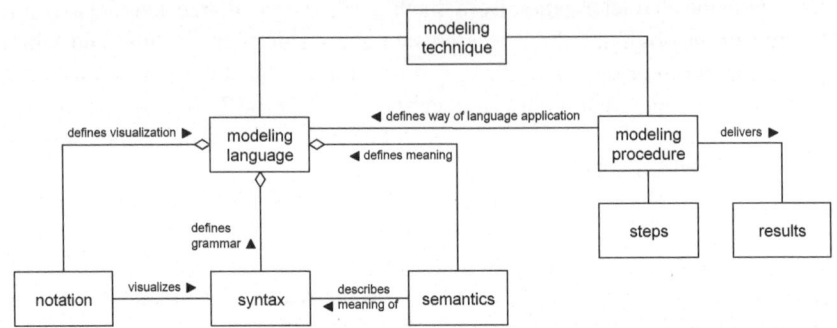

Fig. 1.2 Elements of a Modeling Technique, adopted from [173].

Semantics associates the constructs with a meaning. The *notation* defines a set of symbols for graphically representing the previously specified constructs. Prominent examples for business process modeling languages are, for instance, the Business Process Model and Notation (BPMN) [248], Event-driven Process Chains (EPCs) [86, pp. 258-266], and Petri Nets [257]. The *modeling procedure* defines steps for how the modeling language can be used to create a proper model.

Frederiks and van der Weide [120] present one prominent example for a modeling procedure. They investigate the process of information modeling and present a four-staged approach for creating models of high quality. Since process models are a specific type of information models, this modeling process has been frequently employed for discussing the creation of business process models (e.g., in [193, 286, 56, 259, 223]). Figure 1.3 illustrates the four phases of the modeling process: eliciation, modeling, verification, and validation.

In the *elicitation* phase, the relevant information is collected from the so-called universe of discourse. In the next step, this information is verbalized in natural language. Afterwards, the initial specification is unified and stored in an informal specification. In the subsequent *modeling* phase, the informal specification is transformed into a formal specification. Therefore, the significant modeling concepts and their relationships are identified. Then, the natural language concepts are mapped on modeling concepts, i.e., to constructs of the employed business process modeling language. In the *verification* phase, the formal specification is checked for internal consistency. In process models, for instance, the verification phase covers the assurance of formal properties such as control-flow soundness [8, 110], the correctness of data flow [315, 332, 303], the satisfiability of constraints on the resource perspective [42, 77, 313], and the inter-operability of cross-organizational workflows [9]. The goal of the subsequent *validation* phase is the assurance of the semantic consistency of the formal specification (process model) with the universe of discourse. Frederiks and van der Weide propose to paraphrase the formal specification and then compare it with the informal specification. This suggestion is in line with research from the field of natural language generation, which has proposed techniques for automatically generating natural language texts for validating conceptual models [81].

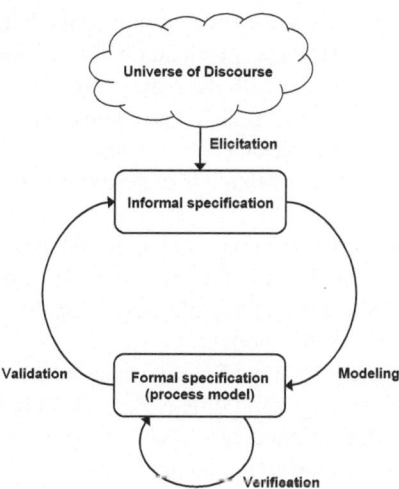

Fig. 1.3 Process of Modeling, adapted from [120]

However, the validation remains a very ambiguous task, which cannot be solved by an algorithm [300].

The challenges illustrated by the process of modeling are also a result of the complementary competencies that are required for creating a model. While the validation is based on a sufficient familiarity with the process, the verification builds on profound knowledge of the employed modeling language. In practice, the problem is that these competencies are often distributed among several persons [285, 102]. In particular, there are typically two roles that are involved in the process of modeling: the domain expert and the process analyst. The *domain expert* has detailed knowledge of the operations of the business process in question. This may, for instance, result from the fact that the domain expert is a process participant [335, p. 16]. The *process analyst* has strong competencies with regard to the activity of business process modeling. This includes, amongst others, knowledge of the modeling language such as BPMN and the ability to adequately organize information in the context of a process model. As a result of this competence distribution, it is necessary that a model is jointly created by a domain expert and a process analyst. However, studies in practice have revealed that this is not always the case. In many projects there are still casual modelers involved that are not sufficiently trained [289].

In order to generally support modelers, the Guidelines of Modeling (GoM) present six principles for creating appropriate models [40, 297, 39]. They include the principles of correctness, relevance, economic efficiency, clarity, comparability, and systematic design. In particular, correctness, relevance, and economic efficiency represent necessary pre-conditions for the quality of models, while clarity, comparability, and systematic design are considered to be optional.

- *Correctness*: When considering model correctness, there are two dimensions: syntactic and semantic. The syntactic correctness requires the modeler to use and combine the modeling constructs of the employed modeling notation solely according to the modeling language specification. The semantic correctness refers to the consistency of the model with the real world. Hence, the semantics of the model should be in line with the modeled problem domain.

- *Relevance*: The principle of relevance postulates that a relevant part of the universe of discourse is selected and that it is represented with an adequate modeling language.
- *Economic Efficiency*: In this context, economic efficiency relates to the trade-off between costs and benefits of including certain aspects into a model. Hence, it might be acceptable to not include all aspects of the real world in order to guarantee the readability of the model.
- *Principle of Clarity*: The principle of clarity requires the model to be well readable and understandable. In general, this is considered to be a highly subjective principle. In practice, for instance, layout conventions provide clear recommendations to accomplish the clarity of a model.
- *Principle of Comparability*: As organizations rarely create a single model, the principle of comparability postulates that all the guidelines should be consistently applied among all models within a modeling project. Thus, for instance, natural language should be applied in a consistent fashion.
- *Principle of Systematic Design*: The principle of systematic design asks for well-defined relationships between models belonging to different views (e.g., data and process models). In particular, there should be a defined approach to integrate the different models.

An alternative perspective on the quality of conceptual models is provided by the Sequal framework [208, 195, 194]. In its initial version the framework proposes to evaluate the quality of conceptual models along three dimensions: syntax, semantics, and pragmatics. Therefore, the Sequal framework defines relations between the model, the domain, the language, and the interpretation of the audience. As a result, the syntactic quality is concerned with the correspondence between the model and the language, i.e., the model should not contain syntactical errors. The pragmatic quality of a model is defined by the degree of correspondence between the model and the interpretation of the audience. Hence, the pragmatic quality of a model is considered as fulfilled if the audience can understand the semantics captured by the model. The semantic quality is concerned with the completeness and correctness of the model with respect to the domain. In this context, correctness is specified as the congruence of the model statements with the domain, i.e., a model should not contain wrong statements. The completeness dimension defines that the statements of the model should cover all relevant aspects of the domain. In order to assure the readability of the model, the authors introduce the notion of *feasible completeness*. A model is considered as feasible complete if adding another statement from the domain has more negative influence on the quality than positive influence.

Reconsidering the introduced conceptualization of a modeling technique, it is apparent that many of the GoM principles as well as the Sequal requirements refer to the syntactic and semantic dimensions. However, the GoM principle of comparability also refers to the use of natural language, which is not included in the introduced modeling technique conceptualization. To clarify the role of natural language in process models, the next section investigates this intersection in detail.

1.3 Role of Natural Language in the BPM Life Cycle

As natural language, we generally understand the language that is produced and spoken by humans. It is distinguished from artificial languages as can be found in computer programming and from constructed languages, which have been consciously designed and did not evolve naturally.[2] Considering the different phases of the previously introduced BPM life cycle, the role of natural language is not particularly obvious. In the following, we take a closer look at each phase and point out where natural language and its analysis come into play:

In the *process identification phase*, the analysis of documents containing information about processes and their interrelations is associated with a considerable amount of work. Hence, natural language processing techniques can significantly reduce this manual workload by automatically discovering key activities or relations between processes. In the *process discovery phase*, natural language plays a particularly important role. The frequently applied process discovery techniques of interviewing and document analysis are both based on natural language analysis. Consequently, natural language processing techniques can be used to automatically extract central concepts, activities, or even entire process models. Also the discovery method of process mining can be enriched with natural technology. An application scenario for such an enrichment is the automatic association of activities with event logs. In the *process analysis phase*, natural language processing can be employed to automatically identify weaknesses such as redundant activities or media disruptions. Moreover, inconsistencies in the control flow can be detected. As an example, consider a job application process, which erroneously allows for rejecting and accepting the application at the same time. An automated analysis could effectively detect such errors. The role of natural language during the *redesign phase* is comparable to the process discovery phase. Using the automated analysis of text documents, potential improvement strategies can be automatically detected. As an example, consider the comparison of different process cases. By analyzing the documented case details, it could be inferred which circumstances lead to the non-successful completion of a process. In the *implementation phase*, natural language processing is particular relevant for workflow-based processes. Here, natural language processing can be used to automatically generate input forms based on the data objects from the process model. In the *monitoring and controlling phase*, natural language technology can complement existing compliance checking techniques such as process mining. For instance, the behavior of employees could be automatically derived from e-mails and system data entries.

---

[2] A well-known example for a constructed language is *Esperanto* [165]. Esperanto has been created with the goal of becoming an internationally spoken language that can foster the understanding between people from all over the world.

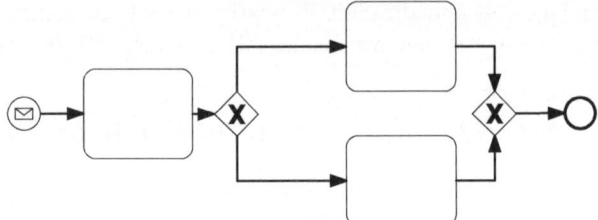

(a) Simple BPMN Model without Natural Language Text Labels.

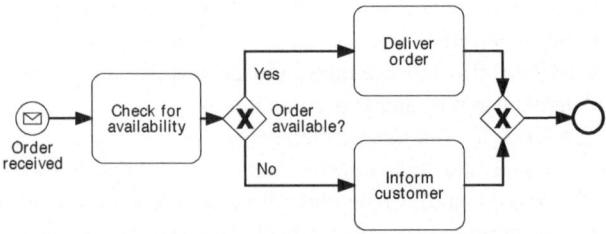

(b) Simple BPMN Model with Natural Language Text Labels.

Fig. 1.4 Semantic Gap Caused by the Absence of Natural Language in Process Models

The consideration of the different life cycle phases already gave an impression of the importance of natural language for business process management. Since many of the discussed aspects are particularly concerned with *process models*, it is worth to have a closer look at the role of natural language in process models and, in particular, at the role of natural language for process model semantics.

To illustrate how much of the overall semantics of a process model is conveyed by natural language, consider the two process models depicted in Figure 1.4. The figure contains two versions of the same model, yet Figure 1.4(a) does not contain any natural language text labels. However, by referring to the syntax and the semantics of the modeling language BPMN, we can at least partially infer a meaning from this model. For instance, we can deduce that the process is triggered by an incoming message since this information is captured by the circle symbol containing an envelope. In addition, we know that after the execution of the first activity, it is only possible to proceed with one of the two activities succeeding the diamond-shaped gateway. Subsequently, the circle with the bold line indicates that the process is finished. In spite of these insights, the process model remains very abstract and does not provide the reader with sufficient semantics. Turning to Figure 1.4(b), it becomes clear how much of the semantics of a model is actually captured by natural language. Only using the text labels, the model reader can infer that this model is representing the processing of an order.

This example illustrates that natural language carries a huge share of the semantics a process model conveys. Thus, the comparison of two process models appears to be hardly possible without considering the natural language text labels. Accordingly, for instance Dijkman et al. [95] and Ehrig et al. [105], propose similarity metrics based on the string edit distance of two natural language labels. In addition, both papers also introduce a similarity metric, which is based on lexical relationships (semantic relationships between words) such as synonymy. In general, it can be stated that natural language may also substantially affect the quality of a process model. If a model contains ambiguous or non-intuitive terms, the model reader might not be able to properly infer its full semantics [317].

Against this background, it is surprising that natural language has not been included in the conceptualization of a modeling technique. Since the distinction between syntactical and semantic aspects of a model has been widely adopted (see e.g., [289, 148, 330, 235, 194, 195]), there exist inconsistent viewpoints regarding the categorization of natural language in this context. For instance, Mendling et al. regard the problem of activity labeling in process models as being part of the semantic or pragmatic dimension [225]. By contrast, Diikman et al. and Ehrig et al. consider structural aspects as syntactical issues [95, 105]. In order to clarify this inconsistency, it is useful to refer to the general structure of natural language.

In essence, a natural language is based on an alphabet, i.e., a finite set of words, which can be used to express a meaning. Syntactic rules define how the words can be combined into sentences. Morphological rules determine how words change in different contexts (e.g., the plural ending -s). Finally, semantics defines the meaning of words. Reconsidering the conceptualization of a modeling technique, it becomes apparent that natural language and modeling language can be considered from the same perspective. Although natural language is more complex in many regards, both share the common properties of having a notation, a syntactic dimension, and a semantic dimension. Hence, natural language is not a concept which is subsumed by the semantic or syntactical dimension of a modeling language, but coexists side by side with it. Accordingly, we propose an extended conceptualization of a modeling technique which is depicted in Figure 1.5.

The key insight from Figure 1.5 is that the overall semantics of a process model is the combination of the modeling and the natural language semantics. Modeling language and natural language are theoretically independent concepts which are combined for the purpose of process modeling. Consequently, the modeling procedure does not only define how to properly use the modeling language, but also how the natural language should be applied. The latter is equally important since natural language constructs in process models do not necessarily represent proper sentences [225].[3]

As a result of this conceptualization, the previous categorization inconsistencies can be reliably resolved. Any aspect which is related to the language structure in a text label falls into the syntactical category of natural language. Thus, for instance, labeling of modeling constructs or naming conventions as requested by the GoM, clearly represent syntactical issues. However, it should be noted that syntactical aspects may have significant implications for the semantics which can be derived from the model. If the absence of naming conventions entails a variety of labeling styles,

---

[3] Also, other conceptual models contain text fragments that do not represent proper sentences. Examples include Entity-Relationship models [67], UML Activity Diagrams [249], and Dependency Diagrams [130].

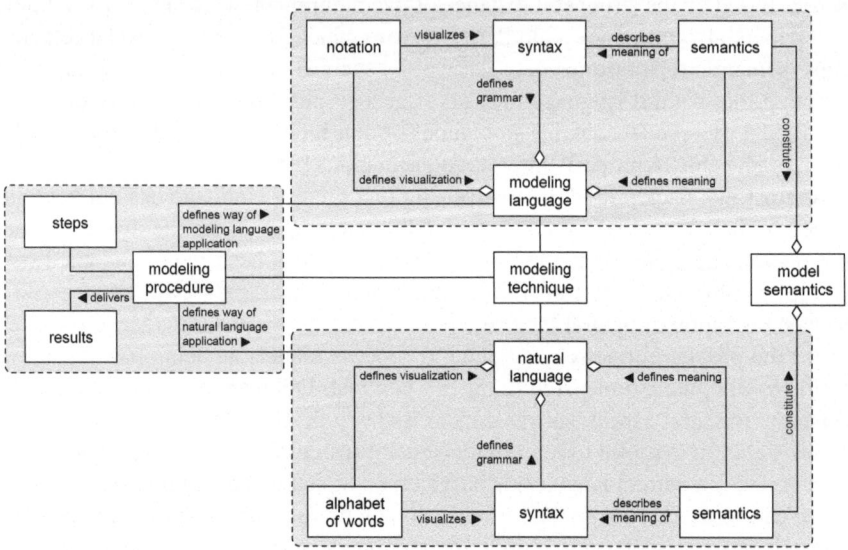

Fig. 1.5 Conceptualization of a Modeling Technique Explicitly Including Natural Language

this can clearly affect the understandability of a model [225]. Aspects such as terminological inconsistencies fall into the semantic category of natural language. As an example, consider synonyms like *bill* and *invoice*. If terms are heterogeneously employed, this may directly affect the ability of a model reader to properly infer the correct semantics.

1.4   Formal Definition of Business Process Models

This section introduces a formal definition for business process models. First, in Section 1.4.1, we propose a canonical format for describing the relevant syntactical process model aspects. Subsequently, in Section 1.4.2 and Section 1.4.3, we formalize the modeling languages EPC and BPMN. Finally, Section 1.4.4 illustrates how these notations can be mapped to the canonical format.

1.4.1   Definition of a Canonical Process Format

As pointed out earlier, business process models can be created with a variety of different modeling languages, including Event-Driven Process Chains, the Business Process Modeling and Notation, and Petri Nets. In this book, we aim at defining techniques which are independent from the notation that is used for representing a model. Hence, we seek to introduce a canonical process model format.

In general, the formalization of process models can be subdivided into a syntactic and a semantic dimension. The first is concerned with the symbols of the notation and how they can be combined. The semantic dimension refers to the execution semantics defining the operational behavior of the model. As we focus on the syntactic dimension of process models in the context of this book, we do not provide a formalization of the execution semantics. However, the execution semantics can be defined by mapping a process model to a Petri Net [3]. Such mappings have been proposed for many common notations such as BPMN [99, 98] or EPCs [4].

Approaches for providing an abstract syntactic definition of a process modeling language have been introduced in different variants. For instance, La Rosa et al. [197] present a UML metamodel for defining a general process format for the purpose of a process model repository. However, they do not provide a formal definition in a mathematical sense. Dijkman et al. [97, 96] introduce a graph-based canonical process format and hence abstract from the specific elements in a process model. Polyvyanyy et al. [263] propose a less abstract format by distinguishing between activities and gateways. Nevertheless, for the purpose of this book we require a more specific definition that explicitly distinguishes between element types such as activities, events, and gateways. Since we refer to the linguistic aspects of a process model as well, we further need to include the text labels which are attached to the different elements of a model. Accordingly, we define the syntax of a process model as follows.

Definition 1.4. (Process Model). A process model $P = (A, E, G, F, R, P, L, \rho, \pi, \lambda, \gamma, \tau)$ consists of six finite sets A, E, G, R, P, L, a binary relation $F \subseteq (A \cup E \cup G) \times (A \cup E \cup G)$, a surjective function $\rho : A \rightarrow R$, a surjective function $\pi : R \rightarrow P$, a partial function $\lambda (A \cup E \cup G \cup F \cup R) \twoheadrightarrow L$, a function $\gamma : G \rightarrow \{and_S, and_J, or_S, or_J, xor_S^D, xor_S^E, xor_J, \}$, and a function $\tau : E_{int} \rightarrow A$ such that

- A is a finite non-empty set of activities.
- E is a finite set of events.
- G is a finite set of gateways.
- We write $N = A \cup E \cup G$ for all *nodes* of the process model.
- F is a finite set of sequence flows. Each sequence flow $f \in F$ represents a directed edge between two nodes.
- R is a finite set of resources.
- P is a finite set of pools.
- L is a finite set of text labels.
- We write $U = N \cup F \cup R \cup P$ for all *units* of the process model which can carry a label.
- The surjective function ρ specifies the assignment of a resource $r \in R$ to an activity $a \in A$.
- The surjective function π specifies the assignment of a resource $r \in R$ to a pool $p \in P$.
- The partial function λ defines the assignment of a label $l \in L$ to a process model unit $u \in U$.

- The function γ specifies the type of a gateway $g \in G$ as and_S, and_J, or_S, or_J, xor_S^D, xor_S^E, xor_J. The subscripts J and S denote joins and splits, and the superscripts D and E denote the distinction between data and event-based split gateways.
- The function τ assigns an intermediate event $e_{int} \in E_{int}$ to an activity (attached event). If such an event occurs, the execution of the respective activity is interrupted.

In order to facilitate a precise characterization of a process model, we define the set of predecessors and successors, the set of incoming and outgoing sequence flows, and the set of labeled elements.

Definition 1.5. (Predecessors and Successors of Nodes). Let N be a set of nodes and $F \subseteq N \times N$ a binary relation over N representing the sequence flows. For each node $n \in N$, we define the set of preceding nodes $\bullet n$ with $\{x \in N \mid (x,n) \in F\}$ and the set of successing nodes $n\bullet$ accordingly with $\{x \in N \mid (n,x) \in F\}$.

Definition 1.6. (Incoming and Outgoing Flows). Let N be a set of nodes and $F \subseteq N \times N$ a binary relation over N representing the sequence flows. For each node $n \in N$, we define the set of incoming flows $n_{in} = \{(x,n) \mid x \in N \wedge (x,n) \in F\}$, and the set of outgoing flows $n_{out} = \{(n,x) \mid x \in N \wedge (n,x) \in F\}$.

Definition 1.7. (Path). Let $P = (A, E, G, F, R, L, \rho, \lambda, \gamma)$ be a process model, and N a set of nodes. There is a path between two nodes $x \in N$ and $y \in N$, denoted with $x \rightsquigarrow y$, if there exists a sequence of nodes $n_1, ..., n_k \in N$ with $x = n_1$ and $y = n_k$ such that for all $i \in 1, ..., k-1$ holds: $(n_i, n_{i+1}) \in F$.

Definition 1.8. (Labeled Elements). Let U be a set of units, L a set of text labels, and λ a partial function assigning units to labels. Accordingly, the set of labeled units U_λ is given by $dom(\lambda)$.

Further, we define several subsets, which are of particular interest for characterizing process models.

Definition 1.9. For a process model $P = (A, E, G, F, R, P, L, \rho, \pi, \lambda, \gamma, \tau)$ we define the following subsets:

- $E_{start} = \{e \in E \mid \bullet e = \emptyset\}$ being the set of start events,
  $E_{int} = \{e \in E \mid \bullet e \neq \emptyset \wedge e\bullet \neq \emptyset\}$ being the set of intermediate events,
  $E_{end} = \{e \in E \mid e\bullet = \emptyset\}$ being the set of end events, and
  $E_\tau = dom(\tau)$ being the set of attached events.
- $J = \{g \in G \mid (\gamma(g) = and_J) \vee (\gamma(g) = xor_J) \vee (\gamma(g) = or_J)\}$ being the set of join gateways,
  $S = \{g \in G \mid (\gamma(g) = and_S) \vee (\gamma(g) = xor_S^D) \vee (\gamma(g) = xor_S^E) \vee (\gamma(g) = or_S)\}$ being the set of split gateways.

- $G_{and} = \{g \in G \mid (\gamma(g) = and_J) \vee (\gamma(g) = and_S)\}$ being the set of and-gateways, $G_{or} = \{g \in G \mid (\gamma(g) = or_J) \vee (\gamma(g) = or_S)\}$ being the set of or-gateways, and $G_{xor} = \{g \in G \mid (\gamma(g) = xor_J) \vee (\gamma(g) = xor_S^D) \vee (\gamma(g) = xor_S^E)\}$ being the set of xor-gateways.
- $J_{and} = \{g \in J \mid \gamma(g) = and_J\}$ being the set of and-joins, $J_{or} = \{g \in J \mid \gamma(g) = or_J\}$ being the set of or-joins, and $J_{xor} = \{g \in J \mid (\gamma(g) = xor_J^D) \vee (\gamma(g) = xor_J^E)\}$ being the set of xor-joins.
- $S_{and} = \{g \in S \mid \gamma(g) = and_S\}$ being the set of and-splits, $S_{or} = \{g \in S \mid \gamma(g) = or_S\}$ being the set of or-splits, $S_{xor}^D = \{g \in S \mid \gamma(g) = xor_S^D\}$ being the set of data-based xor-splits, and $S_{xor}^E = \{g \in S \mid \gamma(g) = xor_S^E\}$ being the set of event-based xor-splits.
- $A_\lambda = \{a \in A \mid a \in dom(\lambda)\}$ being the set of labeled activities, $E_\lambda = \{e \in E \mid e \in dom(\lambda)\}$ being the set of labeled events, $G_\lambda = \{g \in G \mid g \in dom(\lambda)\}$ being the set of labeled gateways, $F_\lambda = \{f \in F \mid f \in dom(\lambda)\}$ being the set of labeled sequence flows, $R_\lambda = \{r \in R \mid r \in dom(\lambda)\}$ being the set of labeled resources, and $P_\lambda = \{p \in P \mid p \in dom(\lambda)\}$ being the set of labeled pools.

In order to be syntactically correct, a process model has to fulfil a set of specific requirements. Accordingly, the following definition summarizes the rules for syntactic correct process models.

Definition 1.10. (Syntactically Correct Process Model). A process model $P = (A, E, G, F, R, P, L, \rho, \pi, \lambda, \gamma, \tau)$ is called syntactically correct if it fulfills the following requirements:

1. A process model contains at least one activity. $|A| \geq 1$.
2. Each node not being a start or end event is on a path from a start to an end event. $\forall n \in (N \setminus (E_{start} \cup E_{end})) : \exists e_{start} \in E_{start}, e_{end} \in E_{end}$, such that $e_{start} \rightsquigarrow n \rightsquigarrow e_{end}$.
3. The latter rule implies that the sets of start and end events are never empty. $e_{start} \neq \emptyset \wedge e_{end} \neq \emptyset$.
4. Start events and attached intermediate events have no incoming and exactly one outgoing flow. $\forall e \in E^{start} \cup dom(\tau) : | \bullet e | = 0 \wedge | e \bullet | = 1$.
5. Non-attached intermediate events have exactly one incoming and one outgoing flow. $\forall e^{int} \in (E^{int} \ dom(\tau)) : | \bullet e^I | = 1 \wedge | e^I \bullet | = 1$.
6. End events have exactly one incoming and no outgoing flow. $\forall e_{end} \in E_{end} : | \bullet e_{end} | = 1 \wedge | e_{end} \bullet | = 0$.
7. Activities have exactly one incoming and one outgoing flow. $\forall a \in A : | \bullet t | = 1 \wedge | a \bullet | = 1$.
8. Gateways either have one incoming and multiple outgoing flows or multiple incoming and one outgoing flow. $\forall g \in G : (| \bullet g | = 1 \wedge | g \bullet | > 1) \vee (| \bullet g | > 1 \wedge | g \bullet | = 1)$.
9. The process model may not contain unlabeled activities. $|A_\lambda| = |A|$.

1.4.2 Formalization of EPCs

EPCs are a widely used process modeling language, which has been initially developed for capturing the reference processes of the SAP R/3 system [79]. Today, EPCs are the core modeling language of the ARIS platform and are supported by a variety of professional modeling tools such as ADONIS, Microsoft Visio, and Signavio. EPCs have been subject to two main extensions: The *eEPC* (extended EPC) notation [295] provides the means for representing additional resources such as systems or organizational roles. The *cEPC* (configurable EPC) notation introduces variation points for the purpose of capturing different process model variants in a single model [7]. By focussing on different aspects of syntax and the execution semantics, EPCs have been formalized in different ways [200, 5, 176, 223]. As we focus on the structural representation of EPCs, we employ the formalization from [223] and adapt it according to the previously introduced canonical format. In particular, we explicitly include text labels and organizational roles as proposed in the context of eEPCs.

Definition 1.11. (EPC). An EPC process model $P_{EPC} = (F, E, C, A, R, O, L, \rho, \pi, \lambda, \gamma)$ consists of six finite sets F, E, C, R, O, L, a binary relation $A \subseteq (F \cup E \cup C) \times (F \cup E \cup C)$, a surjective function $\pi : R \to O$, a surjective function $\rho : F \to R$, a partial function $\lambda : (F \cup E \cup C \cup A \cup R) \twoheadrightarrow L$, and a function $\gamma : C \to \{and, or, xor\}$ such that

- F is a finite non-empty set of functions.
- E is a finite set of events.
- C is a finite set of connectors.
- We write $N = F \cup E \cup C$ for all *nodes* of the EPC.
- A is a finite sets of arcs. Each arc $a \in A$ represents a directed edge between two nodes.
- R is a finite set of roles.
- O is a finite set of organization units.
- L is a finite set of text labels.
- We write $U = F \cup E$ for all *units* of the EPC which can carry a label.
- The surjective function ρ specifies the assignment of a role $r \in R$ to a function $f \in F$.
- The surjective function π specifies the assignment of a role $r \in R$ to a organization unit $o \in O$.
- The partial function λ defines the assignment of a label $l \in L$ to an EPC unit $u \in U$.
- The function γ specifies the type of a connector $c \in C$ as *and*, *or*, or *xor*.

Figure 1.6 visualizes the considered EPC symbol set. EPCs do not provide alternative symbols for different event types. Whether an event is representing a start, intermediate, or end event can only be derived from the incoming and outgoing connectors. Similarly to the canonical format, we further define several important subsets of an EPC.

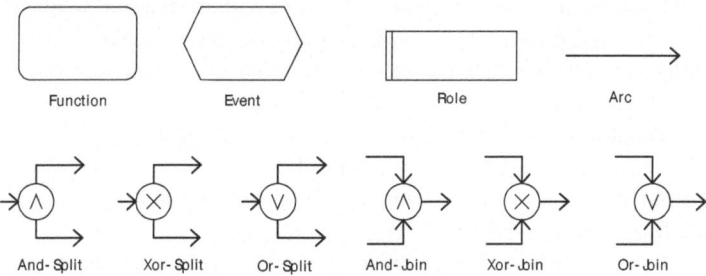

Fig. 1.6 Overview of the Considered Symbol Set of EPCs

Definition 1.12. For an EPC process model $P_{EPC} = (F, E, C, A, R, O, L, \rho, \pi, \lambda, \gamma)$ we define the following subsets:

- $E_{start} = \{e \in E \mid \bullet e = \emptyset\}$ being the set of start events,
  $E_{int} = \{e \in E \mid \bullet e \neq \emptyset \wedge e \bullet \neq \emptyset\}$ being the set of intermediate events, and
  $E_{end} = \{e \in E \mid e \bullet = \emptyset\}$ being the set of end events.
- $J = \{c \in C \mid \mid \bullet c \mid > 1 \wedge \mid c \bullet \mid = 1\}$ being the set of join connectors, and
  $S = \{c \in C \mid \mid \bullet c \mid = 1 \wedge \mid c \bullet \mid > 1\}$ being the set of split connectors.
- $C_{and} = \{c \in C \mid \gamma(c) = and\}$ being the set of and-connectors,
  $C_{or} = \{c \in C \mid \gamma(c) = or\}$ being the set of or-connectors, and
  $C_{xor} = \{c \in C \mid \gamma(c) = xor\}$ being the set of xor-connectors.
- $J_{and} = \{c \in J \mid \gamma(c) = and\}$ being the set of and-joins,
  $J_{or} = \{c \in J \mid \gamma(c) = or\}$ being the set of or-joins, and
  $J_{xor} = \{c \in J \mid \gamma(c) = xor\}$ being the set of xor-joins.
- $S_{and} = \{c \in S \mid \gamma(c) = and\}$ being the set of and-splits,
  $S_{or} = \{c \in S \mid \gamma(c) = or\}$ being the set of or-splits, and
  $S_{xor} = \{c \in S \mid \gamma(c) = xor\}$ being the set of xor-splits.
- $F_{\lambda} = \{f \in F \mid f \in dom(\lambda)\}$ being the set of labeled functions,
  $E_{\lambda} = \{e \in E \mid e \in dom(\lambda)\}$ being the set of labeled events,
  $R_{\lambda} = \{r \in R \mid r \in dom(\lambda)\}$ being the set of labeled roles, and
  $O_{\lambda} = \{o \in O \mid o \in dom(\lambda)\}$ being the set of labeled organizational units.

Traditionally, EPCs have strict requirements in order to be considered as syntactically correct [223, p. 25]. This, for instance, includes the alternation of functions and events and the absence of connector cycles. However, for the purpose of this book, we abstract from these strict requirements and adapt the notion of relaxed syntactical correctness as introduced in [223, p. 26].

Definition 1.13. (Relaxed Syntactically Correct EPC). An EPC $P_{EPC} = (F, E, C, A, R, O, L, \rho, \pi, \lambda, \gamma)$ is called relaxed syntactically correct if it fulfils the following requirements:

1. A process model contains at least one function. $\mid F \mid \geq 1$.

2. Each node not being a start or end event is on a path from a start to an end event.
$\forall n \in (N \setminus (E_{start} \cup E_{end})) : \exists e_{start} \in E_{start}, e_{end} \in E_{end}$ such that $e_{start} \rightsquigarrow n \rightsquigarrow e_{end}$.

3. The latter rule implies that the sets of start and end events are never empty.
$e_{start} \neq \emptyset \wedge e_{end} \neq \emptyset$.

4. Start events have no incoming and exactly one outgoing arc.
$\forall e_{start} \in E_{start} : | \bullet e_{start} | = 0 \wedge | e_{start} \bullet | = 1$.

5. End events have exactly one incoming and no outgoing arc.
$\forall e_{end} \in E_{end} : | \bullet e_{end} | = 1 \wedge | e_{end} \bullet | = 0$.

6. Intermediate events have exactly one incoming and one outgoing arc.
$\forall e_{int} \in E_{int} : | \bullet e_{int} | = 1 \wedge | e_{int} \bullet | = 1$.

7. Functions have exactly one incoming and one outgoing arc.
$\forall f \in F : | \bullet f | = 1 \wedge | f \bullet | = 1$.

8. Connectors either have one incoming and multiple outgoing arcs or multiple incoming and one outgoing arc.
$\forall c \in C : (| \bullet c | = 1 \wedge | c \bullet | > 1) \vee (| \bullet c | > 1 \wedge | c \bullet | = 1)$.

9. The EPC may not contain unlabeled functions or events. $| F_\lambda | = | F |$ and $| E_\lambda | = | E |$.

1.4.3   Formalization of BPMN Process Models

The Business Process Model and Notation is a standardized modeling language for graphically specifying business process models [248]. It has been initially developed by the Business Process Management Initiative (BPMI) and is now maintained by the Object Management Group (OMG). BPMN was designed to support both IT and business users, yet providing the means for representing complex real-world semantics [17, p. 13]. Currently, it is available in version 2.0. A comprehensive (but not complete) formalization of BPMN has been proposed by Dijkman [98]. Due to the extensive symbol set, a complete formalization of BPMN would introduce unnecessary complexity. Hence, we adapt the formalization from [98], focusing on frequently employed elements. Further, we respectively include the aspects of labeling.

Definition 1.14. (BPMN Process Model). A BPMN process model $P_{BPMN} = (A, E, G, F, R, P, L, \rho, \pi, \lambda, \gamma, \varepsilon, \tau)$ consists of six finite sets A, E, C, R, P, L, a binary relation $F \subseteq (A \cup E \cup G) \times (A \cup E \cup G)$, a surjective function $\rho : (A \cup E) \rightarrow R$, a surjective function $\pi : R \rightarrow P$, a partial function $\lambda : (A \cup E \cup G \cup F \cup R) \twoheadrightarrow L$, a function $\gamma : G \rightarrow \{ands, and_J, ors, or_J, xor_S^D, xor_S^E, xor_J,\}$, a function $\varepsilon : E \rightarrow \{plain, timer, message, error, cancellation, escalation\}$, and a function $\tau : E_{int} \rightarrow A$ such that

- A is a finite non-empty set of activities.
- E is a finite set of events.
- G is a finite set of gateways.
- We write $N = A \cup E \cup G$ for all *nodes* of the BPMN model.
- F is a finite set of sequence flows. Each sequence flow $f \in F$ represents a directed edge between two nodes.

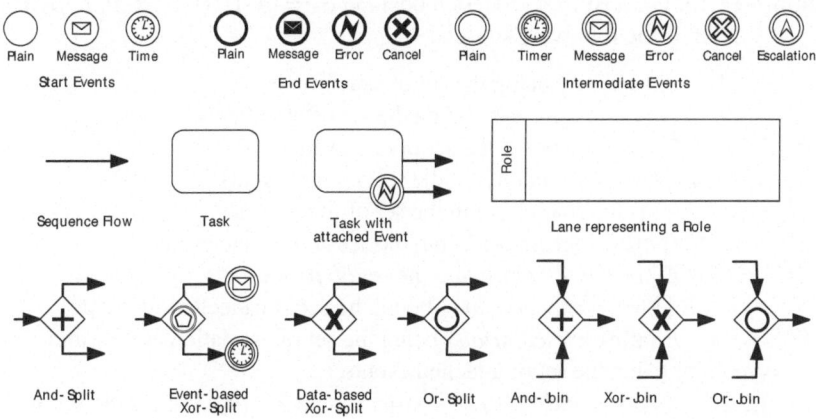

Fig. 1.7 Overview of the Considered Core Subset of BPMN

- R is a finite set of roles.
- P is a finite set of pools.
- We write $U = N \cup A \cup R \cup P$ for all *units* of the BPMN model which can carry a label.
- L is a finite set of text labels.
- The surjective function ρ specifies the assignment of a role $r \in R$ to activities and events $A \cup E$.
- The surjective function π specifies the assignment of a role $r \in R$ to a pool $p \in P$.
- The partial function λ defines the assignment of a label $l \in L$ to a process model unit $u \in U$.
- The function γ specifies the type of a gateway $g \in G$ as and_S, and_J, or_S, or_J, xor_S^D, xor_S^E, xor_J. The subscripts J and S denote joins and splits, and the superscripts D and E denote the distinction between data and event-based split gateways.
- The function ε specifies the type of an event $e \in E$ as *plain, timer, message, error, cancellation*, or *escalation*.[4]
- The function τ assigns an intermediate event $e_{int} \in E_{int}$ to an activity (attached event). If such an event occurs, the execution of the respective activity is interrupted.

Figure 1.7 shows the graphical representation of the considered subset of BPMN. It particularly illustrates the extensive symbol set of BPMN. As opposed to EPCs, BPMN does not only include different event types, but also visually indicates whether an event is a start, intermediate, or end event. As presented for the canonical format and EPCs, we respectively introduce a number of relevant subsets.

---

[4] Note that this does not reflect the entire event symbol set of BPMN.

Definition 1.15. For a BPMN process model $P_{BPMN} = (A, E, G, F, R, P, L, \rho, \pi, \lambda, \gamma, \varepsilon, \tau)$ we define the following subsets:

- $E_{start} = \{e \in E \mid \bullet e = \emptyset\}$ being the set of start events,
  $E_{int} = \{e \in E \mid \bullet e \neq \emptyset \wedge e \bullet \neq \emptyset\}$ being the set of intermediate events,
  $E_{end} = \{e \in E \mid e \bullet = \emptyset\}$ being the set of end events,
  $E^P = \{e \in E \mid \varepsilon(e) = plain\}$ being the set of plain events,
  $E^T = \{e \in E \mid \varepsilon(e) = timer\}$ being the set of timer events,
  $E^M = \{e \in E \mid \varepsilon(e) = message\}$ being the set of message events,
  $E^{Err} = \{e \in E \mid \varepsilon(e) = error\}$ being the set of error events,
  $E^C = \{e \in E \mid \varepsilon(e) = cancellation\}$ being the set of cancellation events,
  $E^{Esc} = \{e \in E \mid \varepsilon(e) = escalation\}$ being the set of escalation events, and
  $E_\tau = dom(\tau)$ being the set of attached events.
- $J = \{g \in G \mid (\gamma(g) = and_J) \vee (\gamma(g) = xor_J) \vee (\gamma(g) = or_J)\}$ being the set of join gateways,
  $S = \{g \in G \mid (\gamma(g) = and_S) \vee (\gamma(g) = xor_S^D) \vee (\gamma(g) = xor_S^E) \vee (\gamma(g) = or_S)\}$ being the set of split gateways.
- $G_{and} = \{g \in G \mid (\gamma(g) = and_J) \vee (\gamma(g) = and_S)\}$ being the set of and-gateways,
  $G_{or} = \{g \in G \mid (\gamma(g) = or_J) \vee (\gamma(g) = or_S)\}$ being the set of or-gateways, and
  $G_{xor} = \{g \in G \mid (\gamma(g) = xor_J) \vee (\gamma(g) = xor_S^D) \vee (\gamma(g) = xor_S^E)\}$ being the set of xor-gateways.
- $J_{and} = \{g \in J \mid \gamma(g) = and_J\}$ being the set of and-joins,
  $J_{or} = \{g \in J \mid \gamma(g) = or_J\}$ being the set of or-joins, and
  $J_{xor} = \{g \in J \mid (\gamma(g) = xor_J^D) \vee (\gamma(g) = xor_J^E)\}$ being the set of xor-joins.
- $S_{and} = \{g \in S \mid \gamma(g) = and_S\}$ being the set of and-splits,
  $S_{or} = \{g \in S \mid \gamma(g) = or_S\}$ being the set of or-splits,
  $S_{xor}^D = \{g \in S \mid \gamma(g) = xor_S^D\}$ being the set of data-based xor-splits, and
  $S_{xor}^E = \{g \in S \mid \gamma(g) = xor_S^E\}$ being the set of event-based xor-splits.
- $A_\lambda = \{a \in A \mid a \in dom(\lambda)\}$ being the set of labeled activities,
  $E_\lambda = \{e \in E \mid e \in dom(\lambda)\}$ being the set of labeled events,
  $G_\lambda = \{g \in G \mid g \in dom(\lambda)\}$ being the set of labeled gateways,
  $F_\lambda = \{f \in F \mid f \in dom(\lambda)\}$ being the set of labeled sequence flows,
  $R_\lambda = \{r \in R \mid r \in dom(\lambda)\}$ being the set of labeled roles, and
  $P_\lambda = \{p \in P \mid p \in dom(\lambda)\}$ being the set of labeled pools.

In comparison to the traditional notion of EPC correctness, BPMN provides the modeler with a lot of freedom. For example, a BPMN modeler may decide to model an and-split without the use of a gateway by introducing an activity with two outgoing flows. In order to avoid unnecessary complexity, we introduce a stricter notion of correctness comparable to the relaxed syntactical correctness of EPCs.[5]

---

[5] Note that this does not imply that the techniques defined in this book are not applicable for standard BPMN models. Every BPMN model complying with the above introduced definition and the correctness requirements of the BPMN specification, can be mapped to a BPMN model fulfilling the above defined correctness criteria.

Definition 1.16. (Syntactically Correct BPMN Process Model). A BPMN process model $P_{BPMN} = (A, E, G, F, R, P, L, \rho, \pi, \lambda, \gamma, \varepsilon, \tau)$ is called syntactically correct if it fulfills the following requirements:

1. A process model contains at least one activity. $|A| \geq 1$.
2. Each node not being a start or end event is on a path from a start to an end event.
   $\forall n \in (N \setminus (E_{start} \cup E_{end})) : \exists e_{start} \in E_{start}, e_{end} \in E_{end}$ such that $e_{start} \leadsto n \leadsto e_{end}$.
3. Start events and attached intermediate events have no incoming and exactly one outgoing flow.
   $\forall e \in E^{start} \cup dom(\tau) : | \bullet e | = 0 \wedge | e \bullet | = 1$.
4. Non-attached intermediate events have exactly one incoming and one outgoing arc.
   $\forall e^{int} \in (E^{int} \ dom(\tau)) : | \bullet e^I | = 1 \wedge | e^I \bullet | = 1$.
5. End events have no incoming and exactly one outgoing flow.
   $\forall e^{start} \in F^{start} : | \bullet e^{start} | = 1 \wedge | e^{start} \bullet | = 0$.
6. Activities have exactly one incoming and one outgoing flow.
   $\forall t \in T : | \bullet t | = 1 \wedge | t \bullet | = 1$.
7. Split gateways have one incoming and multiple outgoing flows.
   $\forall g \in S : (| \bullet g | = 1 \wedge | g \bullet | > 1)$.
8. Join gateways have multiple incoming and one outgoing flow.
   $\forall g \in J : (| \bullet g | > 1 \wedge | g \bullet | = 1)$.
9. An event-based xor gateway must be followed by intermediate message or timer events. $\forall g \in S^E_{xor} : g \bullet \subseteq (E^T \cup E^M)$.
10. The process model may not contain unlabeled activities. $|A_\lambda| = |A|$.

1.4.4 Mapping of EPCs and BPMN to the Canonical Format

In order to employ the canonical process format for discussing the techniques in this book, it is necessary to define a mapping to the BPMN and EPC format. Therefore, we build on the workflow patterns as introduced by van der Aalst et al. [11].[6] The workflow patterns represent a collection of design patterns that can be used in the context of a process model to express the process semantics. The patterns are organized along four perspectives including control flow, data, resource, and exception handling. The goal of the workflow pattern initiative is to provide a basis for evaluating the suitability of modeling languages for a particular modeling purpose. Hence, many languages have been analyzed with regard to their coverage of the defined workflow patterns. Examples include BPMN [338] and many Petri Net based notations [10]. Building on these analyses, it is possible to discuss the semantic equivalence between the modeling constructs of different modeling languages. As a result, we can derive a mapping among the canonical format, BPMN, and EPCs.

Table 1.1 provides an overview of the elements of the canonical process format and their correspondence to the specific elements of EPCs and BPMN process models. The table shows that there are three main differences among the considered

---

[6] http://www.workflowpatterns.com/

Table 1.1 Mapping of Canonical Elements to EPCs and BPMN Models

Canonical Element	(e)EPC	BPMN 2.0
Arc	Arc	Sequence Flow
Activity	Function	Activity
Event	Event	Plain Event, Timer Event, Message Event, Error Event, Cancellation Event, Escalation Event
Attached Event	-	Attached Event
And-Split Gateway	And-Split-Connector	And-Split-Gateway
And-Join-Gateway	And-Join-Connector	And-Join-Gateway
Data-based Xor-Split-Gateway	Xor-Split Connector	Data-based Xor-Split Gateway
Event-based Xor-Split Gateway	-	Event-based Xor-Split Gateway
Xor-Join Gateway	Xor-Join Connector	Xor-Join Gateway
Or-Split Gateway	Or-Split Connector	Or-Split Gateway
Or-Join Gateway	Or-Join Connector	Or-Join Gateway
Resource	Role	Role
Pool	Org. Unit	Pool
Label	Label	Label

modeling languages: coverage of the workflow patterns, names of elements, and the scope of labeling. With regard to the *coverage of workflow patterns*, we observe two differences. First, EPCs do not provide the possibility to express the semantics of attached events. In terms of the workflow patterns, attached events refer to the pattern *Cancel Activity*. As EPCs do not include the possibility to cancel a function, the corresponding mapping is empty. Second, EPCs do not contain event-based xor-splits. While data-based xor-splits refer to the workflow pattern *Exclusive Choice*, event-based xor-splits refer to the pattern *Deferred Choice* as the choice is not made explicitly. Since the EPC xor-connector only refers to the first pattern, there is no correspondence to the canonical format. Concerning the *element names*, we observe two differences: An *activity* in an EPC is referred to as *function* and an *arc* in BPMN is called *sequence flow*. However, these deviations do not imply differences with respect to the semantics of the elements. Finally, there exist differences in regard to the *scope of labeling*. The canonical format and BPMN allow for labeling activities, events, gateways, sequence flows, roles, and pools. EPCs, however, do not provide the possibility to label connectors or arcs.

Altogether, it can be stated that the canonical format covers all concepts of the introduced BPMN and EPC formalization. Hence, we use the canonical process format for discussing the formal aspects of the proposed techniques in the remainder of this book.

1.5 Summary

In this chapter, we gave an overview of business process management. We introduced the main terms and concepts and emphasized the importance of business process models in the BPM life cycle. A deeper investigation of the nature of a modeling technique revealed that the model semantics are the result of combining natural language and modeling language. Further, we clarified that natural language and modeling language can be characterized by the means of syntax, semantics, and notation. In natural language, the syntax determines how words can be combined to sentences and the semantics defines the meaning of words. In a modeling language, the syntax decides on how the notation symbols can be combined in the model and the semantics defines the meaning of these symbols. As a result of this characterization, the inconsistencies in literature concerning the scope of syntax and semantics in a model are resolved. By showing a model without natural language text labels, we further demonstrated the significant role of natural language for the overall model semantics. To facilitate a precise characterization of process models, we presented a formal definition of a process model. In particular, we introduced a canonical process model format and illustrated how this format corresponds to the modeling languages EPC and BPMN. In order to provide the language-related foundations for the subsequent chapters, the following chapter gives an introduction into the field of linguistics.

Chapter 2
Linguistics

This chapter provides an introduction into the field of linguistics. In order to lay the groundwork for the subsequent chapters of this book, we focus on three main aspects. First, Section 2.1 explains the basic concepts of linguistics and introduces the different schools of thought. Then, Section 2.2 gives an overview of theoretical linguistics. In particular, it discusses the different branches of theoretical linguistics such as morphology, syntax, and semantics. Using the insights from this section, we can adequately describe and analyze the natural language phenomena in business process models. Subsequently, Section 2.3 introduces the field of natural language processing. Specifically, it presents theoretical foundations for analyzing natural language in an automated fashion. Finally, Section 2.5 concludes the chapter with a summary.

2.1 Overview and Central Concepts of Linguistics

The importance of natural language in the life of humans can hardly be exaggerated. For instance, the use of natural language allows the exchange of thoughts, expression of feelings, and preservation of knowledge (e.g., in books). The modern philosopher Karl Popper considers natural language as a prerequisite for conducting science: Only through natural language our theories and hypotheses become explicit and hence subject to the criticism of others [266, p. 41].

The discipline of linguistics is concerned with all these aspects of natural language. More precisely, linguistics can be defined as the scientific study of the human language including all its facets such as structure, usage, and history [127]. Linguistics is subdivided into a multitude of sub fields, whereas the major areas are typically *theoretical* and *applied linguistics* [61, pp. 27-28]. Theoretical linguistics is often considered as the core of linguistics and focusses on the description of the basic nature and structure of language. By contrast, applied linguistics is an interdisciplinary field offering solutions to problems in the real world where natural language is involved [74, pp. 5-12]. Examples include language education (how to teach or learn a second language), language assessment (how to assess language

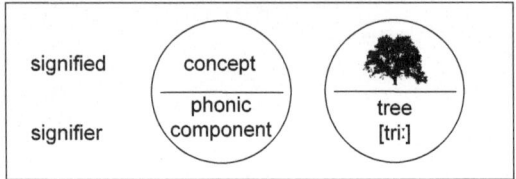

Fig. 2.1 Model of the Linguistic Sign, adapted from Saussure [293, p. 67]

skills in the context of schools or universities), and natural language processing (modeling and analysis of natural language with computational methods).

In the history of linguistics, different approaches have been introduced about how natural language can be conceived. In particular, there are three main schools of thought, which are of prior importance for modern linguistics: structuralism, functionalism, and generative linguistics.

Structuralism was mainly established by the Swiss linguist Ferdinand de Saussure. He proposed to consider language as a system of interrelated elements [46, p. 5]. Thereby, Saussure abstracted from a concrete language (*parole*) and focused on the structure of the language system (*langue*). In this context he also proposed the two-side model of the linguistic sign (see Figure 2.1). According to this model, each linguistic sign consists of two inseparable parts: a phonic component called *signifier* (*signifiant*) and a concept called *signified* (*signifié*) [246, pp. 59-60]. The phonic component represents how the sign is expressed and the concept represents the meaning of the sign. The key insight of Saussure is that there is no internal connection between these two levels. In different languages, the same concept might be referred to by totally different sound patterns. As an example, consider the concept of a *tree*, which is called *Baum* in German and *árbol* in Spanish. Hence, the connection between the two levels is (almost) completely arbitrary and a result of convention.[1]

The school of *functionalism* aims to explain the form and structure of a language by referring to the functions it may carry out [246, p. 181]. This perspective is motivated by the fact that language can be considered as a tool. Hence, functionalists argue that language is best understood by analyzing its functions. A prominent example in this context is the *Organon model* from Karl Bühler, which distinguishes between the expressive function (for expressing feelings), the referential function (for describing the world), and the conative function (for requesting and commanding) [57, 34-37]. It is important to note that there is no objective way of determining the functions of language. Hence, there exists a broad variety of alternative function-based language models (see e.g. [163, 100, 140]).

Especially since the second half of the 20th century, the school of *Generative linguistics* became increasingly important for the linguistic discipline [46, p. 8].

---

[1] The only exceptions are so-called onomatopoeic words such as *cuckoo*. In its spoken form, *cuckoo* refers to the cry of the signified bird [213, p. 101].

Building on the work of Noam Chomsky [68], generative linguistics focuses on describing language in terms of a universal grammar. Such a grammar consists of a finite set of rules that can be applied to construct a theoretically indefinite number of sentences. Thus, generative grammars can characterize a given sentence as grammatically correct or incorrect. Examples for generative grammars include the Head-driven Phrase Structure Grammar (HPSG) [262], Relational Grammar (RG) [167], and the Tree-adjoining grammar [169]. What generative grammars typically have in common is that the outcome of the correctness prediction is simply true or false. In this regard, they differ from stochastic approaches, which compute the likelihood of a given sentence.

In modern linguistics, these schools of thought coexist side by side [190, p. 32]. Considering the introduced linguistic schools in the light of this book, they represent complementary approaches which are integrated by investigating different linguistic aspects of process models. By studying and describing the structure of linguistic fragments, we clearly focus on structural or grammatical problems. Nevertheless, by referring to the expressive power of process models, we also focus on functional aspects. In order to provide the means for adequetely describing the structure of language, the next section introduces the essential concepts of theoretical linguistics.

2.2 Theoretical Linguistics

This section gives an introduction into theoretical linguistics. Section 2.2.1 provides a brief overview of the discipline. Then, the subsequent sections discuss the branches of theoretical linguistics which are of relevance for this book. In particular, Section 2.2.2 discusses morphological aspects, Section 2.2.3 explains the syntax of language, and Section 2.2.4 elaborates on the branch of semantics.

2.2.1 Branches of Theoretical Linguistics

In general, theoretical linguistics is concerned with the form and structure of language. The introduced schools of thought demonstrated that language can be perceived and studied in different ways. Consequently, theoretical linguistics is subdivided into various branches [292, 217, 46]. Since this book is only concerned with written language, we focus on those branches which are relevant for analyzing and describing the written form of language. Accordingly, the following sections introduce the relevant concepts of the following three branches:

- *Morphology*: The study of the structure of words.
- *Syntax*: The study of the structural relationships between words.
- *Semantics*: The study of meaning.

In addition to the considered branches, there also exist subfields focusing on other aspects of language. For instance, *phonetics* and *phonology* study the sounds of human speech, *pragmatics* investigates how context affects the meaning of language [78, p. 2], and *sociolinguistics* studies the relationship between language and society [76, p. 4].

2.2.2 Morphology

Simply speaking, morphology is concerned with the internal structure of words [46, p. 76]. In particular, it includes the study of word structure and how this structure changes in different contexts. In order to properly discuss the morphological aspects, it is necessary to introduce three important linguistic concepts: the lexeme, the lemma, and the word form.

The idea behind a *lexeme* is to abstract from concrete *word forms* and represent a group of different word forms using the lexeme [209, p. 89]. As an example consider the English verb *do*. In natural language texts, *do* may occur in different word forms such as *does*, *did*, and *done*. However, if we look into a dictionary, we will only find the word form *do*. Hence, the word form *do* refers to a lexeme which is representing the entire set of different word forms of *do*. The particular word form that is used to represent a lexeme in a dictionary is called a *lemma*. Typically, a lemma is given by the infinitive form of the verb or the singular form of the noun.

Languages make an important distinction between two word classes: *content words* and *function words* [126, p. 78]. Nouns, verbs, adjectives, and adverbs are *content words*. They, for example, denote objects, actions, and attributes. Often, content words are also called *open class* words as they regularly adopt new members. As examples, consider words like *blog* or *cloud computing*. Several years ago, nobody could have guessed what these words mean. While content words have a clear lexical meaning, this does not necessarily apply to *function words*. Examples for function words include *and*, *or*, *in*, and *of*. These words specify grammatical relations and only have little semantic content. Since function words do not adopt new members, they are also referred to as *closed class* words.

To understand how words change as well as how new words can be created, it is necessary to look at the internal structure of words. In the context of morphology, it is assumed that words are not only composed of sounds, but also of smallest meaning-bearing units, so-called morphemes [46, p. 80]. Such morphemes can be subdivided into two different classes: *free* and *bound* morphemes [250, p. 32]. Free morphemes are called *free* as they do not necessarily need to be combined with other morphemes, they can also stand alone (e.g., *book* or *mail*). In isolation, they represent words with exactly one morpheme. In combination, they may occur in words such as *e-mail* or *textbook*. As opposed to free morphemes, bound morphemes cannot stand alone. They always serve as affixes which are attached to other morphemes. Examples for bound morphemes are *-ment*, *-s*, and *-ing*. Thus, for instance, the word *cooking* consists of the morphemes *cook* and *-ing*.

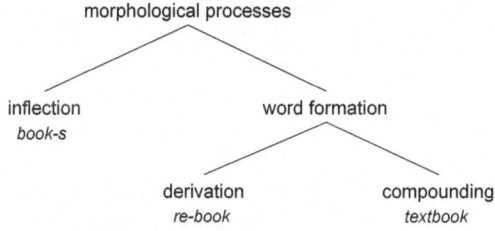

Fig. 2.2 Overview of Morphological Processes, adapted from [46, p. 86]

The provided examples on the usage of morphemes already illustrated how morphemes can be employed for creating and modifying words. In general, there are two main groups of morphological processes (see Figure 2.2): inflectional processes and word formation processes [46, p. 86]. *Inflectional processes* modify words in order to express different grammatical categories. For instance, the singular noun *book* can be transformed into its plural form by adding the suffix -*s*. While this is a very simple example, inflection also includes more complex modifications, where a word is completely replaced. As an example, consider the verb *go*, which turns into *went* in the past tense. As opposed to inflection, *word formation processes* may cause a change in the part of speech of the modified word. Word formation processes are subdivided into two different categories: derivation and compounding. *Derivation* means that prefixes or suffixes are used to create a new lexeme. If we, for instance, add the prefix *re-* to the noun *book*, we obtain the verb *rebook*. A special case of derivation is *conversion*, which is also referred to as *zero-derivation* [240]. Zero-derivation means that a word can be transformed into another part of speech without adding any affixes. Since many English words can represent verb and noun without any modifications, this is a frequent phenomenon in the English language. Examples include *the plan* and *to plan*, *the order* and *to order*, and *the process* and *to process*. *Compounding* is an alternative word formation process and denotes the combination of two or more words for the purpose of creating a new word. If we, for example, combine the nouns *text* and *book*, we obtain the new word *textbook*.

2.2.3 Syntax

While morphology is concerned with the structure of words, syntax studies how words can be combined to phrases, clauses, and sentences [302, p. 143]. As illustrated by Figure 2.3, a sentence may consist of one or more clauses, one clause consists of one or more phrases, and one phrase contains one or more words. For illustrating these concepts, consider the following example sentence:

The students read a book.

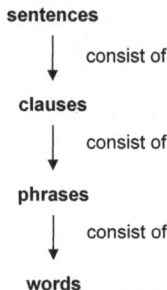

Fig. 2.3 Hierarchy of Sentences, Clauses, Phrases, and Words

At the word level, we can identify different lexical categories, or so-called parts of speech. The main parts of speech include nouns (N), verbs (V), adjectives (Adj), adverbs (Adv), prepositions (Prep), and determiners (Det). Thus, the example sentence can be described as follows:

[$_{Det}$The], [$_N$students] [$_V$read] [$_{Det}$a] [$_N$book].

In addition to the parts of speech, we can further assign grammatical functions to the words. In general, English sentences contain a *subject* and a *predicate*. In the example sentence from above the subject is given by *students* and the predicate by *read*. Typically, sentences are enriched by incorporating *objects* and *adverbials*. Accordingly, the example sentence further contains the object *book* to specify *what* the students actually read. Adverbials such as *yesterday* or *in the library* provide, among others, further details about time and place. Building on the knowledge about lexical categories and grammatical functions, the following paragraphs investigate how sentences, clauses, and phrases are constructed.

As illustrated by Figure 2.3, sentences are decomposed into clauses and phrases. Hence, a sentence can be defined as a the largest syntactic unit which is made up of constituents [250, p. 22]. Based on the number and type of the contained clauses, sentences are categorized as *simple, compound,* or *complex*. A *simple sentence* only contains one clause consisting of a single subject-predicate structure. Consequently, the above introduced example sentence represents a simple sentence. A *compound sentence* contains two or more clauses linked by a coordinating conjunction such as *and* or *but*. If we augment the example sentence with an additional main clause, we can obtain the following compound sentence:

The students read a book and study for the exam.

As opposed to compound sentences, *complex sentences* do not contain another main clause, but one or more subordinate clauses. Typically, subordinate clauses are introduced by subordinating conjunctions such as *although* and *because* or relative pronouns such as *which* and *who* [46, p. 108]. To obtain a complex sentence, we can alter our example sentence as follows:

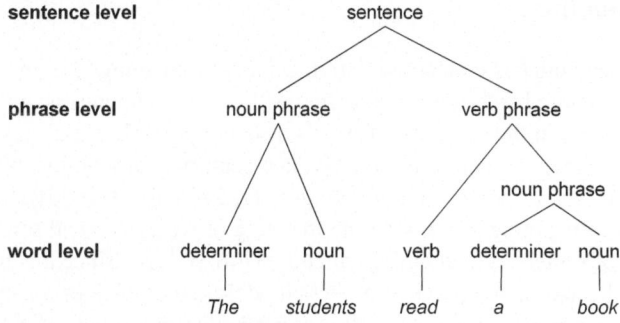

Fig. 2.4 Phrase Structure Tree of Example Sentence

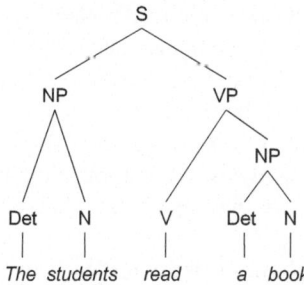

Fig. 2.5 Phrase Structure Tree of Example Sentence According to Linguistic Conventions

The students read a book, although they are supposed to pay attention.

Similar to a clause, a phrase is a group of words with internal cohesion, but by contrast, does not contain a subject-predicate structure [302, 199]. Usually, phrases contain a so-called head word, which defines the type of phrase. To illustrate the phrase concept consider the phrase structure tree depicted in Figure 2.4. The tree visualizes the hierarchical phrase structure of the example sentence and illustrates how phrases relate to the underlying word level. From this figure, we can learn that the sentence consists of one noun and one verb phrase. The head words *students* and *read* determine the type of the top-level phrases. However, the verb phrase does not only contain the verb *read*, but also the noun phrase *a book*. Hence, this noun phrase is included on the underlying phrase level. While the depicted phrase structure tree is appropriate for illustrating the phrasal concept, linguists use abbreviations for referring to lexical categories and phrase types. Specifically, a verb phrase is denoted with *VP* and a noun phrase with *NP*. Figure 2.5 shows the according phrase structure tree complying with linguistic conventions [340, pp. 102-103].

The previously introduced concepts from the field of syntax provide the means for adequately describing the structure of natural language. In fact, this does not only apply to standard natural language texts, but also to language fragments as we typically find in business process models.

2.2.4 Semantics

The field of semantics is concerned with the study of meaning [213, p. 1]. The importance of meaning for the communication with natural language is quite apparent. Without agreeing on the meaning of words, it is not possible for a speaker to convey his or her thoughts. Particularly in the last century, many philosophers studied meaning from various perspectives (see e.g. [121, 290, 288, 337, 23]). Still, the linguistic study of meaning focuses on the meaning of words (lexical semantics) and the meaning of sentences (sentential semantics) [46, p. 128]. Since this book is concerned with the natural language of process models that often does not even include proper sentences, the meaning of words is of particular importance. Hence, we focus on lexical semantics and elaborate on the meaning of words.

In general, the meaning of words can be discussed from a relational perspective, i.e., the meaning is a matter of the relation with other words, or from a local perspective, assuming that a word is self-contained and that its meaning can be described independently [20, p. 242]. Abstracting from these views, it is apparent that words can be semantically related to other words in various ways. Since such sense relations are an important concept of lexical semantics and a predominant issue in the context of natural language analysis, we introduce the most important sense relations in detail. In particular, we investigate the relations of *synonymy*, *homonymy*, *hypernomy*, and *meronymy*.

To illustrate the relation of *synonymy*, consider the words *buy*, *purchase*, and *acquire*. At first glance, it seems to be obvious that these words can bear the same meaning and hence are said to be synonyms. As a result, the clauses *buy a house*, *purchase a house*, and *acquire a house* can reflect the same real-world semantics. However, while *buy* and *purchase* imply a money transaction, that does not equally apply to *acquire*. In general, *acquire* can be employed in a much broader sense. For instance, think of *acquiring a disease* or *acquiring knowledge*. These examples illustrate that many synonyms are not perfect synonyms with exactly the same meaning, but rather share a set of contexts in which they are mutually exchangeable.

The phenomenon of non-perfect synonymy is closely related to the fact that many words have two or more meanings. As an example, consider the word *application*. This word can be used in the context of a *computer application* as well as in the context of a *job application*. The characteristic of a word having more than a single meaning is referred to as *homonymy*. It is important to note that linguists differentiate whether the meanings are semantically related or distinct. In order to illustrate this characteristic, reconsider the different examples of the word *acquire*. In a wider sense, we can say that *acquire* refers to the process of *getting into the possession of something* in all considered examples. Hence, the meanings are semantically related. While words with distinct multiple meanings such as *application* are called homonyms, words with semantically related meanings are referred to as *polysemes*.

The concept of *hyponomy* is concerned with semantic hierarchies among words. For instance a *vehicle* is a more general word for a *car* or a *vegetable* is more general word for a *carrot*. Having such a hierarchical relationship, the superordinate word is referred to as *hypernym* and the subordinate word is called *hyponym*. Another

Table 2.1 Overview of Sense Relations

Sense Relation	Description	Example
Synonymy	words having the same or similar meanings	to buy & to purchase / bill & invoice
Homonymy	a word with multiple unrelated meanings	to order / application
Polysemy	a word with multiple related meanings	to acquire / table
Hyponymy	type-of relationship between words	to build & to create / carrot & vegetable
Meronymy	part-of relationship between words (nouns only)	finger & hand

type of hierarchical relationship is the part-whole relationship. For instance, *fingers* are part of a *hand* or *branches* and a *trunk* are part of a *tree*. Such a relationship, where constituent parts of a concept are considered, is called *meronymy*. Table 2.1 summarizes the introduced sense relations and provides additional examples.

2.3 Natural Language Processing

Natural Language Processing (NLP) is an interdisciplinary research area that is concerned with automatically analyzing natural language [196, p. 1]. The foundations of NLP can be found in various disciplines including computer science, linguistics, artificial intelligence, and psychology [168]. NLP is applied in various domains such as natural language text processing [161, 123], machine translation [155, 55], and speech recognition [269, 166]. Since this book focuses on the analysis of natural language provided in text form, we use this section to introduce the main concepts for natural language text analysis. In Section 2.3.1 we start with discussing text corpora as the foundation for text processing tools. In Section 2.3.2 and Section 2.3.3 we continue by presenting the main concepts from the fields part-of-speech tagging and natural language parsing. Finally, in Section 2.3.4, we introduce the lexical database WordNet as valuable resource for linguistic knowledge.

2.3.1 Text Corpora

A corpus is a large collection of texts, often including many thousands to millions of words. Typically, they are encoded electronically such that they can be automatically processed and used for statistical analyses [30, p. 2].

In many cases corpora are annotated with linguistic knowledge such as part of speech tags or parse trees. Corpora including the latter are also referred to as

Table 2.2 Tagset of the Penn Tree Bank

Tag	Description	Example	Tag	Description	Example
CC	coord. conjunction	*and, or*	RB	adverb	*extremely*
CD	cardinal number	*one, two*	RBR	adverb, comparative	*never*
DT	determiner	*a, the*	RBS	adverb, superlative	*fastest*
EX	existential there	*there*	RP	particle	*up, off*
FW	foreign word	*noire*	SYM	symbol	*+, %*
IN	preposition or sub-conj	*of, in*	TO	"to"	*to*
JJ	adjective	*small*	UH	interjection	*oops, oh*
JJR	adj., comparative	*smaller*	VB	verb, base form	*fly*
JJS	adj., superlative	*smallest*	VBD	verb, past tense	*flew*
LS	list item marker	*1, one*	VBG	verb, gerund	*flying*
MD	modal	*can, could*	VBN	verb, past participle	*flown*
NN	noun, sing. or mass	*dog*	VBP	verb, non-3sg pres	*fly*
NNS	noun, plural	*dogs*	VBZ	verb, 3sg pres	*flies*
NNP	proper noun, singular	*London*	WDT	wh-determiner	*which, that*
NNPS	proper noun, plural	*Azores*	WP	wh-pronoun	*who, what*
PDT	predeterminer	*both, lot of*	WP$	possessive wh-	*whose*
POS	possessive ending	*'s*	WRB	wh-adverb	*where, how*
PRP	personal pronoun	*he, she*			

treebanks. As a result of the annotation, corpora represent a valuable source for large-scale grammatical analyses and can, for instance, provide insights into the frequency of words or the likelihood of a particular part of speech sequence (e.g., how often a noun occurs after a verb). Hence, corpora also play an important role for the development of automatic language processing tools such as taggers and parsers. Using the annotations of corpora, taggers can, for instance, compute the probability of an ambiguous word to occur with a particular part of speech.

To enable the processing of part of speech annotation in an automated fashion, corpora are based on a so-called tag set, i.e., a set of codes which are used to refer to the different parts of speech. Although many tag sets are very similar (e.g., the tag *NN* usually refers to a noun), there exist also notable differences. In order to avoid confusions, we consistently apply the tag set of the *Penn Treebank*. The Penn Treebank is a collection of corpora from different languages, which is frequently employed for training parsers and taggers and often discussed in linguistic literature [216, p. 412],[70, p. 241],[170, p. 404]. Hence, we adopt the Penn Treebank tag set for encoding parts of speech. Table 2.2 gives an overview of the Penn Treebank tag set and provides short examples for each tag. Especially the tags for the main lexical classes including verbs, nouns, adjectives, and adverbs can be easily remembered as they follow a consistent pattern. The first two letters of the tag are used to refer to the base form and the third letter indicates the specific word form. For example, the tag *VB* denotes the base form of a verb, while *VBD* and *VBN* indicate the simple and the past participle form of a verb. Accordingly, tags starting with *NN* denote nouns, tags starting with *JJ* indicate adjectives, and tags beginning with *RB* represent adverbs.

Table 2.3 Examples of Linguistic Corpora

Name	Language	Size in Words	Main Sources
Open American National Corpus (OANC)	English	ca. 14 million	books, academic journals, conversion transcripts
Brown Corpus	English	ca. 1 million	books, newspapers, scientific articles, other documents
Corpus del Español Actual (CEA)	Spanish	ca. 540 million	documents from the European parliament and the United Nations, Wikipedia
Tiger Corpus	German	ca. 900,000	newspapers
Floresta	Portuguese	ca. 1.6 million	newspapers

Annotated text corpora are available in various languages and are, in many cases, publicly available. Table 2.3 gives an overview of five prominent corpora from different languages: the English *OANC* [157], the English *Brown Corpus* [119], the Spanish *CEA* [314], the German *Tiger Corpus* [51], and the Portuguese *Floresta Corpus* [16]. The data from Table 2.3 illustrates that there exists a significant spectrum with regard to the size. However, a bigger size of the corpus does not necessarily imply that the corpus is generally better suited for linguistic analyses. Depending on the task, it is also important to consider the text sources of the corpus. For instance, grammatical constructions like imperatives are not very likely to occur in newspaper articles. Hence, the analysis of a transcribed spoken dialogue with a newspaper-based corpus might not be entirely fruitful. Accordingly, different aspects need to be considered when selecting a corpus for building or training natural language analysis tools.

2.3.2 Part-of-Speech Tagging

Part-of-speech tagging (or *tagging*) is the process of assigning a part of speech to each word in a given text [170, p. 133]. The input for a tagging algorithm is a set of strings and a tag set, specifying the encoding for the different parts of speech. The output of the algorithm is a single tag for each word and for each punctuation mark.[2] To illustrate the concept of part-of-speech tagging, consider the following output of a part-of-speech tagger for the sentence *Process the customer data*:

   Process/VB the/DT customer/NN data/NNS ./.

---

[2] For punctuation marks it is important to differentiate between part-of-word punctuation (as in abbreviations) and end-of-sentence punctuation (period, exclamation mark, etc.). This task is typically performed in the context of the so-called *tokenization* and is not further discussed in the context of this book.

Table 2.4 Tags Returned by the EngCG Tagger (adapted from [170, p. 138])

Word	Returned Tags
Pavlov	**NNP**
had	**VBD** / VBN
shown	**VBN**
that	ADV / DT / WDT / **CS**

For a human it is quite apparent that we face an imperative sentence instructing a person to process the data of the customer. In fact, the automatic assignment of part of speech tags to the words in this sentence is not trivial. One challenge is to assign the correct part of speech tag to the ambiguous word *process*. It could be a verb (as in *to process the data*) or a noun (as in *the process is efficient*). The overall challenge of part-of-speech tagging is to resolve such ambiguities. In general, part-of-speech tagging algorithms can be subdivided into two main categories: rule-based approaches and stochastic approaches [170, p. 135]. In the following paragraphs, we explain the main concepts of each approach.

Rule-based taggers are based on a large set of hand-written disambiguation rules. This means that rule-based taggers do not rely on statistics, but eliminate ambiguous cases by referring to predetermined rules. The work on rule-based tagging mainly builds on three approaches from the sixties and seventies [144, 183, 137]. However, today rule-based approaches employ much bigger rule sets and more comprehensive dictionaries [170, p. 135-137]. The basic architecture of a rule-based tagging algorithm is a two-staged approach. In the first stage, a dictionary is consulted to derive a list of potential part-of-speech tags for each word. In the second stage, the rule set is used to reduce the set of potential parts of speech to a single tag. To illustrate this concept, consider the following phrase:

Pavlov had shown ...

Table 2.4 shows the (simplified) result of the first stage as returned by the rule-based *EngCG tagger* [326, 174]. The correct tags for each word are highlighted using bold font. From these results we can learn that the words *Pavlov* and *shown* can be undoubtedly assigned to a single part of speech. That is because the consulted dictionary only contains one possible part of speech entry for these words. By contrast, *had* and *that* are ambiguous cases, which can be potentially assigned to multiple parts of speech. For example, the word form *had* of the verb *have* may represent the simple past or also the past participle form. The word *that* even suffers from a higher degree of ambiguity. Theoretically, *that* can be employed as adverb (ADV), as determiner (DT), as pronoun (WDT), and as complementizer (CS). To infer that *had* represents a simple past form and the word *that* is used as a complementizer, the rules of the tagger are employed. In total, the EngCG tagger is based

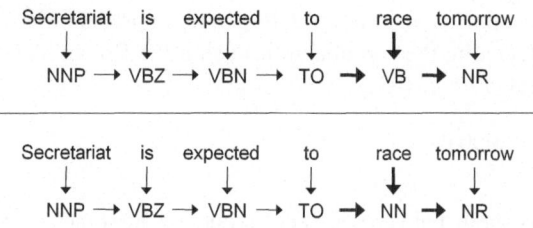

Fig. 2.6 Two Possible Tag Sequences for an Example Sentence, adapted from [170, p. 143]

on 1100 hand-written disambiguation rules. For example, the following (simplified) rule is concerned with deciding about the adverb tag of the word *that* [170, p. 138]:

Input: 'that'
if

(+1 JJ/ADV/QUANT)	/* *If next word is an adjective, adverb, or quantifier,*
(+2 SENT-LIM)	/* *the following is a sentence boundary, and*
(NOT -1 SVOC/J)	/* *the previous word is not a verb taking adjectives as object complements (like 'consider' in 'I consider that odd.')*

then eliminate non-ADV tags
else eliminate ADV tags

   As a result of the application of such disambiguation rules, the set of potential tags for each word can be reduced to a single tag. In this way, rule-based taggers resolve ambiguities and accordingly accomplish the tagging of a given sentence.

   As opposed to rule-based approaches, *stochastic taggers* use statistical methods to compute the best part of speech tag for a given word and a given context. Therefore, stochastic parsers are trained on large corpora such as the OANC, the Brown Corpus, or the Penn Treebank, for instance. Prominent examples for stochastic taggers can be found, for instance, in [93, 69, 80]. One particular and frequently employed stochastic algorithm for part-of-speech tagging is the hidden Markov model (HMM). Since the HMM tagger is well-suited for illustrating the stochastic approach to part-of-speech tagging, we briefly discuss the general approach of HMM taggers. The general strategy of HMM taggers is to compute the most likely sequence of part-of-speech tags for a given sentence [47, p. 71]. As example, consider the two possible interpretations of the sentence *Secretariat is expected to race tomorrow* that are illustrated in Figure 2.6.

   Each arc in Figure 2.6 denotes a probability. In particular, arcs connecting a word and a part of speech tag represent the probability of the word to occur with that specific part of speech. Arcs connecting two part-of-speech tags are referring to the probability of these tags to appear in a sequence. The bold arcs mark the differing probabilities in the two examples. Apparently, the challenge in this example is to decide whether *race* is representing a noun or a verb. To resolve this ambiguity, the HMM tagger compares the three highlighted probabilities: the sequence probabilities $P(NN \mid TO)$ and $P(VB \mid TO)$, the lexical likelihood of *race* being a noun

$P(race \mid NN))$ or verb $P(race \mid VB)$, and the sequence probabilities $P(NR \mid NN)$ and $P(NR \mid VB)$. Calculating these probabilities using the Brown Corpus, we face the following numbers [170, p. 143]:

$$P(NN \mid TO) = .00047$$
$$P(VB \mid TO) = .83$$

These numbers show that verbs are approximately 500 times more likely to occur after the word *to* than nouns. However, looking at the lexical probabilities of *race*, we learn that *race* is more likely to to be used as a noun:

$$P(race \mid NN)) = .00057$$
$$P(race \mid VB)) = .00012$$

The lexical probabilities of *race* emphasize that considering lexical probabilities in isolation is not necessarily very informative. Although *race* is in general more likely to represent a noun, it may still play the role of a verb. In order to derive a complete picture, we have a look at the sequence probabilities for the following word:

$$P(NR \mid NN) = .0012$$
$$P(NR \mid VB) = .0027$$

If we multiply the three probabilities, we obtain the overall likelihood of *race* occurring as noun and as verb for the given context:

$$P(NN \mid TO) * P(race \mid NN) * P(NR \mid NN) = .00000027$$
$$P(VB \mid TO) * P(race \mid VB) * P(NR \mid VB) = .00000000032$$

As a result, we learn that the occurrence of a verb tag is more likely than the occurrence of a noun tag. Hence, the HMM tagger correctly categorizes *race* as a verb.

Although the previously discussed examples either focus on the rule-based or on the stochastic component of taggers, it should be noted that many taggers actually represent hybrids. Also the predominately rule-based EngCG tagger includes probabilistic elements.

2.3.3 Natural Language Parsing

While tagging is concerned with determining a part of speech sequence, parsing aims at working out the grammatical structure of a sentence. Similar to tagging, parsing suffers from the ambiguous nature of language. To illustrate the specific challenges of automatically parsing natural language texts, consider the phrase structure trees depicted in Figure 2.7. Both trees represent valid structural interpretations of the sentence *The boy saw the man with the telescope*. However, they imply significant differences in the semantics. In the first case, shown by Figure 2.7(a), the boy used a telescope to see the man. In the second case, captured by Figure 2.7(b),

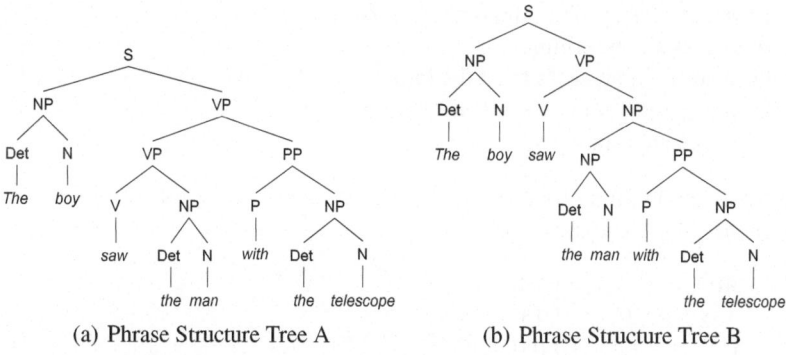

(a) Phrase Structure Tree A   (b) Phrase Structure Tree B

Fig. 2.7 Illustration of Structural Ambiguity, adapted from [126, p. 149]

the boy did not use the telescope, but saw a man who was in the possession of a telescope. This example illustrates that sentences can be structurally ambiguous and that the resolution of such ambiguities is not a straightforward task (sometimes not even for humans).

In order to resolve structural ambiguities, many parsers are based on probabilistic models of syntax [159, p. 237]. Building on such models, it is possible to assign probabilities to parse trees and accordingly decide which parse tree is more appropriate. The most commonly employed syntax model in this context is the probabilistic context-free grammar (PCFG) [170, p. 459]. A PCFG is a probabilistic augmentation of a context-free grammar (CFG) which consists of a set of symbols representing words or phrase structures, and a set of production rules [170, pp. 387-388]. Each of the production rules expresses how symbols of the language can be combined. For example, the following rule expresses that a sentence consists of a noun and a verb phrase.

S → NP VP

The symbols of a CFG are divided into two classes. Those symbols that represent words in the corresponding language are called *terminal symbols*. Symbols expressing groups or generalizations of terminals are referred to as *non-terminal symbols*. In each context-free rule, the left-hand side consists of a single non-terminal symbol, while the right-hand side may contain one or more terminal and non-terminal symbols. In a PCFG, each context-free rule is further associated with a probability of its occurrence. Building on the formalization first introduced by Booth [50], we follow the definition of a PCFG from [170, p. 460]. Accordingly, we define a PCFG as follows.

Definition 2.1. (PCFG). A PCFG is a quadruple (N, Σ, R, S):

− N is a set of non-terminal symbols
− Σ is a set of terminal symbols that are disjoint from N

- R is a set of rules, each of the form $A \rightarrow \beta[p]$,
    where A is a non-terminal,
    β is a string of symbols from the infinite set of strings $(\Sigma \cup N)\star$,
    and p is a number between 0 and 1 expressing $P(\beta \mid A)$
- S is a designated start symbol

As an example for a set of PCFG definitions, consider the following production rules concerning a sentence.

$$S \rightarrow NP\ VP \qquad [.80]$$
$$S \rightarrow Aux\ NP\ VP \qquad [.15]$$
$$S \rightarrow VP \qquad [.05]$$

From these rules we can learn that a sentence can be composed of a noun phrase and a verb phrase, of an auxiliary verb, a noun phrase, and a verb phrase, or also of a verb phrase only. However, if a given sentence is structurally ambiguous, the probabilities allow the parser to select the most likely option. For a complete parse tree T the probability is accordingly given by the product of the probabilities of the n production rules which result from the expansion of all non-terminal nodes. If we refer to each rule i with $LHS_i \rightarrow RHS_i$, the total probability can be expressed as follows [170, p. 462]:

$$P(T,S) = \prod_{i=1}^{n} P(RHS_i \mid LHS_i) \qquad (2.1)$$

To illustrate the application of this procedure, consider the two parse trees and the according production rules of the sentence *Book the dinner flight* in Figure 2.8. The left parse tree corresponds to the meaning of *booking a flight* that *serves dinner*, while the right parse tree represents the senseless meaning of *booking a flight* on behalf of *the dinner*. As both represent theoretically possible parse trees, a natural language parser consequently has to decide about the likeliness of the given options. Multiplying the probabilities of the production rules according to formula 2.1, we obtain the total probabilities for the left (T_{left}) and the right parse tree (T_{right}):

$$P(T_{left}) = .05 * .20 * .20 * .20 * .75 * .30 * .60 * .10 * .40 = \mathbf{2.2 \times 10^{-6}}$$
$$P(T_{right}) = .05 * .10 * .20 * .15 * .75 * .75 * .30 * .60 * .10 * .40 = \mathbf{6.1 \times 10^{-7}}$$

The calculation shows that the probability of the left parse tree is much higher than the probability of the right tree. Hence, the parser would correctly choose the left tree as the correct parse of the sentence.

In order to facilitate such an accurate computation, a parser needs to be trained accordingly. That means that the rules as well as the assigned probabilities need to be learned. This is typically accomplished by training parsers on treebanks containing hand-labeled trees. The variety of PCFG-based parsers is huge and many of them can be freely obtained online. Prominent examples include the Collins' Parser [72], the Berkeley Parser [258], the Charniak & Johnson's Parser [65], and the Standford Parser [181, 182].

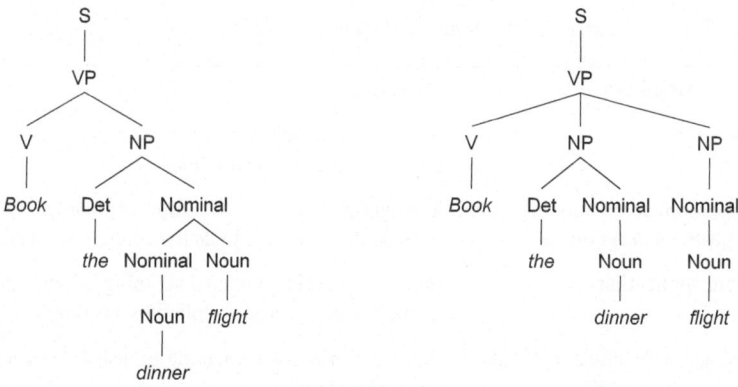

	Rules	P		Rules	P
S	⟩ VP	.05	S	→ VP	.05
VP	→ Verb NP	.20	VP	→ Verb NP NP	.10
NP	→ Det Nominal	.20	NP	→ Det Nominal	.20
Nominal	→ Nominal Noun	.20	NP	→ Nominal	.15
Nominal	→ Noun	.75	Nominal	→ Noun	.75
			Nominal	→ Noun	.75
Verb	→ book	.30	Verb	→ book	.30
Det	→ the	.60	Det	→ the	.60
Noun	→ dinner	.10	Noun	→ dinner	.10
Noun	→ flights	.40	Noun	→ flights	.40

Fig. 2.8 Two Possible Parse Trees for an Ambiguous Sentence and the According Production Rules, adapted from [170, p. 462]

2.3.4 WordNet

WordNet is a lexical database for the English language [232, 233]. It organizes nouns, verbs, adjectives, and adverbs into sets of synonyms, so-called *synsets*, each representing a distinct concept. The synsets are linked via several semantic and lexical relationships. As a result, WordNet represents a net of meaningful related words and concepts. In total, version 3.0 of the database contains 155,287 words which are grouped into 117,659 synsets.

To illustrate the concept of WordNet, reconsider the previously discussed noun *application*. Looking up *application* in WordNet, we can identify seven different synsets containing this word. That is because *application* is homonymous and has, according to WordNet, seven different meanings. Table 2.5 shows the according WordNet entries for the noun *application*. In addition to the members of the synset, WordNet also provides a short description for each synset. Accordingly, we can learn that *application* cannot only be used in the sense of a *job application* (first synset) or a *computer application* (second synset), but also in the sense of a *lotion* (third synset) or for the *act of bringing something to bear* as, e.g., when we *apply*

Table 2.5 WordNet Entries for the Noun *application*

No.	Synset Members	Description
1	application	a verbal or written request for assistance or employment or admission to a school
2	application, application program, applications programme	a program that gives a computer instructions that provide the user with tools to accomplish a task
3	lotion, application	liquid preparation having a soothing or antiseptic or medicinal action when applied to the skin
4	application, practical application	the act of bringing something to bear / using it for a particular purpose
5	application, coating, covering	the work of applying something
6	application, diligence	a diligent effort
7	application	the action of putting something into operation

statistical methods (fourth synset). The WordNet entries for *application* emphasize the necessity of the synset concept. Since almost every word can be used with different meanings, not single words, but rather a particular meaning is the central concept of WordNet. Each meaning is represented by a set of interchangeable words. Thus, if we use *application* in the sense of meaning three, we can employ *lotion* as a synonym. By contrast, if we use it according to meaning number five, we have to use *coating* or *covering*.

Most synsets and also individual words are linked via relationships. In the context of WordNet the relationships between synsets are referred to as *semantic relationships* and relations between words are called *lexical relationships*. The distinction between both is necessary as some relations exist between synsets while other solely exist between words. For instance, the previously discussed relationships such as hypernymy or meronymy are defined between synsets. By contrast, antonymy (the opposite of a word) is defined between words. That is because the antonymy relation does not apply to all members of the synset. As example, consider the words *little* and *small*. Both are part of the same synset, however, the antonym of *little* is given by *big* whereas the antonym of *small* is given by *large*. Another example for a lexical relationship is the derivation relation. It connects words with the same root such as *invent* and *inventor*.

In general, the types of available relationships depend on the part of speech of the synset. The semantic relationships for *nouns* include hyponomy, hypernomy, meronymy, and holonymy. For example, consider the word *finger*. Selecting the synset of *finger* which represents the meaning of a *member of the hand*, we can identify four semantic relationships pointing to a variety of different synsets. Table 2.6 gives an overview of the semantic relations of *finger*. Using the hyponymy relation, we can derive more specific words for *finger* such as the *index finger* or the

Table 2.6 Semantic Noun Relations in WordNet (for the Synset *finger*)

Relationship	Related Synsets
Hyponymy	{thumb, pollex}, {index, index finger, forefinger}, {ring finger, annualry}, {middle finger}, {little finger, pinkie, pinky}
Hypernymy	{digit, dactyl}, {extremity}
Meronymy	{pad}, {fingertip}, {fingernail}, {knuckle, knuckle joint}
Holonymy	{hand, manus, mitt, paw}

Table 2.7 Semantic Verb Relations in WordNet

Relationship	Example
Hypernymy	{fly, wing} → {travel, go, move, locomote}
Troponymy	{fly, wing} → {soar}, {fly, wing} → {hover}
Entailment	{snore, saw wood, saw logs} → {sleep, kip, slumber, log Z's}

thumb. With the hypernymy relation, we learn that *digit* and *extremity* are more general terms for *finger*. Using the meronymy relation, we can infer the subcomponents of a finger. WordNet returns synsets including the words *pad*, *fingertip*, and *fingernail*. Finally, the holonym relation returns those synsets in which finger plays the role of a constituting element. Accordingly, WordNet provides a synset containing the word *hand*.

For *verbs*, the semantic relationships include hypernymy, troponymy, and entailment. Identically to nouns, a hypernym of a verb is a more general description of the considered word. For example, the verbs *to move* and *to travel* represent hypernyms of the verb *to fly*. The troponymy relationship can be best compared with the hyponomy relationship between nouns. Hence, a troponym is a more specific verb. Accordingly, the verbs *to soar* or *to hover* represent troponyms of *to fly*. The entailment relationship refers to the fact that some activities directly imply the execution of other activities. For instance, *snoring* entails the activity of *sleeping*. Hence, *to sleep* is in the set of entailments of *to snore*. Table 2.7 summarizes the semantic verb relations from WordNet.

To access the contents of WordNet, users are provided with different options. In general, WordNet is freely available online and can be downloaded from the website of Princeton University.[3] One of the easiest possibilities to access WordNet is the use of the online interface on the WordNet homepage.[4] For incorporating WordNet in self-developed prototypes, there exists a large set of application interfaces (APIs) for a variety of different programming languages. In the context of this book, we use

---

[3] http://wordnet.princeton.edu/wordnet/download/
[4] http://wordnetweb.princeton.edu/perl/webwn

WordNet for supporting the analysis of natural language in process models. In order to be able to precisely refer to the specific WordNet concepts such as synsets and relations, we subsequently provide a formal definition of the WordNet dictionary. The definition is aimed for representing a formal reference point and focuses on the core aspects of WordNet. In particular, we abstract from the gloss information and the example sentences that are defined for each synset as we do not make use of them in the techniques defined in this book. Building on the sense formalization in [241], we formalize a WordNet dictionary as follows.

Definition 2.2. (WordNet Dictionary). A WordNet Dictionary $D = (W, S, P, L, R, \mu, \lambda, \sigma)$ consists of three sets W, S, and P, a binary relation $L \subseteq W \times P \times W \times P$, a binary relation $R \subseteq S \times S$, a function $\mu : W \times P \to \mathcal{P}(S)$, a function $\lambda : R \to \{antonym, derivation\}$, and a function $\sigma : S \to \{homonym, hypernym, meronym, holonym, troponym, entailment\}$ such that

- W is a finite set of words.
- S is a finite set of synsets.
- $P = \{v, n, a, r\}$ is the set of parts of speech (respectively verbs, nouns, adjectives, and adverbs).
- L is a finite set of lexical relationships between words.
- R is a finite set of semantic relationships between synsets.
- μ is a function assigning a word with a particular part of speech to a number of synsets. We write $\mathcal{P}(S)$ for denoting the powerset of synsets.
- λ is a function categorizing a lexical relation $l \in L$ as antonym or derivation.
- σ is a function categorizing a semantic relation $s \in S$ as homonym, hypernym, meronym, holonym, troponym, or entailment.

Building on this definition we further define several subsets which help to adequately characterize WordNet related concepts.

Definition 2.3. For a WordNet Dictionary $D = (W, S, P, L, R, \mu, \lambda, \sigma)$ we define the following subsets:

- $W_v = \{(w, p) \in dom(\mu) \mid w \in W \wedge p = v\}$ being the set of verbs,
  $W_n = \{(w, p) \in dom(\mu) \mid w \in W \wedge p = n\}$ being the set of nouns,
  $W_a = \{(w, p) \in dom(\mu) \mid w \in W \wedge p = a\}$ being the set of adjectives, and
  $W_n = \{(w, p) \in dom(\mu) \mid w \in W \wedge p = n\}$ being the set of adverbs.
- $W^h = \{(w, p) \in dom(\mu) \mid p \in P \wedge \mid \mu(w, p) \mid \geq 1\}$ being the set of homonymous words.
- $W^m = \{(w, p) \in dom(\mu) \mid p \in P \wedge \mu(w, p) \mid = 1\}$ being the set of monosemous words.

Besides the English WordNet, there also exist lexical databases for other languages. Examples include GermaNet for German [142], WOLF for French [291], and EuroWordNet covering multiple languages such as Dutch, Italian, and Spanish [325]. In addition, there are also more focused linguistic resources available that complement the functionality of WordNet. For example, VerbNet [298] consists of a hierarchy of English verbs based on the English verb classes proposed by Levin [207]. The resource FrameNet [29] provides a collection of semantic frames that, amongst others, define how linguistic concepts are related to events or participants. For instance, the concept of *cooking* usually involves a person that is doing the cooking (the cook). As this book is mostly focusing on syntactic aspects of natural language, WordNet provides sufficient support for implementing the desired functionality.

2.4 Natural Language Processing and Process Models

Due to the free availability of NLP tools such as taggers, parsers, and the lexical database WordNet, natural language processing is applied in a multitude of domains. Since process models contain various natural language information, this also applies to the field of process modeling. In order to develop a precise understanding of the state of the art and the current challenges of NLP in process models, this section investigates this intersection in detail. Recognizing that process models share a lot of commonalities with conceptual models in general, we first take a broader perspective and review existing literature on NLP and conceptual models. Against the background of this literature review, we subsequently discuss the research challenge which is associated with analyzing natural language in process models.

In general, the application of NLP techniques in conceptual modeling often aims for improving the design of these models. In particular, the literature reveals two main directions that have been considered for accomplishing this goal: approaches applying NLP on *external text material* to infer useful information about the design of the model, and approaches applying NLP on the text of the *model elements* in order to facilitate different kinds of analyses. The differences between the two directions become clear if we consider how NLP techniques are employed in each scenario.

Many of the approaches applying NLP techniques on *external text material* aim for the automatic inference of conceptual models. Examples include the (semi-) automatic creation of process models [125, 19, 132, 131, 305], conceptual dependency diagrams [130], entity-relationship models [135, 251], and UML diagrams [28, 89, 90, 236]. Some authors also propose inference approaches which are not limited to a single model type but can be adapted for different kinds of conceptual models [114, 234]. Works which are not concerned with the extraction of conceptual models typically aim for supporting the model designer in different ways. For instance, Richards et al. propose a technique for visualizing natural language requirements in order to better compare multiple viewpoints [284]. Bolloju et al. go a step further by introducing a technique which automatically indicates inconsistencies with requirement documents [49]. Lahtinen and Peltonen complement UML tools with a speech interface such that the conceptual models can be easily edited via spoken language [198]. In some cases, the extraction of the conceptual models is only an intermediate step: Tseng and Chen propose a methodology for mapping natural language constructs into SQL statements via the inference of UML class diagrams [321]. Similarly, Tseng et al. map natural language constructs into relational algebra via the extraction of entity-relationship models [320]. The important advantage that all these works have in common is that they can apply standard NLP tools such as taggers, parsers, or speech recognition to infer the required information from written or verbal sources. Because such sources usually contain grammatically rich sentences, the authors obtain satisfying results with this strategy.

Techniques applying NLP tools on *a conceptual model itself* have to meet different requirements. Typically, conceptual models do not contain full and grammatically correct sentences. As a result, authors restrain from employing traditional NLP tools as parsers and taggers. Some authors explicitly recommend to avoid the application of NLP tools because of these issues [35, 187]. However, there are several attempts to make use of the natural language in conceptual models. For instance, Becker et al. propose an approach for enforcing naming conventions in process models [38, 37]. Other authors also look at the terminology used in conceptual models to improve the overall quality [52, 192, 191, 118, 324]. Going beyond the syntactic quality dimension of process models, Gruhn and Laue employ a Prolog based algorithm that is capable of identifying semantic errors in process model labels [138]. Bögl et al. use rules to perform a semantic annotation of EPCs in order to detect common modeling practices. For achieving the best possible semantic congruence with the modeled domain, some authors use the natural language of models to generate human-readable texts. The first methods that introduced the text generation for conceptual models were Object-Role Modeling (ORM) and its predecessor NIAM [323, 243]. A key feature of ORM is a direct mapping from data models to natural language text called *verbalization*. Other authors introduced natural language generation for UML class diagrams [229], object models [202], and conceptual models in general [81]. While many works applying NLP in conceptual models are concerned with model quality, there are also approaches aiming at discovering knowledge that is implicitly captured by the models. Examples include the identification of activity correspondences between models [105, 36], the discovery of services [186], and the elicitation of process patterns [128].

Table 2.8 summarizes the discussed approaches from both use-case classes. The double line separates the approaches applying NLP on text material (first half) from those applying NLP directly on the models (second half). The table highlights that NLP tools for eliciting the syntactical structure of sentences such as parser and taggers are only employed by approaches that work on text material. In fact, none of the previously mentioned approaches applying NLP on model elements, makes use of parsers or taggers. Instead, they either assume a certain format of the language in the model [229, 81, 202] or they ignore the syntax. In the latter case, the approaches typically remove stop words such as articles and conjunctions and then use the remaining words for their analyses. While this might be sufficient for some use cases, it yet inhibits the precise usage of natural language in conceptual models. For example, consider the process model activities *Create Invoice for Customer* and *Invoice Creation for Customer*. Apparently, both activities convey the same meaning. However, the syntactical form is different. While the first text label contains an imperative verb in the beginning, the second label does not contain a verb at all.

Table 2.8 Overview of Approaches Applying NLP

Approach	Author	NLP Tools
Construction of Models		
BPMN Model from Text	Friedrich et al. [125]	Parser, WordNet
BPMN Model from Group Stories	Goncalves et al. [19]	Parser
BPMN Model from Textual Sources	Ghose et al. [132, 131]	Parser
BPMN Model from Use Cases	Sinha et al. [305]	Parser
Dependency Diagram from Text	Gangopadhyay [130]	Parser
ER-Model from Text	Gomez et al. [135]	Parser
ER-Model from Text	Omar et al. [251]	Tagger, Parser
UML Class Model from Text	Bajwa & Choudhary [28]	Tagger, Parser
UML Model from Text	More & Phalnikar [236]	Tagger, Parser
UML Model from Text	Deeptimahanti & Babar [89, 90]	Parser, WordNet
Conceptual Model from Requirements	Fliedl et al. [115]	Tagger, Parser
Conceptual Model from Requirements	Montes et al. [234]	Tagger, Parser
Designer Support		
Visualization of Use Case Descriptions	Richards et al. [284]	Parser
Consistency of Object Models	Bolloju et al. [49]	Parser
Speech Recognition for UML	Lahtinen & Peltonen [198]	Speech Analysis
Construction of Formal Specification		
SQL Statements	Tseng and Chen [321]	Parser
Relational Algebra	Tseng at al. [320]	Parser
Quality Assurance		
Term Inconsistency Detection in PMs	Koschmider & Blanchard [191]	WordNet
User Support for PMs	Koschmider et al. [192]	WordNet
Linguistic Consistency Checking of CMs	van der Vos et al. [324]	WordNet
Naming Convention Enforcement in PMs	Becker et al. [38, 37]	Domain Thesauri
Reducing Linguistic Variations in PMs	Breuker et al. [52]	WordNet
Semantic Annotation of BPMN PMs	Francescomarino & Tonella [118]	WordNet
Detection of Semantic Errors in EPCs	Gruhn and Laue [138]	Proprietary
Semantic Annotation of EPCs	Bögl et al. [48]	Proprietary
Generation of Text		
Generation from UML Class Diagrams	Meziane et al. [229]	WordNet
Generation from Object Models	Lavoie et al. [202]	Proprietary
Generation from Data Models	Verheijen & van Bekkum [323]	Proprietary
Generation from Data Models	Nijssen & Halpin [243]	Proprietary
Generation from Conceptual Models	Dalianis [81]	Proprietary
Information Elicitation		
Service Discovery from CMs	Knackstedt et al. [186]	WordNet
Detection of Process Patterns	Gacitua-Decar & Pahl [128]	WordNet
Similarity Measurement in PMs	Ehrig et al. [105]	WordNet
Process Activity Mappings	Becker et al. [36]	Proprietary

Nevertheless, both activities instruct to create an invoice. We simply observe different grammatical representations of the same meaning. This example illustrates that the syntactical structure of a label as well as the role of each word is a valuable source of information. A sophisticated analysis of process models can only be accomplished if we are able to address the problem of recognizing the syntactical structure of process model element labels.

2.5   Summary

In this chapter, we provided an introduction into the field of linguistics. In particular, we gave an overview of the different linguistic schools of thought and discussed the relevant concepts from theoretical linguistics. As this book is solely concerned with written language, we accordingly focused on the branches of morphology, syntax, and semantics. In addition, we introduced the foundations of natural language processing as required for the automated analysis of natural language texts. Specifically, we discussed the different approaches to part-of-speech tagging and parsing and highlighted the differences between rule-based and stochastic approaches. Moreover, we emphasized the role of text corpora and WordNet as valuable resources for natural language text analysis. Using corpora, it is possible, for example, to train taggers and parsers and to infer information on word usage and frequencies. WordNet provides users with the possibility to lookup different word meanings, to determine lexical relations like synonymy, and to infer semantic relations such as hypernomy and holonymy. Finally, we investigated the intersection between research on natural language processing and conceptual modeling. The review revealed that there are currently no approaches that can adequately deal with the syntactic structures of element labels. Existing approaches either ignore aspects related to natural language or apply heuristics to infer relevant words. Against the background of this research gap, we turn to the analysis of natural language in processes models in the next chapter.

Chapter 3
Parsing and Annotating Process Model Elements

The aim of this book is to provide the means for exploiting and analyzing the linguistic information that is captured by process models. This chapter represents the first step in this direction by introducing a technique for automatically parsing and annotating process models. The technique can deal with the specific challenges of process model element labels and uses insights about grammatical structures and a tailored disambiguation algorithm to yield accurate results.

In order to highlight the challenges that need to be addressed by such an annotation technique, Section 3.1 reflects on the task of labeling and investigates the specific difficulties of applying NLP in process models. As the precise annotation requires a thorough understanding of the structure of process model element labels, Section 3.2 discusses typical grammatical patterns. Using the insights on these structures, Section 3.3 presents the annotation algorithms for activities, events, and gateways. Subsequently, in Section 3.4, we test the presented technique on three large process model collections from practice. Section 3.5 gives an outlook on how the annotation technique can be adapted to languages other than English. Finally, Section 3.6 summarizes the chapter.

3.1 Labeling of Process Model Elements

This section gives an overview of the activity of labeling in the context of process models. Section 3.1.1 introduces the general concept of labeling and illustrates its implications using a process model from practice. Then, Section 3.1.2 highlights the challenges that are associated with applying NLP in process models.

3.1.1 Concept of Labeling

In general, the activity of *labeling*, often also referred to as naming, is concerned with tagging an entity with natural language text. In process models, that is, amongst others, required for activities, events, and roles. In other conceptual models it is, for instance, necessary to provide names for features or goals. As an application

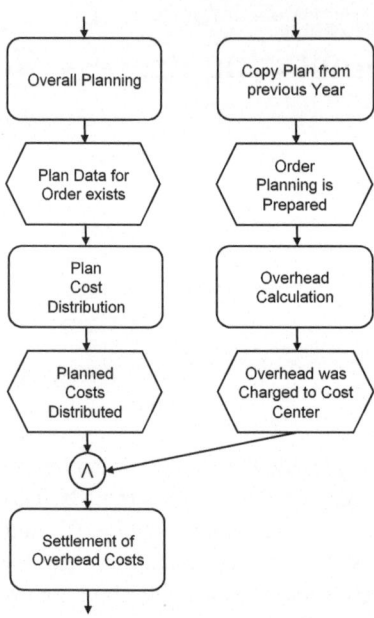

Fig. 3.1 Fragment from the SAP Reference Model

scenario outside the domain of conceptual modeling, consider the labeling of methods in source code of programming languages. A general characteristic of such labels is that they are subject to a certain degree of variation in terms of structure and wording. As natural languages provide various possibilities for expressing the same semantics, text labels may follow entirely different structures.

Figure 3.1 illustrates this problem for process models. It captures a part of a cost planning process from the SAP Reference Model [176]. Analyzing the model, one can see that it is easy to misinterpret the label *Plan Cost Distribution*. If the preceding and succeeding events were ignored, a model reader might erroneously conclude that this activity instructs to *plan* the *cost distribution*. As the preceding activity instructs to conduct the *overall planning*, and the activity at the top right uses the verb *copy* in the first position of the label, it is not unlikely that *plan* is perceived as action. However, as *Plan Cost Distribution* simply follows a different style, the label does not start with a verb, but with the business object *plan cost*. Another activity starting with a business object is given by *Overhead Calculation*. For the activity *Settlement of Overhead Costs*, we observe an additional style. Here, the action is provided as a noun in the first position of the label. Altogether, this example demonstrates the high ambiguity that stems from the style of labeling. In one case the first word is a verb instructing the reader to perform an action, in other cases the first word is a noun representing a business object.

Table 3.1 Overview of Approaches Concerned with Syntactic Aspects of Labeling

Approach	Author
Studies on the Effect of Labeling	
Activity Labeling in Process Models	Mendling et al. [225]
Identifier Naming in Source Code	Lawrie et al. [203]
Guidelines for Labeling Elements	
Process Models	Mendling et al. [224]
Process Models	Sharp and McDermott [301]
Process Models	MIT Process Handbook [214]
Use Case Diagrams	Cockburn [71]
Feature Diagrams	Lee et al [205]
Goal Models	Rolland et al [287]
Ontologies	Schober et al. [296]
Java Source Code	Sun Microsystems [230]
Source Code	Relf [283]
Checking of Labeling Structures	
Naming Conventions Process Models	Becker et al. [38, 37]
Identifier Names in C++ Source Code	Duby et al. [101]
Identifier Names in Source Code	Deissenboeck and Pizka [91]

As a result of such arbitrary labeling practices, guidelines for process models typically recommend a verb-object labeling structure [301, 214, 224]. The negative effect of ignoring conventions has been demonstrated by Mendling et al. [225]. They showed that arbitrarily mixing labeling styles leads to a significant decrease of the understandability of a process model. Similarly, Lawrie et al. showed the negative influence of inadequate identifier naming on source code understandability [203]. The latter study highlights that the importance of proper labeling is not only recognized for process models. In fact, labeling recommendations can be also found for the elements of ontologies [296], the names of methods and classes in source code [230, 283], and many other conceptual models including use case diagrams [71], feature diagrams [205], and goal models [287]. The problem of such guidelines is that they are typically not fully respected in practice. Consequently, many authors introduced techniques for automatically enforcing such conventions. For instance, Becker et al. present a technique for automatically enforcing naming conventions for process model activities [38, 37]. However, they do not adequately deal with the problem of zero-derivation ambiguity. Hence, the structure of labels suffering from this phenomenon cannot be recognized correctly. The complexity of properly addressing ambiguity is also reflected by other contributions that are concerned with checking structural label aspects. For instance, techniques for enforcing source code conventions typically abstract from the accurate checking of the recommended verb-noun structure for methods [101, 91]. Deissenboeck and Pizka even explicitly admit that they cannot deal with the problem of zero-derivation [91]. As a consequence, none of the previously discussed approaches provides a solution to the problem of properly recognizing the syntactic structure of text labels. Table 3.1 gives a summarizing overview of the previously discussed work concerned with syntactic aspects of text labels.

3.1.2   Challenges for Analyzing Process Models Labels

The discussion of existing work addressing syntactic aspects of labeling and the review of approaches applying NLP in conceptual models in the last chapter illustrated that the automated analysis of the text structure in process models is associated with considerable challenges. Aiming for the automated annotation of process models, we have to address two main problems: the non-applicability of standard NLP tools and the linguistic complexity impeding the grammatical disambiguation of terms.

The *non-applicability of standard NLP tools* is mainly caused by the shortness of process model element labels. Typically, linguistic parsers employ statistical methods for computing the most likely part of speech using a manually pre-tagged corpus. Thus, they require a certain degree of context to perform well [181, 319]. Further, they are usually trained with corpora consisting of book texts and newspaper articles. Hence, corpora often do not contain the specific word sequences we find in process models. As a result, tagging algorithms do not have the possibility to find an according match in a corpus.

The *linguistic complexity* of the target language influences how well information can be extracted from short fragments like process model labels. As pointed out by McWhorter, the complexity of a language can be assessed from four different angles: phonology (sounds of the language), syntax (structure of the sentences), semantics (meaning of words), and morphology (structure of word forms) [221]. For the identification of parts of speech in process model elements, especially the morphological complexity is of major importance: the more complicated the morphological rules of the target language, the more different word forms are available to differentiate words and their parts of speech from each other. If a language is poor in terms of morphological changes, many words suffer from the zero-derivation ambiguity as discussed in Chapter 2. Examples are words like *the order* and *to order* or *the plan* and *to plan*. Particularly in English, this is a frequently occurring phenomenon. As the resolution of such cases requires an appropriate disambiguation, it is important to be aware of the morphological complexity of the target language. Different authors tried to adequately assess this characteristic with different metrics [177, 45, 73]. The bottom line is usually that English is one of the languages with the least morphological complexity. German and also Slavic languages can be found at the other end of the scale. For the analysis of process models this means that English is one of the biggest challenges. Especially for English, sophisticated disambiguation algorithms must be introduced.

Table 3.2 Activity Labeling Styles

Labeling Style	Core Structure	Example
Verb-Object VO	A(imperative) + O	Create invoice
Action-Noun AN(np)	O + A(noun)	Invoice creation
Action-Noun AN(of)	A(noun) + 'of' + O	Creation of invoice
Action-Noun AN(gerund)	A(gerund) + [article] + O	Creating invoice
Action-Noun AN(irregular)	*anomalous*	LIFO: Valuation: Pool level
Descriptive DES	[role] + A(3P) + O	Clerk creates invoice
No-Action NA	*anomalous*	Error

3.2 Process Model Element Styles

Considering the findings of the previous section, it becomes clear that the design of appropriate algorithms requires a thorough understanding of the use of natural language in process models. As pointed out in [225], every activity label can be characterized by three components: an action, a business object on which the action is performed, and an optional additional information fragment which is providing further details. As an example, consider the activity label *Forward Request to Insurance Department*. This label contains the action *forward*, the business object *request*, and the additional information fragment *to Insurance Department*. However, to gain a deep understanding of labeling practices across element types, we manually analyze three large process model collections from practice. In total, the collections include 1,450 models with almost 30,000 element labels. In addition, they cover different domains and vary with respect to labeling quality. For further details, please refer to Table 3.7. In the following, we focus on labeled elements with syntactical variations. Hence, we investigate activities, events, and gateways.

3.2.1 Activity Labeling Styles

The activity labeling styles can be categorized in four classes based on how the action is captured in the label. The focus on the action is particularly important for activity labels as they instruct the model reader to perform a business-related activity. Table 3.2 shows an overview of the observed activity labeling styles. It shows the core structure of each style and an example. Note that we abstract from additional information fragments such as *for customer* in the label *Create invoice for customer* and focus on the core structure consisting of action and business object.

In the first of the four classes, the action is given as a verb. In *verb-object* labels, the verb is given as an imperative verb in the beginning of the label, followed by the business object. As examples, consider *Create invoice* or *Notify Customer*.

In labels belonging to the second class, the action is captured as a noun. In particular, four different styles can be observed. The first is the *action-noun style (np)*. In such activities, the nominalized action is provided at the end of the label as in *Invoice creation*. Another frequent pattern is the *action-noun style (of)* where the preposition *of* is used to separate the nominalized action from the business object. As examples, consider *Creation of invoice* or *Notification of customer*. The *action-noun style (gerund)* contains a gerund in the beginning of the label as in *Creating invoice*. All labels which contain a nominalized action, but cannot be assigned to one of the three previously introduced styles, are categorized as *action-noun (irregular)*.

The third class contains the *descriptive labeling style*. In such labels, the provided action is a verb in the third person form. In many cases a role is mentioned in the beginning of the label. Examples are the labels *Clerk creates Invoice* or *Customer approves order*.

All labels which do not contain any action are assigned to the *no-action style*. Examples are usually given by single nouns such as *Error* or *Protocol*.

3.2.2   Event Labeling Styles

While activity labels instruct the reader to do something, event labels indicate a state. As this can be expressed in different ways, we derived five different event labeling styles. Four of them follow a regular structure. Note that some events are also labeled using activity styles. Nevertheless, as they have already been presented in the previous subsection we do not revisit them here.

Table 3.3 shows an overview of the observed event labeling styles. The first event labeling style is the *participle style*, which contains a business object followed by a participle verb. In some cases an auxiliary verb is inserted before the participle verb form. Examples are *Invoice created* or *Customer notified*. In general, the *modal style* is quite similar to the participle style. However, labels of the modal style always contain a modal verb such as *can*, *must*, or *shall*. This modal verb is then followed by an auxiliary and a participle verb as in *Invoice must be created*. Labels following the *adjective style* are characterized by an adjective at the end of the label. In some cases an auxiliary verb is used to obtain a correct sentence. Examples are *Invoice correct* or *Status is ok*. The last regular style is the *categorization style* that is characterized by the usage of two nouns that are associated with each other. As an example, consider the label *Customer is member*.

Besides these regular event labeling styles, we also observed *irregular* labels. In many cases these labels contain a single noun such as *Inquiry*.

3.2.3   Gateway Labeling Styles

The role of gateway labels is to properly indicate what kind of decision must be made in order to follow a particular path in a model. Hence, gateway labels usually

Table 3.3 Event Labeling Styles

Labeling Style	Core Structure	Example
Participle PS	O + [aux. verb] + A(participle)	Invoice created
Modal MS	O + A(modal verb construction)	Invoice must be created
Adjective AS	O + [aux. verb] + adjective	Invoice correct
Categorization CS	O + aux. verb + noun	Customer is member
Irregular	anomalous	Inquiry

Table 3.4 Gateway Labeling Styles

Labeling Style	Core Structure	Example
Participle-Question PQ	O + [aux. verb] + A(participle)	Invoice created?
Infinitive-Question IFQ	A(infintive) + O	Approve contract?
Adjective-Question AQ	O + [aux. verb] + adjective	Parts available?
Equation-Question EQ	O + logical construction + no.	Amount is greater than € 200?
Irregular	anomalous	Result?

end with a question mark to explicitly show that a decision must be made. From this analysis, we derived four regular gateway label patterns.

Table 3.4 shows an overview of the observed gateway labeling styles. Labels following the *participle-question style* can be considered to be participle state style labels with a question mark at the end. Accordingly, they consist of a business object which is followed by an action in the participle verb form. Examples are *Invoice created?* or *Customer notified?* The *infinitive-question style* is the question counterpart of the verb-object activity style. The infinitive verb is typically positioned in the first position of the label as in *Approve Contract?* Gateway labels of the *adjective-question style* are characterized by an adjective at the end of the label. Hence, they are the question counterpart of the adjective event style. As examples consider *Parts available?* or *ID valid?* While the previously introduced styles can be associated with event or activity styles, the *equation-question style* is gateway specific. Such labels contain a logical evaluable statement, in many cases by using logical operators such as '$>$' or '$<$'. An example is given by the label *Amount $>$ €200?* However, in some cases the logical operator is replaced by a verbal construct. Thus, the given example could be also written as *Amount is greater than €200?*

As with all investigated model elements, some gateway labels also do not follow a regular structure. Such *irregular* labels usually contain a single word such as *Result?*

Table 3.5 Non-Terminal Symbol Set of the Process Model Grammar

Symbol	Description	Symbol	Description
NP	noun phrase	CD	cardinal number
VP	verb phrase	QM	question mark
PP	prepositional phrase	L_{VO}	label, verb-object style
VB	verb, base form	L_{AN}^{np}	label, action-noun (np) style
VBG	verb, gerund	L_{AN}^{of}	label, action-noun (of) style
VBZ	verb, 3-sg	L_{AN}^{ing}	label, action-noun (ing) style
VBN	verb, past participle	L_{DES}	label, descriptive style
VBD	verb, simple past	L_{NA}	label, no-action style
VBP	verb, non-3-sg	L_{PS}	label, participle style
NN	noun, singular	L_{MS}	label, modal style
NNS	noun, plural	L_{AS}	label, adjective style
ADJ	adjective	L_{CS}	label, categorization style
DT	determiner	L_{PQ}	label, participle question
IN	preposition	L_{IFQ}	label, infinitive question
CC	coordinating conjunction	L_{AQ}	label, adjective question
MD	modal	L_{EQ}	label, equation question
REL	relational sign		

3.2.4 Labeling Style Formalization

Having discussed the existing labeling styles and some typical examples, it will be useful to describe the natural language contained by process models in a more formal manner. As discussed in Chapter 2, language can be described by the means of formal grammars such as the CFG. The advantage of such grammars is that they facilitate a precise and compact, yet comprehensive description of language. Hence, we provide a formal characterization of the language in process models. Following the CFG definition, the description of such a process model element grammar requires the specification of a set of non-terminal symbols, a set of terminal symbols that are disjoint from the latter, a set of CFG rules, and a designated start symbol.

Table 3.5 gives an overview of the employed non-terminal symbols. Where possible, we adapt the tags from the Penn Treebank tag set. For explicitly referring to punctuation and specific symbols, we additionally introduce the non-terminals QM for a question mark and REL for relational signs such as '$<$' or '$>$'. For defining the terminal symbols, we refer to the English vocabulary. As we do not want to make any assumptions on the words used in process models, we specify this set generically. By abstracting from rules assigning terminals to non-terminal symbols and by defining L as the start symbol, we can define a CFG grammar that formalizes the typical language phenomena in process models. Table 3.6 summarizes the comprised CFG rules.

It is important to note that this grammar definition does not cover all possible variations that may occur in process models; in particular, irregular styles are not captured. However, the grammar definition represents a compact formal overview

Table 3.6 Grammar of English Process Model Elements

Rules		Example / Explanation
NP	$\rightarrow$ NN | NNS	data, documents
NP	$\rightarrow$ DT NN | DT NNS	the data, the documents
NP	$\rightarrow$ NP CC NP	data and documents
PP	$\rightarrow$ IN NP	of the customer
NP	$\rightarrow$ NP PP	data of the customer
VP	$\rightarrow$ VBP | VBZ | VPD	checked, checks
NP	$\rightarrow L_{VO} \mid L_{AN} \mid L_{AN}^{ing} \mid L_{AN}^{of} \mid$ $L_{DES} \mid L_{NA}$	label can be activity label,
NP	$\rightarrow L_{PS} \mid L_{AS} \mid L_{MS} \mid L_{CS}$	event label,
NP	$\rightarrow L_{PQ} \mid L_{AQ} \mid L_{IQ} \mid L_{ES}$	or gateway label
L_{VO}	$\rightarrow$ VB | VB NP	verify, verify data of customer
L_{AN}^{np}	$\rightarrow$ NP	verification, data verification
L_{AN}^{ing}	$\rightarrow$ VBG | VBG NP	verifying, verifying data of customer
L_{AN}^{of}	$\rightarrow$ NN of NP	verification of data
L_{DES}	$\rightarrow$ VBZ | VBZ NP	verifies, verifies data of customer
L_{NA}	$\rightarrow$ NN	data
L_{PS}	$\rightarrow$ NP VBN | NP VP VBN	data of customer was verified
L_{MS}	$\rightarrow$ NP MD VB VBN	data of customer must be verified
L_{AS}	$\rightarrow$ NP ADJ | NP VP ADJ	data of customer is correct
L_{CS}	$\rightarrow$ NP VB NP	person is employee
L_{PQ}	$\rightarrow$ NP VBN QM | NP VP VBN QM	data of customer was verified?
L_{IFQ}	$\rightarrow$ VB NP QM	verify data?
L_{AQ}	$\rightarrow$ NP ADJ QM	data of customer is correct?
L_{EQ}	$\rightarrow$ NP VP CD QM | NP REL CD QM	data is greater than 100 MB, data $>$ 100 MB

capturing the majority of the language structures in process models. The presented grammar definition comprises three blocks. In the *first block*, we define the general legitimate grammar structures. We specify a set of rules for each non-terminal symbol. Where applicable, we use a horizontal line to compactly denote alternative rules. However, in order to maintain a structured presentation, we generally use multiple lines to define alternative rules for a non-terminal. As an example definition, consider the rules specified for a noun phrase (NP). In the first rule concerning the noun phrase, we specify that a noun phrase may consist of a singular or a plural noun. Further, we define that a noun phrase may also be composed of two noun phrases linked by a coordinating conjunction, or of a noun phrase and a preposition phrase. These definitions illustrate that CFG rules are also applied recursively. For example, the structure *NP CC NP PP* can be constructed from the rules *NP* $\rightarrow$ *NP PP* and *NP* $\rightarrow$ *NP CC NP*. The *second block* specifies the possible definitions for the start symbol *L*. Each line represents the assignments for a particular process model element type. The first line defines the activity label structures, the second the event label structures, and the third the gateway label structures. Finally, in the *third block*, we specify the actual grammatical structure of the different labeling styles. Following the same order as in the second block, we start with the activities, and subsequently define events and gateways.

3.3 Automatic Process Model Element Annotation

This section introduces a technique for the automatic annotation of process model elements. The basic rationale behind the approach is to assign a given label to one of the presented labeling styles. By using insights into the structure of the detected style, it is then possible to determine and annotate the label components. In the subsequent sections, we present the specific steps for the annotation of process model activities, events, and gateways. For each element class we accordingly discuss the two phases *style recognition* and *component derivation*.

3.3.1 Annotation of Activity Labels

Among the considered process model elements, activities represent the biggest challenge. Due to the fact that they typically capture the action in the base form of the verb, they most of all suffer from the zero-derivation ambiguity. In order to address this challenge, we design a specific approach that is tailored to the requirements of process model activities.

3.3.1.1 Labeling Style Recognition

To adequately and reliably recognize the style of process model activities, we introduce an algorithm exploiting the context of activity labels. In particular, we investigate four levels of context: 1) the activity label itself, 2) the process model containing the activity, 3) the process model collection, and 4) the knowledge on word frequencies (see Figure 3.2). These levels are organized in a sequence from the most local context towards most generic. The algorithm tries to classify an activity label starting from the most local context, i.e., the label, and broadening the context, once the previous level is insufficient. If required it takes more generic, yet increasingly uncertain information into account. The overall rationale of this approach is to resolve ambiguity by utilizing all available information from the process model collection. We assume that local information is more related to the considered activity and hence should be prioritized. Once the information from the model does not help to decide on the labeling style, we make a probabilistic decision based on linguistic features of the investigated word. Against this background, the labeling style recognition is organized into four subordinate stages.

- *Stage 1:* Label Analysis
- *Stage 2:* Model Analysis

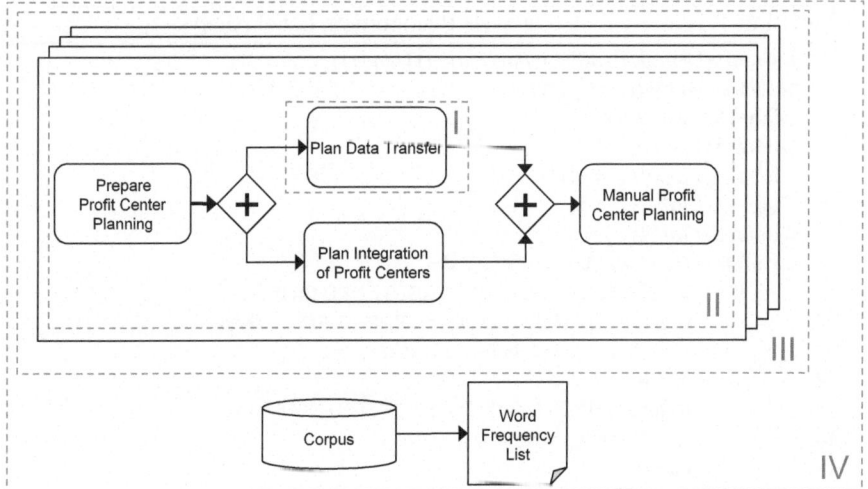

Fig. 3.2 Disambiguation Using Four Levels of Context

- *Stage 3:* Model Collection Analysis
- *Stage 4:* Natural Language Analysis

Using these four levels of context, it is possible to decide whether a given activity label is a verb-object, action-noun, or descriptive label. In the following paragraphs, we elaborate on each phase in detail. Subsequently, we discuss how the action-noun labels can be further assigned to the according action-noun sub-styles.

Stage 1: Label Analysis. This step tries to assign each activity label either to the verb-object style, any of the action-noun styles, or the descriptive style. The algorithm's input is a set of activity labels from a process model collection. The core idea of the algorithm is to reject a hypothesis that a label is following the verb-object style. Furthermore, the global set of verbs and nouns is populated for later usage. Algorithm 1 illustrates the steps of the first stage.

Algorithm 1 starts by applying a set of structural rules against the considered label which doubtlessly indicate the used labeling style (line 9). We included the following rules as a part of the *getStyleByRule* function to predetermine the labeling style:

- *Of Rule*: The usage of the preposition *of* in the second position of the label requires the first word to be a noun representing the action. In case a phrasal verb is used, the *of* can consequently be found in the third position of the label. As examples, consider the labels *Approval of concept* or *Notification of Customer* which can be, based on this rule, directly assigned to the action-noun style.
- *If Rule*: The usage of *if* at the second or, in case of a phrasal verb, at the third position of the label implies an imperative action as the first word. The algorithm classifies such labels, as, for instance, *Check if customer is satisfied*, as verb-object labels.

Algorithm 1. Activity Labeling Style Recognition, Label Analysis

---

1: **recognizeUsingLabel**(Set *modelActivityLabels*)
2:   Set *unrecognizedLabels* = ∅;
3:   **Global** Set *verbs* = ∅;
4:   **Global** Set *nouns* = ∅;
5:   **Global** Set *labels$_{vo}$* = ∅;
6:   **Global** Set *labels$_{an}$* = ∅;
7:   **Global** Set *labels$_{des}$* = ∅;
8:   **for all** *label* ∈ *modelActivityLabels* **do**
9:       **if** getStyleByRule(*label*)!=UNCLASSIFIED **then**
10:          **if** getStyleByRule(*label*) == VERB-OBJECT **then**
11:              *labels$_{vo}$* = *labels$_{vo}$* ∪ {*label*};
12:          **end if**
13:          **if** getStyleByRule(*label*) == ACTION-NOUN **then**
14:              *labels$_{an}$* = *labels$_{an}$* ∪ {*label*};
15:          **end if**
16:          **if** getStyleByRule(*label*) == DESCRIPTIVE **then**
17:              *labels$_{des}$* = *labels$_{des}$* ∪ {*label*};
18:          **end if**
19:       **else if** isVerb(*label*.words[1]) **then**
20:          **if** isInfinitive(*label*.words[1]) **then**
21:              **Set** *potentialVerbs* = getOtherPotentialVerbs(*label*);
22:              **if** *potentialVerbs* == ∅ **then**
23:                  *verbs* = *verbs* ∪ {*label*.words[1]};
24:                  *labels$_{vo}$* = *labels$_{vo}$* ∪ {*label*};
25:              **else**
26:                  *unrecognizedLabels* = *unrecognizedLabels* ∪ {*label*};
27:              **end if**
28:          **else**
29:              *nouns* = *nouns* ∪ {*label*.words[1]};
30:              *labels$_{an}$* = *labels$_{an}$* ∪ {*label*};
31:          **end if**
32:       **else**
33:          *nouns* = *nouns* ∪ {*label*.words[1]};
34:          *labels$_{an}$* = *labels$_{an}$* ∪ {*label*};
35:       **end if**
36: **end for**
37: recognizeUsingModel(*unrecognizedLabels*)

- *Condition Rule*: Some labels provide extensive information by using a combination of a main and a subordinate clause. This is, for instance, the case if a condition for the instructed action is stated. Such conditions are frequently introduced by fragments such as *in case of*, *in the event of*, or *if*. These subordinate clauses are then succeeded by a main clause starting with an imperative verb. Hence, labels as *In case of continuous delay escalate* are directly assigned to the verb-object style.

Algorithm 2. Activity Labeling Style Recognition, Model Analysis

---

```
 1: recognizeUsingModel(Set labels)
 2: Set unrecognizedLabels = ∅;
 3: for all label ∈ labels do
 4:     assigned = false;
 5:     Set processModelLabels = label.getProcessModel().getActivityLabels();
 6:     for all pmLabel ∈ processModelLabels do
 7:         if pmLabel.words[1] == label.words[1] ∧ pmLabel ∈ VOLabels then
 8:             verbs = verbs ∪ {label.words[1]};
 9:             labelsᵥₒ = labelsᵥₒ ∪ {label};
10:             assigned = true;
11:         end if
12:         if pmLabel.words[1] == label.words[1] ∧ pmLabel ∈ ANLabels then
13:             nouns = nouns ∪ {label.words[1]};
14:             labelsₐₙ = labelsₐₙ ∪ {label};
15:             assigned = true;
16:         end if
17:     end for
18:     if !assigned then
19:         unrecognizedLabels = unrecognizedLabels ∪ {label};
20:     end if
21: end for
22: recognizeUsingModelCollection(unrecognizedLabels)
```

- **Descriptive Rule**: Stage 1 also uses rules to detect descriptive labels. As descriptive labels are fragments of natural language text, we analyze them by means of the Stanford Parser. In this way, labels without an actor, such as *writes down annual fee*, and also labels with actor, such as *Seller processes order*, can be allocated to the descriptive style. Once the Parser recognizes the first possible verb in the label as a third-person form of a verb, the label is categorized accordingly.

If no structural rule applies to the label, Algorithm 1 proceeds by considering potential verbs at different positions. First, it checks whether the first word of the label is a potential verb (line 19). If this is the case, we investigate whether the first word also equals the respective imperative of the verb it may represent. As the imperative in English always equals the infinitive, we implement this check using WordNet. If this assumption is confirmed, we consider a case of zero-derivation ambiguity and proceed with further analysis steps. To reliably decide on the zero-derivation labels, the algorithm detects other potential verbs in the label (line 21). As an example, consider the label *Order System*. The word *order* suffers from zero-derivation ambiguity and without examining the rest of the label, an automatic decision is impossible. However, if we assume facing an action-noun label, we are able to figure out that *system* cannot be an action. Thereafter, the only potential verb in this label is given by *order*. In this case the label is assigned to the verb-object style (lines 23-24). Nevertheless, if multiple potential verbs are identified, the classification decision is

---

Algorithm 3. Activity Labeling Style Recognition, Model Collection Analysis

---

1: **recognizeUsingModelCollection**(Set *labels*)
2: **Set** *unrecognizedLabels* = ∅;
3: **for all** *label* ∈ *labels* **do**
4:      **if** *label*.words[1] ∈ *verbs* ∧ *label*.words[1] ∉ *nouns* **then**
5:          *labels_{vo}* = *labels_{vo}* ∪ {*label*};
6:      **else if** *label*.words[1] ∈ *nouns* ∧ *label*.words[1] ∉ *verbs* **then**
7:          *labels_{an}* = *labels_{an}* ∪ {*label*};
8:      **else**
9:          *unrecognizedLabels* = *unrecognizedLabels* ∪ {*label*};
10:     **end if**
11: **end for**
12: recognizeUsingLanguage(*unrecognizedLabels*)

---

handed over to the second stage of labeling style analysis: we add the label to the set of unrecognized labels (line 26).

If the first word of a label is not an infinitive, the label is assigned to the action-noun style and the precise style is determined later on (line 29). Similarly, the label is classified as action-noun once its first word is not a verb (line 33). After every label in the set was processed, unrecognized labels are passed as input to Algorithm 2 (line 37).

Stage 2: Model Analysis. Algorithm 2 implements the second stage of the activity labeling style recognition. It takes information on labeling styles in the whole model into account. Its input is the set of labels that have not been recognized in Stage 1. To classify a label, the algorithm inspects the process model in which the activity label is observed. In particular, for each label to be classified the algorithm checks its first word. All the labels of the activities in this model that start with the same word are investigated. If the process model includes such an activity that was already assigned to a style, the current label is allocated respectively (lines 7–11, 12–16). If the label was not assigned using this strategy, it is added to the newly created set of unrecognized labels. After every label in the set was processed, the Stage 3 of recognition is triggered (line 22).

Stage 3: Model Collection Analysis. Stage 3 is described by Algorithm 3. The input of the algorithm is the set of labels unrecognized in Stage 2. Algorithm 3 broadens the context from the model to the process model collection level. Technically, this context is captured by sets of *verbs* and *nouns*, created in the preceding stages. These two sets contain the first words of verb-object and action-noun labels of the process model collection. Inspecting the sets of *verbs* and *nouns*, the algorithm checks if the first word of an unrecognized label has been considered a verb or a noun earlier. If the word is exclusively contained in one of these sets, the label is assigned to the respective labeling style (lines 5 and 7). Labels that are not classified within the first three algorithm stages are handled by Stage 4 (line 12).

Algorithm 4. Activity Labeling Style Recognition, Natural Language Analysis

```
 1: recognizeUsingLanguage(Set labels)
 2: for all label ∈ labels do
 3:     int verbFrequency = getVerbTagsInCorpus(label.words[1])
 4:     int nounFrequency = getNounTagsInCorpus(label.words[1])
 5:     if verbFrequency ≥ nounFrequency then
 6:         labels_vo = labels_vo ∪ {label};
 7:     else
 8:         labels_an = labels_an ∪ {label};
 9:     end if
10: end for
```

Stage 4: Natural Language Analysis. Algorithm 4 finalizes labeling style recognition. In order to decide upon the labeling style, it is necessary to disambiguate the first word and decide whether it represents an action. In Stage 4, we exploit insights on the usage of the English language. In particular, we build on the analysis of large natural language text collections to learn about the frequencies of words. Therefore, we consult a frequency list derived from the Corpus of Contemporary American English [85]. This list contains 500,000 words with their parts of speech and the respective frequencies in the corpus. Having this information at hand, we learn for each word how often it occurs with a particular part of speech. If the verb frequency is higher or equal to the noun usage count, the label is allocated to the verb-object style. If it is lower, the label is consequently assigned to the action-noun style. In this way, every remaining label is assigned to a labeling style. As an example, consider the label *Credit Check* in which both words can be used as verbs as well as nouns. In order to decide about the labeling style we access the frequency list and consider the part of speech related occurrences for the word *credit*. As a result, we receive 7,169 occurrences for *credit* as a verb and 36,784 for *credit* as a noun. Consequently, we assume *credit* to be a noun and assign the label *Credit Check* to the action-noun style.

Analysis of Action-Noun Labels. Once the activity labels are separated into verb-object, descriptive labels, and action-noun labels, it is necessary to determine the exact style of the latter group. Based on this classification, we directly infer the position of verbs and business objects in the label. For determining the labeling style, there is a set of rules to be considered:

- If the label contains irregular characters, the style is set accordingly.
- If conjunctions or prepositions are found, we store the position of their first occurrence.
- If the label starts with a gerund, we check whether it really represents an action. As an example, consider the label *Planning scenario processing Planning* is a gerund, but it can also be a part of a business object. For resolving this ambiguity, we analyze surrounding events or activities preceding and succeeding the considered activity with the inspected label. We might find that the activity is

connected to an event labeled with *Planning scenario is processed*. A part of
speech analysis identifies *planning* and *scenario* as nouns and *process* as a verb.
Therefore, we assume that *processing* defines the action. The label is classified
as *action-noun AN (ing)*.

- If the label contains prepositions and the first one is an *of*, the label is qualified
as *action-noun AN (of)*.
- Otherwise, the label is assumed to be *action-noun AN (np)*.

3.3.1.2   Automatic Component Derivation

At this stage, all the information is available for deriving the action and the business object from the label. Algorithm 5 defines a derivation method for verb-object,
action-noun (np), action-noun (of), action-noun (ing), and descriptive labels. Labels
of irregular style are not addressed. Algorithm 5 also abstracts from labels that contain coordinating conjunctions and phrasal verbs as for instance *set up*. The input
of the algorithm is an activity label *label* and a corresponding *LabelProperties* object *prop* storing the classification properties of the prior steps. The output of the
algorithm is the object *prop* with the respective values for the properties *action*,
bObject, and *addition*.

The algorithm starts with an analysis of labels following the verb-object, action-
noun, or gerund style. If the label contains a prepositional phrase, it is stored as
an addition and is subsequently removed from the label (lines 4–8). If the label is
a single word such as *Verify*, *Verification* or *Verifying*, this word is classified as an
action. Otherwise, the decision on the action is depending on the specific labeling
style. In case of verb-object or gerund labels, the action is given by the first word
in the label. The remaining words constitute the business object (lines 12–15). In
case of an action-noun label, the action is given by the last word of the label. The
business object is accordingly derived from the words in the beginning of the label
(lines 16-19).

Algorithm 5 proceeds with the analysis of activity labels following the *action-
noun (of) style* (lines 21–30). The label part preceding the preposition *of* is recognized as action. The label part between preposition *of* and the next preposition is
treated as business object. The remaining words are stored as addition.

Finally, Algorithm 5 concludes with the analysis of descriptive labels (lines 31–
44). In order to illustrate the subsequent steps, we consider the two descriptive labels
Buyer informs seller to cancel and *Checks process model*. While the first label specifies the role *buyer* for performing the given task, the second label only states the
task from a third person perspective. As already indicated by the two examples, the
verb position in descriptive labels is not predefined. However, as descriptive labels
were assigned to its style using the Stanford Tagger, the assigned tags can be used
to identify the verb. Accordingly, the first step of the derivation is to identify the
occurrence of the first verb tag in the label. Beginning with the first word, each tag
of the label is considered (lines 32–37). If the current word carries a verb tag, it
is saved as action to the *prop* record and the loop is terminated (lines 33–35). As
the business object directly follows the action, the remaining words are saved as

---

Algorithm 5. Derivation of an action and a business object from a label

---

 1: **deriveActionAndBusinessObject**(Label *label*, LabelProperties *prop*)
 2: *size* = *label*.words.size;
 3: **if** *prop*.style == VERB-OBJECT ∨ *prop*.style == ACTION-NOUN
    ∨ *prop*.style == GERUND **then**
 4:     **if** *prop*.hasPrepositions **then**
 5:         *prop*.addition = *label*.words[*prop*.pIndex] + ... + *label*.words[*size*];
 6:         *label* = *label*.words[1] + ... + *label*.words[*prop*.pIndex - 1];
 7:         *size* = *label*.words.size;
 8:     **end if**
 9:     **if** *size* == 1 **then**
10:         *prop*.action = *label*.words[1];
11:     **else**
12:         **if** *prop*.style == VERB-OBJECT *vee* *prop*.style == GERUND **then**
13:             *prop*.action = *label*.words[1];
14:             *prop*.bObject = *label*.words[2] + ... + *label*.words[*size*];
15:         **end if**
16:         **if** *prop*.style == ACTION-NOUN **then**
17:             *prop*.action = *label*.words[*size*];
18:             *prop*.bObject = *label*.words[1] + ... + *label*.words[*size* - 1];
19:         **end if**
20:     **end if**
21: **else if** *prop*.style == PREPOSITION_OF **then**
22:     *prop*.action = *label*.words[1] + ... + *label*.words[*pIndex* - 1];
23:     *pPhrase* = *label*.words[*pIndex* + 1] + ... + *label*.words[*size*];
24:     **if** *pPhrase* contains prepositions **then**
25:         *nIndex* = index of the next preposition after *pIndex*;
26:         *prop*.bObject = *label*.words[*pIndex* + 1] + ... + *label*.words[*nIndex* - 1];
27:         *prop*.addition = *label*.words[*nIndex*] + ... + *label*.words[*size*];
28:     **else**
29:         *prop*.bObject = *label*.words[*pIndex* + 1] + ... + *label*.words[*size*];
30:     **end if**
31: **else if** *prop*.style == DESCRIPTIVE **then**
32:     **for** *i* = 1 → *size* **do**
33:         **if** *label*.words[i].getTag() == VERB **then**
34:             *prop*.action = *label*.words[i];
35:             **break**;
36:         **end if**
37:     **end for**
38:     *prop*.bObject = *label*.words[*i*+1] + ... + *label*.words[*size*];
39:     **if** *prop*.bObject contains preposition **then**
40:         *pIndex* = index of the next preposition after *i*;
41:         *prop*.bObject = *label*.words[*i*+1] + ... + *label*.words[*pIndex* - 1];
42:         *prop*.addition = *label*.words[*pIndex*] + ... + *label*.words[*size*];
43:     **end if**
44: **end if**
45: **return** *prop*;

---

business object (line 38). If this business object contains a preposition, the business object is accordingly split into business object and addition (lines 39–43).

Algorithm 5 does not explicitly deal with irregular action-noun labels, conjunctions, and phrasal verbs. Therefore, we provide an outlook on how such labels are analyzed. For irregular labels, we first identify all potential actions in the label. Then we select the most likely action by investigating surrounding events or activities. For conjunction labels, the first step is to identify if the conjunction coordinates actions or business objects. This can be achieved using information about the labeling style and the position of the conjunction in the label. Afterwards, an algorithm can be used for deriving actions and business objects from coordinated components of the label. Notice that a conjunction may appear in the optional prepositional phrase, as in *Creation of proposal for sales and profit planning*. In this case, the conjunction is ignored, as it neither coordinates actions nor business objects. For the analysis of labels with *phrasal verbs*, we make use of WordNet. Knowing the position of the verb, it is straightforward to check whether a phrasal verb is included in the label. If we, for instance, analyze the verb-object label *Set up IT infrastructure*, we can consult WordNet to verify that not only the first word represents a verb, but also the combination of the first and the second word.

3.3.2 Annotation of Event Labels

As opposed to activity labels, the annotation of event labels does not require the complex grammatical disambiguation of words. The reason for the lower complexity stems from the fact that events are often characterized by past participle verbs or adjectives at the end. As these words do not suffer from the verb-noun zero-derivation ambiguity, the annotation can be accomplished in a less complex fashion. In particular, we can use the detection of characterizing features, as for instance the existence of a modal verb, to accomplish the categorization.

3.3.2.1   Labeling Style Recognition

Algorithm 6 defines the derivation method for regular event labels. Analogously to Algorithm 5, we abstract from labels with coordinating conjunctions and phrasal verbs. The input of the algorithm is an event label *label* and the corresponding *LabelProperties* object *prop*. The output of the algorithm is the record *prop* containing the values for *action*, *bObject*, and *addition*.

Algorithm 6 starts with checking for an optional prepositional phrase. If a prepositional phrase is detected, it is omitted (lines 9–12). Subsequently, the algorithm checks for modal verbs such as *can*, *must*, and *shall*. If the label includes modal verbs, it is assigned to the modal style (lines 13–16). Otherwise, the last word of the label is investigated. In case the last word is a past participle, the label is classified as a participle-style label (lines 18–19). If the last word is an adjective, the considered event is assigned to the adjective style (lines 20–21). Finally, the label is checked for the descriptive style. If the first or the second word represent a third-person verb that is not derived from the verb *be*, the label is allocated to the descriptive style

---

Algorithm 6. Event Labeling Style Recognition

1: **recognizeEventStyle**(Set $modelEventLabels$)
2:   **Global** Set $labels_{ps} = \emptyset$;
3:   **Global** Set $labels_{ms} = \emptyset$;
4:   **Global** Set $labels_{as} = \emptyset$;
5:   **Global** Set $labels_{cs} = \emptyset$;
6:   **for all** $label \in modelEventLabels$ **do**
7:       $assigned$ = **false**;
8:       $size = label$.words.size;
9:       **if** $prop$.hasPrepositions **then**
10:          $label = label$.words[1] + ... + $label$.words[$prop$.pIndex-1];
11:          $size = label$.words.size;
12:       **end if**
13:       **if** $prop$.hasModalVerb **then**
14:          $labels_{ms} = labels_{ms} \cup \{label\}$;
15:          $assigned$ = **true**;
16:       **end if**
17:       **if** !$assigned$ **then**
18:          **if** isParticipleVerb($label$.words[$size$]) **then**
19:             $labels_{ps} = labels_{ps} \cup \{label\}$;
20:          **else if** isAdjectiveVerb($label$.words[$size$]) **then**
21:             $labels_{as} = labels_{as} \cup \{label\}$;
22:          **else if** is3PSVerb($label$.words[1]) $\wedge$ $label$.words[1].getInf() != 'be' **then**
23:             $labels_{des} = labels_{des} \cup \{label\}$;
24:          **else if** is3PSVerb($label$.words[2]) $\wedge$ $label$.words[2].getInf() != 'be' **then**
25:             $labels_{des} = labels_{des} \cup \{label\}$;
26:          **else**
27:             $labels_{cs} = labels_{cs} \cup \{label\}$;
28:          **end if**
29:       **end if**
30: **end for**

(lines 22–25). If none of the latter options applies, the event is assigned to the categorization style (line 27).

3.3.2.2 Automatic Component Derivation

Building on the recognized event labeling styles, Algorithm 7 defines the required steps for deriving the event label components. As input, it requires an event label *label* and the property object *prop*. As a result, the algorithms returns the object *prop* containing the according values for *action*, *bObject*, and *addition*. The algorithm starts with checking for an optional prepositional phrase. If a prepositional phrase is identified, it is stored as *addition* and is subsequently removed from the label (lines 3–7). Afterwards, action and business object are derived from the different styles. In participle-style labels the action is determined by the last word of the label. Accordingly, the words in the beginning constitute the business object (lines

---

Algorithm 7. Derivation of Components from Event Label

1: **deriveComponentsFromEventLabel**(Label *label*, LabelProperties *prop*)
2: *size = label*.words.size;
3: **if** *prop*.hasPrepositions **then**
4:       *prop*.addition = *label*.words[*prop*.pIndex-1]+ . . . + *label*.words[*size*];
5:       *label = label*.words[1] + . . . + *label*.words[*prop*.pIndex-1];
6:       *size = label*.words.size;
7: **end if**
8: **if** *prop*.style == PARTICIPLE **then**
9:       *prop*.action = *label*.words[*size*];
10:       *prop*.bObject = *label*.words[1] + . . . + *label*.words[*size*-1];
11: **else if** *prop*.style == ADJECTIVE **then**
12:       *prop*.action = **empty**;
13:       *prop*.bObject = *label*.words[1] + . . . + *label*.words[*prop*.auxVerbIndex];
14: **else if** *prop*.style == MODAL **then**
15:       *prop.action = label.words*[*size*];
16:       *prop*.bObject = *label*.words[1] + . . . + *label*.words[*prop*.modalVerbIndex];
17: **else if** *prop*.style == CATEGORIZATION **then**
18:       *prop*.action = **empty**;
19:       *prop*.bObject = *label*.words[1] + . . . + *label*.words[*prop*.auxlVerbIndex];
20: **end if**
21: **return** *prop*;

8–10). For adjective-style labels the action is specified as empty since the label only contains auxiliary verbs. Analogously to participle style labels, the business object is derived from the words in the beginning (lines 11–13). Afterwards, the algorithm analyzes modal-style labels. In such labels the action is positioned at the end, while the business object is positioned before the modal verb. Hence, we use the index of the modal verb to appropriately derive action and business object (lines 14–16). Finally, the algorithm derives the components from categorization-style labels. Since they only contain an auxiliary verb, the action is defined as empty. The business object is determined with the word before the auxiliary verb (lines 17–19).

3.3.3   Annotation of Gateway Labels

Like events, gateways only rarely suffer from zero-derivation ambiguity. In fact, the grammatical constructions of gateways are often very similar to those of events. Whether a gateway label is perceived as a question or as an event, typically depends on the existence of a question mark. Hence, the algorithms for the gateway-style recognition and component derivation are analogous to the event annotation algorithms. We build on the detection of style characteristics to accomplish the recognition.

Algorithm 8. Gateway Labeling Style Recognition

1: **recognizeGatewayStyle**(Set *modelEventLabels*)
2: **Global** Set *labels*$_{pq}$ = ∅;
3: **Global** Set *labels*$_{ifq}$ = ∅;
4: **Global** Set *labels*$_{aq}$ = ∅;
5: **Global** Set *labels*$_{eq}$ = ∅;
6: **for all** *label* ∈ *modelGatewayLabels* **do**
7:      *assigned* = **false**;
8:      *eqKeyWords* = { '>',' <', '=', 'greater', 'more than', 'below', 'smaller', 'under', 'between', 'within' }
9:      *size* = *label*.words.size;
10:     **if** *prop*.hasPrepositions **then**
11:         *label* = *label*.words[1] + ... + *label*.words[*prop*.pIndex-1];
12:         *size* = *label*.words.size;
13:     **end if**
14:     **If** *label* contains an element *k* in *eqKeyWords* **then**
15:         *labels*$_{eq}$ = *labels*$_{eq}$ ∪ {*label*};
16:         *assigned* = **true**;
17:     **end if**
18:     **if** !*assigned* **then**
19:         **if** isParticipleVerb(*label*.words[*size*]) **then**
20:             *labels*$_{pq}$ = *labels*$_{pq}$ ∪ {*label*};
21:         **else if** isAdjectiveVerb(*label*.words[*size*]) **then**
22:             *labels*$_{aq}$ = *labels*$_{aq}$ ∪ {*label*};
23:         **else if** isInfinitiveVerb(*label*.words[1]) **then**
24:             *labels*$_{ifq}$ = *labels*$_{ifq}$ ∪ {*label*};
25:         **end if**
26:     **end if**
27: **end for**

3.3.3.1 Labeling Style Recognition

Algorithm 8 defines the derivation steps for regular gateway labels. As for activities and events, we abstract from labels with coordinating conjunctions and phrasal verbs in order to avoid unnecessary complexity. The input of the algorithm is a gateway label *label* and a corresponding *LabelProperties* object *prop*. The output of the algorithm is the object *prop* containing the according values for *action*, *bObject*, and *addition*.

Algorithm 8 starts with checking for an optional preposition phrase. If such a phrase is identified, it is stored as addition and is removed (lines 10–13). Afterwards, the algorithm parses the given label for symbols or words indicating an equation-question. The complete set of signal words is stored in the set *eqKeyWords*. If an element from this set is found in the label, the label is classified as equation-question (14–17). Otherwise, the algorithm continues by checking the last word of the label. If it is a participle verb, the label is categorized as a participle-question (lines 19–20). In case the last word is an adjective, the label is classified as an adjective-question.

Algorithm 9. Derivation of Components from Gateway Label

1: **deriveComponentsFromGatewayLabel**(Label *label*, LabelProperties *prop*)
2:    *size* = *label*.words.size;
3: **if** *prop*.hasPrepositions **then**
4:       *prop*.addition = *label*.words[*prop*.pIndex-1]+ ... + *label*.words[*size*];
5:       *label* = *label*.words[1] + ... + *label*.words[*prop*.pIndex-1];
6:       *size* = *label*.words.size;
7: **end if**
8: **if** *prop*.style == EQUATION-QUESTION **then**
9:       *prop*.action = **empty**;
10:      *prop*.bObject = *label*.words[1] + ... + *label*.words[*prop*.keyWordIndex-1];
11: **else if** *prop*.style == PARTICIPLE-QUESTION **then**
12:      *prop*.action = *label*.words[*size*];
13:      *prop*.bObject = *label*.words[1] + ... + *label*.words[*size*-1];
14: **else if** *prop*.style == ADJECTIVE-QUESTION **then**
15:      *prop*.action = **empty**;
16:      *prop*.bObject = *label*.words[1] + ... + *label*.words[*prop*.auxVerbIndex];
17: **else if** *prop*.style == INFINITIVE-QUESTION **then**
18:      *prop*.action = *label*.words[1];
19:      *prop*.bObject = *label*.words[2] + ... + *label*.words[*size*];
20: **end if**
21: **return** *prop*;

Finally, the first word of the label is considered. If it represents an infinitive verb, the label is assigned to the set of infinitive-question labels (lines 23–24).

3.3.3.2 Automatic Component Derivation

Based on the knowledge about gateway styles, Algorithm 9 specifies the method for deriving the components from gateway labels. It requires a gateway label and the *LabelProperties* object *prop* as input and returns the *prop* object with the values for action, business object, and addition. Analogously to the derivation algorithms for activities and events Algorithm 9 first checks whether the label contains a preposition phrase. If that is the case, the preposition phrase is saved as addition and removed from the label (lines 3–7). Subsequently, the algorithm derives the remaining components for each style. For equation-questions, the action is specified as empty. Either such labels do not contain a verb or they only include auxiliary verbs. The business object is given by the label part before the key word (lines 8–11). For participle-question labels, the action is determined with the first word of the label and the business object is derived from the remaining words (lines 11–13). In case of an adjective-question, the action is specified as empty. Since the label only contains auxiliary verbs, no meaningful action can be derived. The business object is defined using the word before the adjective (lines 14–16). Finally, for infinitive-question labels, the action is given by the first word. The business object is respectively derived from the remaining words (lines 17–19).

3.4 Evaluation

To demonstrate the capability of the presented technique for annotating process models, we conduct an evaluation with real-world data. Section 3.4.1 gives an overview of the process model collections we utilize. The goal of the evaluation is to learn how well the proposed algorithms approximate a human interpretation and a manual annotation of process model elements. Accordingly, we study different dimensions of the evaluation. Section 3.4.2 investigates our approach from a runtime performance perspective. Section 3.4.3 discusses the results from the recognition experiment illustrating how well the presented technique detects labeling styles. Finally, Section 3.4.4 presents the results from the annotation experiment.

3.4.1 Test Collection Demographics

In order to achieve a high external validity, we include process model collections which vary in multiple dimensions as, for instance, the domain, modeling language, and the distribution of labeling styles. We designed a test sample that includes three different real-world process model collections and the human interpretation for each process model element label. Table 3.7 summarizes the main features of the considered process model collections. They include:

- *SAP Reference Model (SAP)*: The SAP Reference Model represents the business processes of the SAP R/3 system in its version from the year 2000 [176, pp. 145-164]. It contains 604 Event-driven Process Chains (EPCs) which are organized in 29 functional branches such as sales and accounting.
- *Insurance Model Collection (CH)*: The insurance model collection contains 328 EPCs dealing with the claims handling activities of an Australian insurance company. The insurance model set contains rather large processes with a high density of events.
- *Academic Collection (AC)*: The Academic Collection includes 518 process models created with the Business Process Model and Notation (BPMN). The models stem from academic training and cover diverse domains.

With respect to the differences between the model collections, we emphasize three dimensions of diversity: labeling style distribution, modeling language, and modeling experience.

The most significant feature of the considered collections is the opposed distribution of *labeling styles*. While the majority of the activity labels in the SAP Reference Model follow the action-noun style and only a small share belongs to the verb-object style, the labeling style distribution in the insurance and academic collections is the opposite. This fact is important, as a small share of action-noun labels requires the algorithm to work with a high precision in terms of style recognition. A similar situation can be observed for event labels. The academic collection contains much more event labels following activity labeling styles and fewer labels of the participle style. To demonstrate the capability of the annotation algorithm to cover different

Table 3.7 Details about Used Model Collections

	SAP	CH	AC
Number of Models	604	328	518
No. of Activities	2,433	4,414	4,109
Average No. of Activities per Model	4.03	13.45	7.93
Average No. of Words per Label	3.50	5.59	3.66
Minimum No. of Words. per Label	1	1	1
Maximum No. of Words per Label	12	19	15
AN Labels	81%	9%	9%
VOS Labels	11%	80%	74%
DES Labels	0 %	1%	6 %
NA Labels	8%	10%	11%
No. of Events	6,933	10,292	553
Average No. of Events per Model	11.48	31.38	1.07
Average No. of Words per Label	5.37	4.74	2.78
Minimum No. of Words per Label	2	1	1
Maximum No. of Words per Label	13	19	11
PS Labels	59%	60%	38%
MS Labels	27%	6%	7%
AS Labels	4%	7%	0%
CS Labels	0%	3%	1%
Activity Style Labels	5%	17%	31%
Irregular Labels	5%	7%	23
No. of (Labeled) Gateways	-	-	235
Average No. of Gateways per Model	-	-	0.45
Average No. of Words per Label	-	-	2.57
Minimum No. of Words per Label	-	-	1
Maximum No. of Words per Label	-	-	9
PQ Labels	-	-	30%
IFQ Labels	-	-	25%
AQ Labels	-	-	16%
EQ Labels	-	-	4%
Irregular Labels	-	-	25%
Notation	EPC	EPC	BPMN

extremes in terms of style distribution, the selected process model collections can be considered to be well suited.

As the extensiveness of the information content varies among different *modeling languages*, we also chose process models which differ in this regard. EPCs contain, by definition, numerous events which can be used for inferring information or to validate assumptions about words and their parts of speech in activity labels. By contrast, the event information in BPMN can be very sparse. Furthermore, BPMN models contain labeled gateways. To show that our approach does not rely on

Table 3.8 Computation Performance

	SAP	CH	AC
All Activities (ms)	26,209	42,021	40,556
Single Activity (avg. ms)	10.77	9.52	9.87
All Events (ms)	54,701	78,631	3,815
Single Event (avg. ms)	7.89	7.64	6.90
All Gateways (ms)	-	-	1,384
Single Gateway (avg. ms)	-	-	5.89

modeling language specific information, we cover two widely adopted modeling languages.

When process models are created in practice, it cannot be assumed that the involved modelers have extensive *modeling experience* or can be considered modeling experts. While the SAP Reference Model and the insurance model collection were created in a professional environment, the academic process model collection was mainly created by students as course assignments. In order to cover the aforementioned real-world scenario of heterogeneous modeling quality, we studied both professional and non-professional process model collections.

By mixing the characteristics of the included process model collections along these dimensions, we aim to increase the external validity of the conclusions drawn from our evaluation.

3.4.2 Performance Results

The annotation algorithm represents the basis for a variety of techniques than can support modelers in practice. Thus, the computation time should be adequately fast. For this reason, we investigate the response time for each model collection in total, and also for one single model element.

We tested the execution on a MacBook Pro with a 2.26 GHz Intel Core Duo processor and 4GB RAM, running on Mac OS X 10.6.7 and Java Virtual Machine 1.5. In order to exclude one-off setup times, we executed the algorithm twice and measured the second run only. Table 3.8 summarizes the results for the three process model collections by showing the execution times for each of the process model collections and for one single element on average. From the numbers we can learn that the execution times vary considerably among the different element types. In particular, the results for activities indicate that the disambiguation algorithm entails longer execution times. However, the longest average annotation time for a process model element is roughly 10 ms. Thus, within one second a process model with almost 100 element labels can be completely annotated. Consequently, we consider the annotation technique to be well suited in terms of execution time.

3.4.3 Recognition Results

We assess the recognition performance of the algorithm using precision, recall, and f-measure. In our context, the *precision value* is the number of correctly recognized labels of a given style divided by the total number of labels retrieved by the algorithm. The *recall* is the number of correctly recognized labels of a given style divided by the total number of labels belonging to this style. As our goal is to obtain considerable recall and precision values at the same time, we also compute the *f-measure*, the harmonic mean of precision and recall [26].

In order to be able to assess the computed results, we created a benchmark using the human interpretations of the process model element labels. In particular, this benchmark includes the manual assignment of each process model element to a labeling style. This information is stored in a spreadsheet, which can then be read by an application in the evaluation phase.

Table 3.9 shows the recognition results for each element type, style, and investigated process model collection. In general, the results show that the style recognition works satisfactory. However, there are notable differences among the element types. Despite the complex disambiguation algorithm, activity labels apparently remain the biggest challenge. The differences between the action-noun and verb-object f-measures highlight that the activity style distribution is an influencing factor. In collections such as the SAP models that only contain a few verb-object labels, the recall and precision values for verb-object labels are lower while the results for action-noun labels are reliably high. In collections such as the insurance or the academic collection, we observe the exact opposite. The results for verb-object labels are much higher than the results for action-noun labels. Nevertheless, the results show that the algorithm yields appropriate results in both extremes. For gateways and events we generally receive more stable results. Since the gateway and event recognition is hardly affected by zero-derivation, the f-measure for these process model elements is consistently high. Here, the major factor negatively influencing the results is given by the mix of event and activity labeling styles. This is also reflected by the numbers in the table. The higher degree of style mix in the insurance and the academic collection entails lower recall and precision values.

Based on the results of this analysis, we investigated the reasons for misclassification. In total, we identified four main reasons why a label was correctly assigned to its labeling style:

- *Erroneously Resolved Ambiguity:* As extensively discussed in this book, the proper resolution of ambiguous words is one of the major challenges. Although the technique works reliably, ambiguity still represents a major source of error. Whether labels such as *Plan data transfer* are correctly assigned depends heavily on the available model context. In order to resolve the remaining ambiguity problems, text corpora could be used to identify common combinations of words. For example, a corpus could reveal that the word *transfer* in combination with *plan data* indicates that *transfer* is likely to represent a verb.
- *Typographic Errors:* If words in the labels contain typographic errors, it is not possible to find them using WordNet or text corpora. Hence, they are often

Table 3.9 Recognition Results

			SAP	CH	AC
Activities	VOS Style	Recall	80.0%	99.9%	97.9%
		Precision	77.8%	99.9%	96.6%
		F-Measure	78.9%	99.9%	97.2%
	AN Style	Recall	95.1 %	83.5%	87.4%
		Precision	97.9%	87.3%	87.7%
		F-Measure	96.5%	85.4%	87.5%
	DES Style	Recall	-	96.0%	93.2%
		Precision	-	92.3%	81.8%
		F-Measure	-	95.1%	87.2%
Events	PS Style	Recall	98.8%	95.1%	93.6%
		Precision	99.7%	95.1%	98.6%
		F-Measure	99.2%	95.1%	96.1%
	AS Style	Recall	99.7%	93.3%	92.3%
		Precision	92.5%	92.9%	86.2%
		F-Measure	95.9%	93.1%	89.2%
	MS Style	Recall	98.5%	97.2%	-
		Precision	100%	97.2%	-
		F-Measure	99.2%	97.2%	-
	CS Style	Recall	-	92.5%	100%
		Precision	-	87.8%	100%
		F-Measure	-	90.1%	100%
Gateways	PQ Style	Recall	-	-	100%
		Precision	-	-	93.3%
		F-Measure	-	-	96.6%
	IFQ Style	Recall	-	-	91.4%
		Precision	-	-	97.1%
		F-Measure	-	-	94.2%
	AQ Style	Recall	-	-	94.8%
		Precision	-	-	94.8%
		F-Measure	-	-	94.8%
	EQ Style	Recall	-	-	100%
		Precision	-	-	100%
		F-Measure	-	-	100%

erroneously classified. As an example, consider the label *Parts avalable*. Here, the missing *i* could cause a misclassification of the label. In order to resolve this problem, we may employ the Levenshtein string edit distance [206] and allow words to slightly deviate from the terms in the word list. For instance, with a

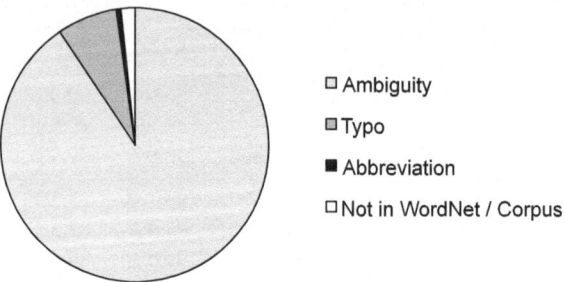

□ Ambiguity

▨ Typo

■ Abbreviation

□ Not in WordNet / Corpus

Fig. 3.3 Distribution of Error Sources

Levenshtein distance of 1, the word *avalable* with a missing *i* could be correctly associated with the word *available* in a corpus. However, for bigger mistakes, this strategy cannot be employed. If we, for instance, allow for a Levenshtein distance of 2, the word *test* could also be associated with its participle *tested* or even completely different words as *tear*. As a solution for such cases, we propose to refine the Levenshtein metric. By including the closeness of keys on the keyboard for instance, the metric could be improved to better reflect errors which really stem from typing mistakes.

- *Abbreviations:* Similar to typographic errors, most abbreviations will not be found in WordNet or corpora. Thus, labels containing such abbreviations cannot be reliably assigned to the correct labeling style. Standard abbreviations are usually not a problem as they are in many cases also included in WordNet or the employed corpora. However, non-standard abbreviations always result in a misclassification. An example for an arbitrarily abbreviated label is given by *Inf. Customer*. Here, the verb *inform* is simply abbreviated after the third letter. Although such cases are rare, they can lead to a decrease of the overall performance. As a solution for this problem, we propose to identify the abbreviated word in corpora using a substring match. For the introduced example, the search for *Inf.* would accordingly result in a match. In case of multiple matches, the context of the label could be used to select the most likely option.

- *Word not in WordNet or Corpus:* Apart from typos and abbreviations, we also found elements solely consisting of completely correct words which were not correctly assigned to the according labeling style. The main problem in this context are modern or domain-specific words. In many cases, WordNet and corpora do not contain words such as *sublicense* that have just been recently added to standard dictionaries. For domain specific words, as for instance system terms (e.g SAP or ECPA), the problem is similar. To resolve this problem, WordNet or corpora could be complemented with a list of domain-specific terms. As many companies maintain such lists, we consider this to be a reasonable solution.

Figure 3.3 illustrates the distribution of the error sources. It illustrates that ambiguity is the major problem among the considered reasons for misclassification.

Table 3.10 Annotation Results

	SAP	CH	AC
Activities	99.8%	99.8%	99.7%
Events	99.6%	99.7 %	99.4%
Gateways	-	-	99.1%

Approximately 90% of the misclassification reasons were caused by erroneously resolved ambiguous cases. Nevertheless, reconsidering the numbers from Table 3.9, we can still conclude that we are capable to deal with the problem of ambiguity. Future work for improving the technique should, however, focus on the refinement of the disambiguation algorithm.

3.4.4 Annotation Results

Building on the recognized labeling styles, the label components can be accordingly derived and annotated. For evaluating the annotation performance, we compare the result of the algorithm with the manual annotation of the investigated process model collections. The manually created benchmark consists of three mappings: A mapping from an element label to an action, a mapping from an element label to a business object, and a mapping from an element label to an addition. Table 3.10 summarizes the results from the annotation evaluation by showing the shares of correctly annotated process model elements.

The results illustrate that the annotation is accomplished with high accuracy. Since the labeling style reliably indicates the position of the different components, the share of correctly annotated process model elements is consistently close to 100%. Remaining annotation errors mainly stem from the adjective-noun ambiguity and from compound business objects containing prepositions. As an example for the *adjective-noun ambiguity*, consider the activity label *Manual verification*. The recognition phase correctly categorizes this label as an action-noun (np) label. Hence, the annotation algorithm returns the action *verify* and the business object *manual*. While the action is correctly derived from the noun at the end of the label, the business object is erroneously determined with *manual*. Although the word *manual* may theoretically represent a noun, it actually plays the role of an adjective. Thus, the returned annotation record is not entirely correct. To avoid this type of error, the most likely part of speech could be identified using a corpus. For the given example, the combination of the adjective *manual* and the noun *verification* is in fact more likely than the combination of both words as nouns. The second error source in the context of annotation is *business objects containing prepositions*. Typical examples for such business objects are *bill of exchange* or *scope of work*. If the business object cannot be found in WordNet or the employed corpus, the annotation algorithm accordingly assumes that the preposition is introducing a prepositional phrase. Thus, the business object *bill of exchange* is split up into the business object *bill* and the addition *of work*. This error type can be avoided by maintaining a list of compound business objects. As such an endeavour represents a one-time effort, we consider this as a reasonable solution. All in all, it can be stated that the annotation works very satisfactory once the correct labeling style has been determined.

3.5   Adaptation to Other Languages

In the previous sections, we discussed the annotation of a process model that contain English element labels. Since companies typically model their processes using their local language, the possibility of adapting the presented technique to other languages represents an important feature. Hence, we use this section to provide an outlook on how the annotation technique can be adapted to other languages. Essentially, the adaptation of the annotation technique requires two steps: the identification of the labeling styles of the target language and the replacement of language-specific NLP tools.

The *identification of the labeling styles* of the target language is mainly concerned with detecting structures that deviate from the English styles. Since the algorithm uses knowledge on labeling styles, this is an important step. However, an analysis of three German and three Portuguese model collections revealed that the labeling styles from these languages are almost completely identical to the English styles. Table 3.11 illustrates how the activity styles for German and Portuguese models complement Table 3.2 from Section 3.2.1.

Table 3.11 illustrates that the typical English activity label structures such as the verb-object and the action-noun style also occur in German and Portuguese. Nevertheless, there are two additional styles that are not included in English models. The first non-English structure is the *infinitive style*, which is characterized by an infinitive verb in the beginning of the label. This style is not present in English models since the infinitive of English verbs is always identical to the imperative. Hence, English infinitive style labels could not be differentiated from English verb-object labels. As examples for infinitive style labels, consider the German activity *Erstellen Rechnung* and the Portuguese activity *Criar nota fiscal* (both mean *Create invoice*). A second non-English structure is the *object-infinitive style*. This style is the most typical pattern for German activities and provides the action as infinitive verb at the end of the label. An example is given by the activity *Rechnung erstellen* (literally *Invoice create*). The similarities concerning the activity labeling styles emphasize that the presented annotation technique is not dependent on a specific language. Once the labeling styles of the target language are known, the style recognition algorithms can be accordingly adapted. In this context, it should be also noted that English represents one of the biggest challenges in terms of ambiguity. As discussed in Section 3.1.2, English has a low morphological complexity. Thus, many English words are structurally ambiguous. The examples for German and Portuguese labels from Table 3.11 illustrate that this does not equally apply to these languages.

Table 3.11 Activity Labeling Styles For English, German, and Portuguese

Labeling Style	Core Structure	Example	Lang.
Verb-Object VO	A(imperative) + O	Create invoice	EN
		Erstelle Rechnung	GER
		Crie nota fiscal	PT
Infinitive Style IS	A(infinitive) + O	Erstellen Rechnung	GER
		Criar nota fiscal	PT
Objective-Infinitive OI	O + A(infinitive)	Rechnung erstellen	GER
Action-Noun AN(np)	O + A(noun)	Invoice creation	EN
Action-Noun AN(of)	A(noun) + 'of' + O	Creation of invoice	EN
Action-Noun AN(gerund)	A(gerund) + [article] + O	Creating invoice	EN
		Erstellung der Rechnung	GER
Action-Noun AN(irregular)	*anomalous*	LIFO: Valuation: Pool level	EN
Descriptive DES	[role] + A(3P) + O	Clerk creates Invoice	EN
		Mitarbeiter erstellt Rechnung	GER
No-Action NA	*anomalous*	Error	EN
		Protokoll	GER

For German and Portuguese, it is much easier to determine the according labeling style as they are only a few cases where a verb and a noun are represented by the same syntactical word.

The second step for adapting the annotation technique is the *replacement of language specific tools*. As discussed in Section 3.3, we employ language specific resources such as WordNet and the Stanford Tagger for determining the part of speech of words. While parsers and taggers can be obtained for many languages, this is not the case for WordNet. Although there exist many WordNet solutions for various languages,[1] these tools significantly vary with respect to completeness, quality, and availability. For instance, the English Wordnet covers 155,287 words, while the German *GermaNet* only covers 93,407 words. In addition, many WordNet solutions do not always cover morphological rules. Hence, a word will only be found in the database if it is given in the base form, i.e., a noun in the singular or a verb in the infinitive. On top of that, most WordNet databases for other languages cannot be freely accessed. In order to overcome these restrictions, we propose to replace the employed NLP tools with a corpus. By checking the content of a corpus, the potential parts of speech of a word can be appropriately determined. With the help of the introduced disambiguation algorithm, ambiguous words can be assigned to the correct part of speech. As a result, the annotation technique can also annotate non-English process models.

---

[1] http://www.globalwordnet.org/gwa/wordnet_table.html

3.6 Summary

In this chapter, we introduced a technique for automatically annotating process model elements with their comprised components. The technique is based on a study of typical labeling structures and uses a tailored disambiguation algorithm to resolve ambiguous parts of speech. An evaluation with three large process model collections from practice indicated that the presented techniques have a high accuracy. In particular, we achieved recall values between 80% and 100% for the recognition algorithm and an annotation accuracy of over 99% for all three collections. An analysis of the results revealed that the remaining errors are caused by erroneously resolved ambiguity, typographic errors, non-standard abbreviations, and words that are not contained in the corpus or by WordNet. However, ambiguity in particular turned out to remain as a major source of error. While the concepts presented in this chapter are mainly applicable for English models, we also illustrated that the annotation algorithm can be adapted to languages other than English. Therefore, a labeling style topology for the target language must be created and the linguistic resources must be replaced. In light of the benefits provided by the presented technique, we consider this to represent a reasonable effort. All in all, the technique presented in this section represents the basis for an advanced linguistic process model analysis. Contrary to prior research, it enables the explicit usage of the language and hence creates completely new possibilities to exploit the linguistic information captured by process models. In the next chapter, we discuss how the techniques for parsing process models can support the automatic detection and correction of linguistic guideline violations.

Chapter 4
Detecting and Correcting Linguistic Guideline Violations

Due to the huge size of modeling initiatives in practice, many companies struggle with assuring the quality of their process model collections. While many model properties can already be checked automatically, there is a notable gap concerning techniques for checking linguistic aspects such as naming conventions for process model elements. In this chapter, we aim at closing this gap by introducing techniques for automatically detecting and correcting linguistic guideline violations. The presented approaches build on the parsing techniques defined in the last chapter and facilitate a reliable and flexible detection and correction of guideline violations.

In order to highlight the necessity for such techniques, Section 4.1 discusses the essential aspects of process modeling guidelines and points out which aspects can already be automatically checked with existing tools. Afterwards, Section 4.2 introduces an approach for automatically checking linguistic guidelines. Then, in Section 4.3, we present a technique for automatically correcting detected violations. Subsequently, Section 4.4 demonstrates the applicability of both techniques using three large process model collections from practice. Since many companies model their processes using the local language, Section 4.5 investigates how the violation detection and correction techniques can be adapted to languages other than English. Finally, Section 4.6 summarizes the chapter.

4.1 Process Modeling Guidelines and Their Enforcement

Process modeling guidelines aim at assuring the quality and consistency of process models which are created by different and heterogeneously skilled users. They capture best practices which have proven to be beneficial to support readers in understanding the models [122, 304, 17]. In their simplest forms, they can be formulated as rules such as 'A model must have one start event' or 'A model should not make use of complex gateways'. The rationale behind such guidelines is the insight that some modeling practices are easier to understand and hence are superior in terms of clarity.

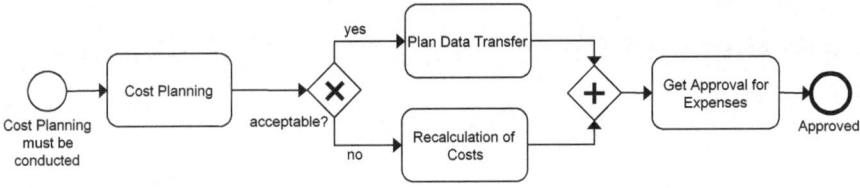

Fig. 4.1 Example Model

Guidelines refer to different aspects of process models. Four of the major aspects are formal model properties, model layout, the use of modeling elements, and the use of natural language. *Formal model properties* refer to the correctness of the model structure. It is often suggested to keep a model as structured as possible [224] and to avoid deadlocks [6]. The *model layout* discusses the proper arrangement of the elements. Good layout typically minimizes the number of crossing arcs and utilizes a clear direction of flow either from left to right or from top to bottom [301]. The *usage of modeling elements* dimension defines which elements should or should not be used. Since languages like BPMN offer different options to express the same behavior [277], one option might be preferred over the other. Elements with complicated semantics might be forbidden in order to guarantee a good model understanding also for inexperienced model readers [304]. The *usage of natural language* can be considered from two perspectives. The first refers to the set of terms which can be used in the model. Some guidelines try to ensure the term consistency by introducing glossaries [256] or forbidden unspecific verbs [301]. The second perspective is concerned with the structure in which these terms are presented in the label. Guidelines usually suggest certain naming conventions as for instance the verb-object style for activities [225].

In order to illustrate these dimensions and to discuss in how far they can be checked automatically, we consider the exemplary BPMN process model from Figure 4.1. The process starts with a start event which is then followed by the activity *Cost Planning* and proceeds with an xor-split gateway. Accordingly, either the activity *Plan Data Transfer* or the activity *Recalculation of Costs* is conducted. Afterwards, the control is passed to the and-join gateway. This diamond-shaped element with a plus sign synchronizes both incoming branches and hence waits for both of them to complete. Once both branches have been executed, the process continues with the activity *Get Approval for Expenses* before the process is terminated. It is quite apparent that this exemplary process model contains some considerable weaknesses which may prevent a reader from understanding it correctly.

Starting with the formal properties perspective, we might want to check whether the process model suffers from structural errors as deadlocks. In fact, such formal issues are well-understood and can be efficiently checked in an automatic way using Petri-net concepts [110].

Further techniques are available for checking the correctness of the data flow [315, 332, 303] or the satisfiability of resource constraints [42, 77, 313]. Automatic techniques for refactoring the model structure have also been defined [331, 263]. The layout of the model can be discussed in terms of flow direction and crossing arcs. The model appears to be well organized according to these criteria. Poorly arranged models can be laid out using concepts from graph drawings [34] which have been customized for process models [104]. The usage and exclusion of certain model elements is intensively discussed for BPMN [238, 304]. We observe that the example model from Figure 4.1 only uses a basic set of elements and does not contain any symbols that are typically considered to be problematic. Technically, checking for the inclusion and exclusion of elements is trivial.

If we consider the usage of the natural language in the model, we can observe two main problems. The first is concerned with inconsistent terms. While two activities refer to the word *costs*, the last activity mentions the word *expenses*. To avoid such inconsistencies, an approach for automatically creating and enforcing the usage of glossary terms has been proposed [256]. The second problem is the inconsistent usage of labeling styles. While a verb-object labeling is typically suggested [304, 224, 17], the example model of Figure 4.1 shows different deviations. The activities *Cost Planning* and *Recalculation of Costs* capture the actions *plan* and *recalculate* as nouns at different positions in the label. The activity *Get Approval for Costs* is compliant with the verb-object requirement. As a result of the style mix, the activity *Plan Data Transfer* can be easily misinterpreted. It could either advise to *plan* a *data transfer* or to *transfer* a record of *plan data*. Also the event and gateway labels can be improved. The gateway label *acceptable?* lacks a reference to a business object, and also the end event label *Approved* does not precisely define the result of the process execution.

The significance of these linguistic problems is emphasized by various process modeling guidelines [301, 224, 122, 304, 17]. Different research has been conducted to at least partially tackle the problems concerning labeling. Table 4.1 gives an overview of approaches addressing the checking of linguistic aspects in process models. The table reveals that the majority of existing approaches focus on the word level, i.e., they are using WordNet to check for synonyms or related inconsistencies. As this does not necessarily require the detection of the syntactic structure, they also do not address this aspect. The only approach that is not building on WordNet is the technique proposed by Gruhn and Laue [138] who use Prolog to anaylze activity labels. However, they also abstract from the syntax as they simply remove stop words from the label and use the residual words for their analysis.

Approaches that are concerned with recognizing the syntax of process model labels are provided by Bögl et al. and by the research group of Becker et al. [38, 92]. The goal of Bögl et al. is to semantically annotate a process model in order to detect common labeling practices. Becker et al. explicitly pursue the goal of enforcing naming conventions. The strategy of both approaches for accomplishing their goals is quite similar. Both build on the modeling of linguistic rules. They differ, however, with respect to the tool they use for evaluating the compliance with these rules. While Bögl et al. employ WordNet, Becker at al. build on a parser. What both approaches have in common is that they abstract from the problem of zero-derivation ambiguity. As an example, consider the activity *Plan Reconciliation*. Although this

Table 4.1 Overview of Approaches Enforcing Linguistic Guideline Aspects

Approach	Solution Concept
Focus on Words	
Term Inconsistency Detection [191]	WordNet
Linguistic Consistency Checking [324]	WordNet
Reducing Linguistic Variations [52]	WordNet
Semantic Annotation [118]	WordNet
Detection of Semantic Errors [138]	Prolog-based Algorithm
Focus on Syntax and Words	
Semantic Annotation [48]	WordNet & Rule Definition
Naming Convention Enforcement [38, 92]	Parser & Rule Definition

label complies with the verb-object requirement, it is not yet clear whether the word *plan* actually represents a verb. By abstracting from this fact, these approaches are not capable of resolving such ambiguous cases. Hence, they also cannot be employed for checking modeling guidelines. In order to close this research gap, the subsequent sections introduce techniques for automatically detecting and correcting linguistic guideline violations.

4.2 Detecting Linguistic Guideline Violations

In this section, we present a technique for automatically detecting naming convention violations in process models. In Section 4.2.1, we describe the manual preparation steps that are required. In Section 4.2.2, we introduce the technique on a conceptual level and discuss the comprised components in detail.

4.2.1 Requirements for Detecting Guideline Violations

In order to automatically detect naming convention violations, we first need to operationalize the verbally described rules provided by guidelines. In particular, we have to convert the rules into a pattern than can be checked in an automatic fashion. Hence, the preparation phase includes the transformation of the given rules into so-called linguistic patterns. As linguistic pattern, we understand a sequence of parts of speech. In order to illustrate this step, consider the following naming conventions that are frequently suggested for English process models [224, 231, 214]:

1. Activities must start with an imperative verb which is followed by a business object, e.g., *Send Documents* or *Inform Customer*.
2. Events must start with a business object which is followed by a passive verb construction or a verb in the past tense, e.g., *Customer is informed* or *Documents were sent*.

3. Gateways must represent a question which is starting with a verb, followed by a business object and an adjective, e.g., *Is customer informed?* or *Were documents sent?*

Having such naming conventions at hand, we can manually transform them to a sequence of required part-of-speech tags. Using the tags defined in Section 3.2.4, we derive the following linguistic patterns for the above stated rules:

1. Activity Pattern: *VB NN*
2. Event Pattern: *NN VB VBN*
3. Gateway Pattern: *VB NN VBN QM*

As these formal representations of linguistic guideline rules can be automatically compared against existing process model elements, they form the basis of the technique. However, before the derived linguistic patterns are defined as a benchmark, we propose an exploratory analysis of the targeted process model collection. Without knowing about existing patterns, it is hard to decide about minor deviations which would not be considered to violate the above defined rules. As an example, consider the event label *Document of customer sent*. In comparison to the defined event pattern, we can identify two essential differences. First, the label contains an additional information fragment which is introduced by the preposition *of*. Second, the label does not contain an auxiliary verb before the participle *sent*. We may encounter a similar situation with activity labels. For instance, the activity label *Notify Customer of Rejection* contains an additional information fragment introduced by the preposition *of*. Also gateways might be complemented with an additional fragment. For example, consider the label *Were documents of customer sent?*. In general, it is essential to be aware of such deviations in order to decide whether they should be considered as violation or not. Hence, by analyzing and classifying the labels in the considered process model collection, the linguistic patterns can be extended and adapted to the actual needs. Allowing for the introduced deviations for events, activities, and gateways, we replace the *NN* tag with a *NP* tag as defined in Section 3.2.4, and define the auxiliary verb in events as optional:

1. Activity Pattern: *VB NP*
2. Event Pattern: *NP VB VBN | NP VBN*
3. Gateway: *VB NP VBN QM*

Once the valid linguistic patterns have been determined, they serve as input for the automatic violation detection approach.

4.2.2 Conceptual Approach

Based on a set of required linguistic patterns, we define a technique for automatically detecting naming convention violations. Figure 4.2 provides an overview of

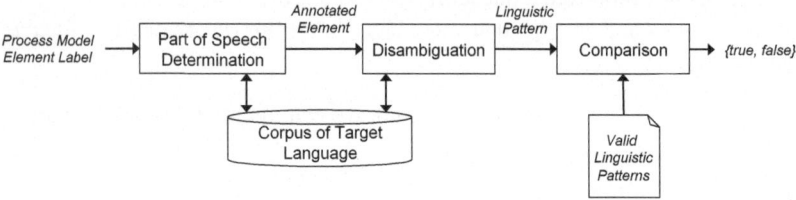

Fig. 4.2 General Architecture

the architecture. The core idea is to use a corpus to assign the corresponding part-of-speech tags to a given process model element. In case the label contains ambiguous words, and hence can be represented by multiple linguistic patterns, the subsequent disambiguation component resolves the ambiguity and decides the correct pattern. By comparing the linguistic pattern from the process model element with the required linguistic patterns from the preparation phase, violations can be automatically detected. The key difference to the concepts defined in Chapter 3 is the focus on linguistic patterns and the usage of a corpus. The advantage of the linguistic patterns is the possibility to freely define compliant or non-compliant patterns. Depending on the requirements of organizations such patterns may deviate from the standard labeling styles we previously identified. The usage of a corpus facilitates the part of speech determination for a wide range of words. As many corpora contain more word entries than WordNet, they represent an adequate choice for implementing the part of speech determination and disambiguation. Further, they can be easily replaced such that languages other than English can also be supported. In the following, we introduce each component in detail.

4.2.2.1   Part of Speech Determination

The goal of the part of speech determination component is the automatic annotation of the given process model element with the according part of speech tags. Therefore, words with multiple possible parts of speech are annotated with all potential tags.

Figure 4.3 illustrates how a text corpus can be used for determining the parts of speech of words. The strategy is to derive two data tables from the corpus: a part of speech table and a verb table. The *part of speech table* contains a list of all verbs from the corpus and how often they occur as verb, noun, adjective, and adverb. As text corpora have been manually tagged by humans, this information can be easily and automatically inferred. The *verb table* includes all verbs from the corpus and the according conjugation forms. In order to completely obtain this information, the verb data in the corpus is complemented with additional information. In particular, we employ conjugation rules of the target language to compute all required verb forms. In addition, we use an exception list for appropriately determining the form of irregular verbs. We are aware that the complexity of the verb conjugation varies

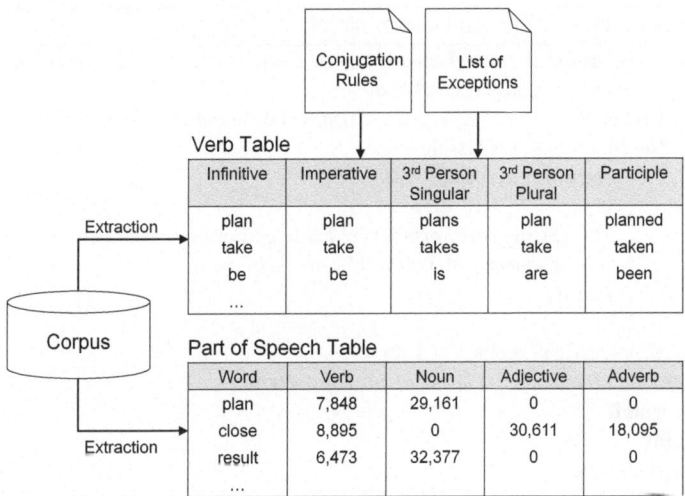

Fig. 4.3 Generation of Part-of-Speech Tagging Sources

from language to language. However, the conjugation rules and a list of exceptions are available in many resources including language books for instance.

Using the data of these tables, two important goals can be achieved. First, all possible parts of speech of a given word can be determined. This is accomplished by checking the different entries in the part of speech tables. As an example, consider the word *plan*. Figure 4.3 shows the occurrences from the *OANC*. From the numbers in the illustrated table, we learn that *plan* has 7,848 occurrences as a verb and 29,161 occurrences as noun. Hence, plan could be a verb as well as a noun. Second, in addition to the determination of the possible parts of speech, the verb table provides the possibility to reliably decide the word form of a given verb. Since naming conventions typically ask for specific verb forms such as participles or imperatives, this is a key task for detecting violations.

Algorithm 10 formalizes the usage of this technique. It requires a process model element and the two created tables as input. As a result, the algorithm returns the element with the derived part-of-speech tags as annotation. The algorithm consists of a loop which iteratively goes through the element label and tags each word (lines 2-14). Therefore, we first use the part of speech table to infer all possible part-of-speech tags (line 3). Subsequently, we annotate the considered word with each tag from the derived list (line 5). In case the considered tag represents a verb, the verb table is further used to derive the according verb form (line 7). The inferred verb form is then added to the annotation of the word (line 8). Finally, if the derived part of speech list contains more than a single entry, the variable *hasMultipleTags* is set to *true* (line 12).

Algorithm 10. Part of Speech Determination

 1: **tagProcessModelElement(Label** *element*, **Table** *posTable*, **Table** *verbTable*)
 2: **for** i=0 to $i <$ *element*.getLength() **do**
 3:         **List** *posList* = *posTable*.getPartOfSpeeches(*element*.get(i));
 4:         **for each** *tag* $\in$ *posList* **do**
 5:                 *element*.get(i).addPOS(*tag*);
 6:                 **if** *tag* = 'VERB' **then**
 7:                         String *verbForm* = *verbTable*.getForm(*element*.get(i));
 8:                         *element*.get(i).setVerbForm(*verbForm*);
 9:                 **end if**
10:         **end for**
11:         **if** *posList*.getLength() > 1 **then**
12:                 *element*.get(i).*hasMultipleTags* = **true**;
13:         **end if**
14: **end for**
15: **return** *element*;

4.2.2.2   Ambiguity Resolution

The ambiguity resolution component aims for adequately resolving cases where one word of the element label is associated with multiple part-of-speech tags. This is a crucial step as the compliance of a given label with the required linguistic pattern is based on their parts of speech. As an example, consider the English activity pattern. If the first word in the label (e.g., *plan*) can be classified as a verb and as a noun, a wrong classification leads to a wrong decision with regard to its compliance with the naming convention.

For the solution of this problem, we adapt the disambiguation technique we introduced in Chapter 3. The core idea is to use different stages of label context for determining the part of speech of a given word. In the beginning, the algorithm tries to use the information which is included in the label. If we, for instance, consider the label *Test of hardware*, the word *test* can be doubtlessly recognized as a noun since it is succeeded by the preposition *of*. If the information in the label is not sufficient for disambiguating the considered word, the scope is broadened to the process model. For instance, the English word *plan* could be identified as noun since the process model contains several other activities using the business object *plan*. Similarly, the whole process model collection can be checked for the typical part of speech of the considered word. If the process model collection is still not sufficient to disambiguate a word, we employ knowledge about the frequency of each part of speech. By consulting the part of speech table we derived from the text corpus, we can easily learn how often a part of speech occurs for a word. For instance, the *OANC* corpus contains 226 occurrences for *credit* as verb and 1,672 as noun. Accordingly, we can derive that *credit* is, in general, more likely to be a noun.

Algorithm 11 illustrates the derivation of the linguistic pattern from the element and its annotation. After creating a string variable for the linguistic pattern (line 2), each word of the input element is investigated in the context of a loop (lines 3–8).

Algorithm 11. Derivation of Linguistic Pattern

1: **deriveLinguisticPattern**(**Label** *element*)
2:   String *linguisticPattern* = **new** String();
3:   **for** *i*=0 **to** *i* < *element*.getLength() **do**
4:       **if** *element*.get(*i*).*hasMultipleTags* = **true then**
5:            String *actualPOS* = resolveAmbiguity(*element*.get(*i*));
6:            *linguisticPattern* = *linguisticPattern* + *actualPOS*;
7:       **end if**
8:   **end for**
9:   **return** *linguisticPattern*;

If the considered word carries more than a single part of speech tag, the above introduced technique is used to decide on the actual part of speech (line 5). Afterwards, the derived tag is added to the linguistic pattern variable (line 6). Once all words have been investigated and the linguistic pattern was constructed, the pattern is returned (line 9). This pattern then serves as input for the comparison component.

4.2.2.3 Comparison

In the comparison component we check whether the linguistic pattern from the input element is equivalent to the required linguistic pattern from the naming convention. Therefore, we iteratively go through the label and check the compliance of the current part of speech with the linguistic pattern. Algorithm 12 formalizes this procedure.

The algorithm requires two input parameters: the labeled element which needs to be checked and the linguistic pattern that has been derived from the naming convention. In the beginning of the algorithm, the boolean variable *correct* is set to *true* and the index variables for the element and the convention are initialized (line 2-4). If the required part of speech belongs to an optional element in the linguistic pattern and the current and the required part of speech do not match, the index of the convention string is increased (lines 8-12). As a result, the next iteration of the loop compares the same word from the element string with the subsequent word in the convention string. In case the required part of speech belongs to a mandatory element, the current and the required part of speech have to match. Otherwise, a violation is detected and the variable *correct* is set to *false* (lines 13-16). If the two parts of speech match, the subsequent lines handle the occurrence of composite nouns (lines 17-19). This is important as composite nouns are often not represented by a single word, but by a sequence of words. As an example, consider the English noun *service order*. Accordingly, the function *containsCompositeNouns* checks whether the current word and the subsequent words from the element string represent a composite noun (line 17). If that is the case, the index of the element string is adjusted to the first word after the composite noun (line 18). Otherwise, if no composite noun is detected, both indexes are increased by one (lines 21-22). As long as the index of the element

---

Algorithm 12. Checking of Naming Conventions

1: **fulfillsNamingConvention(String** *element*, **String** *convention*)
2: **boolean** correct = **true**;
3: **int** *elemIndex* = 1;
4: **int** *convIndex* = 1;
5: **while** *elemIndex* ≤ *element*.getLength() **do**
6:     String *requiredPOS* = *convention*.get(*convIndex*);
7:     List *currentPOSList* = getPartOfSpeech(*element*.get(*elemIndex*));
8:     **if** *convention*.get(*convIndex*).isOptional() **then**
9:         **if** *requiredPOS* ≠ *currentPOS* **then**
10:             *convIndex* = *convIndex*+1;
11:         **end if**
12:     **else**
13:         **if** *requiredPOS* ≠ *currentPOS* **then**
14:             *correct* = **false**;
15:             *break*;
16:         **end if**
17:         **if** *currentPOS* = 'NOUN' ∧
        containsCompositeNoun(*elemIndex*,*element*.getLength()) **then**
18:             *elemIndex* =
            getEndOfCompositeNoun(*elemIndex*,*element*.getLength())+1;
19:             *convIndex* = *convIndex*+1;
20:         **else**
21:             *elemIndex* = *elemIndex*+1;
22:             *convIndex* = *convIndex*+1;
23:         **end if**
24:     **end if**
25: **end while**
26: **return** *correct*;

---

string has not reached the last word, the next iteration is triggered. Finally, the value of the variable *correct* is returned (line 26).

All in all, it can be stated that the pattern formalization is a preparatory step that has to be conducted once. The technique with its three-step part of speech determination, disambiguation, and comparison can then be applied in an automatic fashion to analyze large collections of process models.

4.3 Correcting Linguistic Guideline Violations

While the detection of naming convention violations can indicate improvement opportunities in process models, the effort for correcting the models is still left to the modeler. Thus, a technique for automatically correcting violating labels would even further reduce the maintenance effort. In this section, we address this problem by introducing an approach for automatically correcting process model elements. Section 4.3.1 discusses the requirements for the correction of element labels, then Section 4.3.2 presents the conceptual approach.

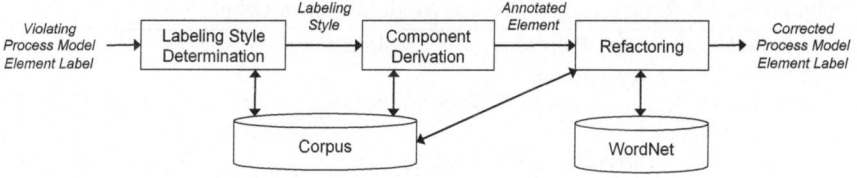

Fig. 4.4 Architecture of Correction Approach

4.3.1 Requirements for Correcting Guideline Violations

Process model labels violating linguistic guidelines can only be corrected automatically if they contain at least an action and a business object. If one of these components is missing, the label cannot be corrected in an automated fashion.

To illustrate this problem, consider the activity label *Invoice creation* and the event label *Customer is member*. The activity label *Invoice creation* contains the action *create* and the business object *invoice*. Hence, it can be refactored to any activity labeling style consisting of action and business object. For example, the label could be converted to the verb-object label *Create invoice* by rearranging action and business object and by deriving the verb *create* from the noun *creation*. For the event label *Customer is member*, the situation is different. Since this label only contains a business object and an auxiliary verb, it is not possible to rearrange these components according to a style containing an action. Since guidelines typically ask for labeling styles containing an action and a business object, the existence of these components is an essential prerequisite.

4.3.2 Conceptual Approach

For those element labels containing an action and a business object, we introduce an automated correction technique that transforms labels into the desired labeling style. Figure 4.4 depicts the general architecture of the correction approach. The input for the approach is a label violating a given naming convention. Building on the techniques from Chapter 3, the input label is assigned to a labeling style and accordingly annotated with its components. Subsequently, the refactoring implements the correction of the label to the desired format.

Algorithm 13 formalizes the refactoring steps. The input is a *LabelProperties* object *prop* containing the annotated components from the considered label, and the object *targetStyle* capturing the component positions of the target labeling style. The algorithm starts with creating a new label object (line 2). Subsequently, the verb form required by the target style is derived from the annotated action (line 3). The details of the transformation are implemented by the function *transformToVerbForm*. Essentially, the function distinguishes between two cases. If the action is given as a verb and the target style requires another verb form, the function

---

Algorithm 13. Refactoring of Process Model Element Label

```
 1: refactorLabel(LabelProperties prop, LabelingStyle targetStyle)
 2: Label label = new Label();
 3: String newAction = transformToVerbForm(targetStyle.getActionVerbForm(),
    prop.action);
 4: for i=1 to i < targetStyle.getLength() do
 5:     if targetStyle.getComponentAtPosition(i) == 'action' then
 6:         label.add(newAction);
 7:     else if targetStyle.getComponentAtPosition(i) == 'bo' then
 8:         label.add(prop.bo);
 9:     else if targetStyle.getComponentAtPosition(i) == 'addition' then
10:         label.add(prop.addition);
11:     else
12:         label.add(targetStyle.getComponentAtPosition(i));
13:     end if
14: end for
15: return label;
```

---

consults the verb table introduced in Section 4.2.2. In case the action is given as a noun, the function employs the lexical database WordNet to transform the noun into a verb. Once the according verb form has been derived, the algorithm iteratively goes through the *targetStyle* object (lines 4-14). For each position, the algorithm checks which element is required by the target style. Accordingly, action, business object, and addition are added to the label in the corresponding order (lines 5-10). If the target style contains additional elements such as prepositions or auxiliary verbs, these elements are added analogously (lines 11-12). After all components have been added, the label is returned (line 15).

Once the refactoring step is completed, a given label has been transformed to the desired labeling style. As a result, a detected guideline violation has been automatically corrected.

4.4 Evaluation

To demonstrate the capability of the presented techniques for checking and correcting naming conventions, we conduct an evaluation experiment. We test both techniques on three large process model collections from practice. The goal of the experiment is to learn how well the automatically recognized violations and corrections match a manually created benchmark. Section 4.4.1 describes the general setup of the experiment. Afterwards, Section 4.4.2 provides an overview of the utilized process model collections. Then, Section 4.4.3 investigates the technique from a runtime performance. Finally, Section 4.4.4 and Section 4.4.5 discuss the overall experiment results from detecting and correcting linguistic guideline violations.

Table 4.2 Allowed Naming Conventions for the Evaluation Experiment

Element Type	Guideline Compliant	Guideline Violation
Activities	VO	AN, DES, NA
Events	PS, MS, AS	CS, Irregular
Gateways	PQ, IQ, AQ, EQ	Irregular

4.4.1 Setup

The setup of the evaluation consists of a prototypical implementation of the presented algorithms and a manually created benchmark. In order to test the presented techniques, we implemented the algorithms in the context of a Java prototype. For realizing the part of speech determination, we used the publicly available corpus *OANC*. We developed a simple parser for automatically extracting the part of speech and the verb table from the corpus. We complemented the verb table by implementing the according conjugation rules with a complete list of exceptions. The information required for this implementation can be easily obtained online.[1] For discussing the further setup details, we first consider the violation detection technique before we subsequently turn to the guideline violation approach.

For the proper assessment of the *violation detection technique*, we created a benchmark for the test collection. Therefore, we manually inspected each label in the test collection and derived the linguistic pattern. In addition, we categorized each label as *guideline compliant* or as *naming convention violation*. In order to decide on the required naming conventions, we employed two sources. First, we used existing guidelines and recommendations from research and practice [224, 304, 17, 225]. Second, we consulted different industry partners who provided us with their process model collections. From their internal process model guidelines we were able to derive specific naming conventions.

Table 4.2 gives an overview of the compliant and non-compliant naming conventions for the evaluation experiment. Note that this configuration can be flexibly adapted to the preferences of organizations. In general, the table illustrates that guidelines for activities are very strict while events and gateways can be labeled more divergently. For activities, there are several guidelines and recommendations available suggesting the use of the verb-object style [224, 304, 17, 225]. For events and gateways, the requirements from practice and academia are usually less specific. Silver [304] suggests that event labels should refer to a state and must be clearly separable from activities. For gateways, the consensus is rather that they should be named with a question that can be logically evaluated. Consequently, we consider all structured gateway question styles to be valid.

For the evaluation of the *guideline violation correction* technique we complemented the aforementioned benchmark with a manual correction of the guideline violating labels. Since only the non-compliant activity styles fulfill the requirements

---

[1] http://www.usingenglish.com/reference/irregular-verbs/

Table 4.3 Details about Used Model Collections

	SAP	CH	AC
Number of Models	604	328	518
No. of Activities	2,433	4,414	4,109
Share of Naming Convention Violations	88.7%	40.2%	25.8%
No. of Events	6,933	10,292	553
Share of Naming Convention Violations	40.4%	35.9%	67.1%
No. of (Labeled) Gateways	-	-	235
Share of Naming Convention Violations	-	-	46.8%
Notation	EPC	EPC	BPMN

of containing an action and a business object, the correction is only applicable for activity labels. Table 4.2 illustrates that the non-compliant event and gateway styles are either irregular or do not contain an action. Hence, the evaluation of the correction technique focusses on activity labels. As the verb-object style is the only activity style that is considered to be guideline compliant, we accordingly transform violating activity labels into the verb-object style. Since activities are the most important process model element, we consider the activity correction to provide relevant insights.

4.4.2   Test Collection Demographics

For the evaluation of the presented techniques, we employ the test sample from the experiment in Chapter 3. Since this collection does not only differ in terms of domain and modeling language, but also in regard to the share of labels violating the naming conventions defined in the previous section, we consider this collection to be well-suited. Table 4.3 gives a brief overview of the main characteristics of the model collections utilized. For further details on the collection, please refer to Table 3.7.

4.4.3   Performance Results

We designed the introduced techniques to support modelers in the context of a modeling tool. Hence, the implementation must be adequately fast such that naming convention violations can be immediately indicated or corrected. Accordingly, we measure the computation time for each investigated model collection. We tested the computation on a MacBook Pro with a 2.26 GHz Intel Core Duo processor and 4 GB RAM, running on Mac OS X 10.6.8 and Java Virtual Machine 1.5. In order to

Table 4.4 Computation Performance

		SAP	CH	AC
Detection	All Activities (ms)	134,722	168,262	169,617
	Single Activity (avg. ms)	55.37	38.12	41.27
	All Events (ms)	412,445	538,477	35,984
	Single Event (avg. ms)	59.49	52.32	153.12
	All Gateways (ms)	-	-	6,461
	Single Gateway (avg. ms)	-	-	27.49
Correction	All Activities (ms)	34,198	51,688	46,858
	Single Activity (avg. ms)	14.06	11.71	11.40

avoid distortions due to one-off setup times, we ran the algorithms twice and measured the second run only. Table 4.4 summarizes the total and average execution times of the naming convention violation detection for each element type and the total and average execution times for the violation correction of activities.

The numbers illustrate that the execution time for the *violation detection* is mainly depending on the share of guideline violations. This is especially emphasized by the events of the English Academic Collection. The share of 67.1% of convention violations results in a significant increase of the overall computation time. The reason for this relates to the algorithm design. In order to classify a given label as *violation*, all other possibilities have to be excluded. This is also the main reason for the performance difference from the technique in Chapter 3. In addition, the querying of the verb and the part of speech table consumes more time. However, all in all, the detection algorithm yields execution times which are well suited for supporting modelers during the modeling process. Even the worst average execution time of 153 milliseconds is fast enough for directly indicating a violation. The execution times for the *correction* are even smaller. Since the labeling style determination and the refactoring are very efficient, the average correction time for an activity label is between 10 and 15 milliseconds. Hence, we consider the implementation to have a sufficient performance in terms of computation time.

4.4.4 Guideline Violation Detection Results

In order to assess the naming violation detection performance, we employ the metrics precision, recall, and f-measure. In this context, the precision value is the number of correctly identified violations divided by the number of retrieved violations. The recall is the number of correctly identified violations divided by the total number of violations in the considered model collection. As it is important for our scenario that both metrics yield sufficiently high values, we also calculate the f-measure, which is the harmonic mean of precision and recall [26].

Table 4.5 Evaluation Results

		SAP	CH	AC
Activities	Recall	98.0%	96.6%	90.0%
	Precision	95.5%	99.7%	93.7%
	F-Measure	96.7%	98.1%	91.8%
Events	Recall	99.3%	93.0%	99.5%
	Precision	98.2%	98.7%	99.0%
	F-Measure	98.7%	95.8%	99.2%
Gateways	Recall	-	-	97.3%
	Precision	-	-	95.5%
	F-Measure	-	-	96.4%

Table 4.5 summarizes the results of the automatic violation detection for the three considered process model collections. In general, the numbers show that the technique for detecting naming convention violations works satisfactory. Even the lowest obtained f-measure is above 91%. However, we also observe notable differences among the model collections. For example, the activities in the CH collection yield an f-measure of 98.1% while the f-measure for the AC collection is only 91.8%. Such differences can be explained with the different modeling style and emphasizes the importance of including different collections in the evaluation experiment. Depending on the modeling style, ambiguous labels are more or less frequent. As the AC collection was mainly created by students, these models contain more ambiguous cases, which in turn results in a slightly poorer performance. Nevertheless, still 90% of all naming convention violations could be successfully detected. Surprisingly, there is no notable effect of the process model element type. In some cases the f-measure for activities is higher than the corresponding event value, in other cases we observe the opposite. For example, the f-measure for events in the academic collection is significantly higher than the corresponding activity value. By contrast, the activity f-measure in the CH collection is higher than the value for the events.

In order to learn about possible improvement opportunities, we investigated the reasons for misclassification. Since the naming convention violation technique directly builds on the parsing algorithms we defined in Chapter 3, we accordingly encounter the same problems. The majority of the errors can be traced back to erroneously resolved ambiguity. In addition, typographic errors, the use of non-standard abbreviations, and the use of modern or domain-specific words caused the misclassification of element labels. However, altogether, the guideline checking algorithm yields good and reliable results and can hence effectively support the quality assurance of process models.

4.4.5 Guideline Violation Correction Results

As already discussed in Section 4.4.1, the guideline violating labeling styles of events and gateways do not contain action and business object. Hence, they cannot be automatically corrected. Accordingly, we test the correction algorithm using activities and transform guideline violating activity labels into the verb-object style.

To evaluate the quality of the final labeling-style correction, we consider two aspects: first, that labels are properly corrected, and second, that labels can also be erroneously corrected. As a baseline for this discussion, we consider the set of action-noun labels ($labels_{AN}$) and the set of descriptive labels ($labels_{DES}$). Together they define the set of all labels that *should be* corrected:

$$labels_{AN+DES} = labels_{AN} \cup labels_{DES} \qquad (4.1)$$

Furthermore, we consider the set of labels that *are actually* corrected. These are either properly or erroneously corrected:

$$labels_c = labels_{c-proper} \cup labels_{c-erroneous} \qquad (4.2)$$

$$labels_{c-proper} = labels_c \cap labels_{AN+DES} \qquad (4.3)$$

$$labels_{c-erroneous} = labels_c \setminus labels_{AN+DES} \qquad (4.4)$$

Based on these sets, we introduce two metrics: correction gain and correction effect. While the correction gain captures the relative share of properly corrected labels, the correction effect also takes into account that labels can be erroneously corrected. We consider it to be important that both metrics yield satisfying results. On the one hand, we aim to maximize the share of mediocre labels that are corrected (correction gain). On the other hand, we also want to minimize the damage caused by the erroneous correction of good labels (correction effect).

$$\text{Correction Gain } CG = \frac{|\ labels_{c-proper}\ |}{|\ labels_{AN} \cup labels_{DES}\ |} \qquad (4.5)$$

$$\text{Correction Effect } CE = \frac{|\ labels_{c-correct}\ | - |\ labels_{c-erroneous}\ |}{|\ labels_c\ |} \qquad (4.6)$$

The correction gain CG is the share of labels which has been properly corrected in relation to the labels to be corrected, i.e., action-noun and descriptive labels. This metric ranges between 0 (no label is properly corrected) and 1 (all required labels are properly corrected). The correction effect CE takes into account the damage of misclassification. It ranges from -1 (all corrected labels are erroneous) and 1 (all labels have been properly corrected).

Figure 4.5 shows the results for both metrics and for each stage of context that has been used to recognize the labeling style. In Figure 4.5(a) we can see that the *correction gain* ranges between 64% and 77% in the different phases for the three collections. The growth of the curves reflects a corresponding increase in the recall of action-noun labels. For all the three collections about 75% of the action-noun

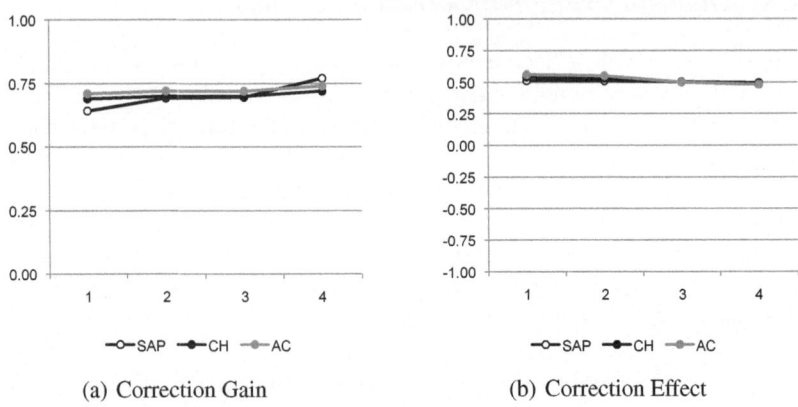

(a) Correction Gain   (b) Correction Effect

Fig. 4.5 Results of Guideline Violation Correction

and descriptive labels have been properly corrected into verb-object labels. In order
to assess the overall *correction effect*, we balance the correct and erroneous corrections.

Following on this analysis, we investigated the cases of misclassification. Altogether, we observe 14% erroneously corrected action-noun labels for the SAP, 12%
for the CH, and 14% for the AC collection. The sources for this wrong correction
can be divided into three classes:

- *Compound Words:* In some cases the algorithm does not recognize compound
  words and treats them as isolated words. For instance, consider the label *New
  User Registration*. In this label, we find the compound noun *new user* and the
  action *register*. However, the algorithm has only limited contextual information
  available to determine whether *new* is an adjective of the business object *user* or
  an adjective characterizing the nominalized action *registration* which should be
  transformed to an adverbial conjunct in the corrected label. Although this case is
  quite clear to humans, the algorithm determines the corrected label *Register user
  newly* and not *Register new user*. By contrast, if we examine the label *Informal
  Sales Conversation*, it becomes clear why this decision is non-trivial. Both labels
  have the same structure. Although the adjective relates to the business object in
  the first case, it is used to qualify the action in the latter case. Hence, the label
  does not require the process participant to *converse* about *informal sales*, but to
  informally converse about *sales*.
- *Adjective-noun Ambiguity*: We have already discussed the problem of zero-
  derivation ambiguity between nouns and verbs. However, the ambiguity problem
  also arises between nouns and adjectives. This becomes critical if we try to identify adjectives which are specifying verbs since the former must be transformed
  into adverbial conjuncts in the corrected label. For instance, in the label *Good
  Receipt* we apparently face the receipt of goods. However, for the algorithm it

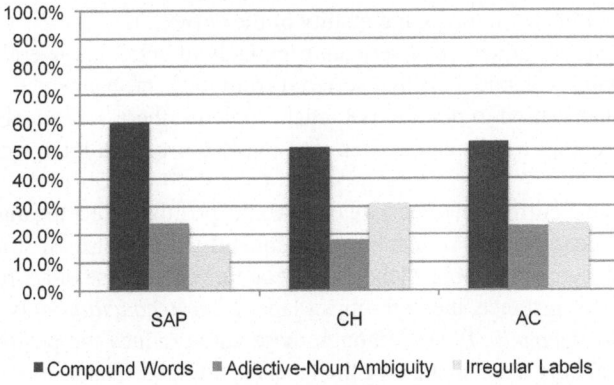

Fig. 4.6 Distribution of Correction Error Sources

is not possible to disambiguate *good*. Hence, the correction of the label is not
determined with *Receive goods* but with *Receive well* due to misinterpretation.

- *Irregular Labels*: Although this problem only applies to a minor share, the investigated collections also contain labels following an arbitrary labeling style. For
these labels such as *LIFO: Group Formation: Change*, it is challenging to infer
the action correctly and also to agree on how an adequate correction of these labels should be defined. Therefore, many of the corrected results of these irregular
labels have been assessed to be improper, either because the action was not correctly inferred or because the structure of the corrected label was not satisfying.

Figure 4.6 illustrates the distribution of the introduced error classes among the
three considered model collections. It shows that compound words are the most frequent error source. The share of labels being erroneously corrected due to compound
words ranges from 51% in the CH collection to 60% in the SAP collection. However, in the three model collections the adjective-noun-ambiguity and the irregular
labels also affect the overall correction result. In order to overcome these problems
in the future, we propose the following strategy.

All three error classes are based on the problem of ambiguity: For one label, theoretically two or even more interpretations are possible. In order to resolve these
ambiguities, we suggest the incorporation of a text corpus. As a result, the most
likely solution can be identified. As an example, consider the above introduced label *New User Registration*. If we look up the words *new user*, we will most likely
obtain more matches than if we search for the word combination *user newly*. Based
on the frequency of the word combination in the corpus, we can identify action
and business object and hence obtain a proper correction. The same strategy can be
applied for irregular labels. As the lack of structure permits the reliable determination of action and business object, all possible action - business object combinations
must be identified. Then, the corpus can be consulted to determine the most likely
combination. An additional solution is the involvement of the user. Being aware

of the fact that a heuristic decision will be made, the feedback of the user can be incorporated to further improve the quality of the correction.

Although the discussed error sources negatively affected the overall correction effect, the share of noun labels that suffered from these problems was quite small. If the algorithm is used to point to potential problems, these shortcomings will not affect the modeling results as the user can simply correct the interpretation of the algorithm.

Turning to the correction effect, we observe the positive effect the algorithm creates in the process model collection. Consequently, this metric also includes the drawback that some verb-object labels might be flawed because of a wrong classification. Thus, for instance, the verb-object label *Plan Reconciliation* is erroneously corrected into *Reconcile Plan*. Although these cases reduce the positive effect of our correction, only a small share of the labels is affected. This is also reflected by the overall correction gain. The final numbers after phase 4 amount to 50% for the SAP Reference Model, 49% for the CH models, and 48% for the AC collection. The development of the metric among the different collections is slightly different. While the correction effect for the SAP collection starts with 51% and hence remains constant, it decreases by 5 and 8 percentage points in the CH and the AC collections. This development can be explained by the combination of the phase concept of our approach and the different labeling style distribution in the affected model collections. Concerning the phases, we can generally state that the certainty of the classification declines with each phase. Thus, if the algorithm is applied on a model collection with only a few action-noun labels, the number of erroneously corrected labels may exceed the number of properly corrected labels and lead to an overall decrease of the correction effect. However, the trade off between a high-correction gain and a suitable correction effect can be explicitly reached by reasonably defining the number of phases. Altogether, we can state that the correction gain and effect show that our approach significantly improves the labeling quality in the considered process models collections. Although some labels may be flawed, these can be easily and quickly corrected by the user as the amount is relatively small.

In summary, it can be stated that the correction approach performs satisfactory on the three model collections. A great share of labels can be corrected by the help of the algorithm and only a manageable amount of labels requires further inspection.

4.5   Adaptation to Other Languages

As opposed to structural quality checks, algorithms for linguistic analysis are, at least to some extent, always bound to a target language. In the following, we discuss the possibility of the guideline violation detection and correction techniques to be adapted to languages other than English.

The *guideline violation detection* algorithm presented in this chapter was designed to be easily adaptable to other languages. Since the approach does not build on any linguistic tools, the adaptation is possible without larger restrictions. In particular, two essential steps are required: the formalization of the linguistic guidelines of the target language and the generation of the required part-of-speech tagging sources from a suitable corpus.

For English process models for instance, it is necessary to *formalize the linguistic guidelines* of the considered target language. For each process model element type, the rules must be transformed into a linguistic pattern. Depending on the language, these rules may strongly deviate from the English patterns. For example, the verb-object recommendation for activities does not apply for German or Portuguese models. A guideline from a large German health insurer suggests to employ the object-infinitive style. As the German language has two different imperative modes, the object-infinitive style conveys the information in a more neutral manner. A similar observation can be made for Portuguese models. A guideline from a large Brazilian Energy Corporation also asks for the application of the object-infinitive style. In general, this step represents a necessary one-time effort for each language. Since it can be accomplished in a reasonable amount of time, we do not consider it as a restriction for the adaptation of the guideline-checking approach.

In addition to the formalization, it is necessary to provide the *part-of-speech tagging sources* for the algorithm. In particular, that includes a text corpus of the target language and the according verb and part of speech tables. In general, text corpora are easily obtainable for various languages. As examples, consider the *Corpus del Español* (Spanish), *Floresta* (Portuguese), and the *Tiger Corpus* (German). Since text corpora are the basis for a variety of linguistic tools, they are also available for less frequently spoken languages. Similarly, irregular verb lists and conjugation rules are readily available online.[2,3,4] As a result, the required resources for adapting the guideline-checking technique can be easily obtained. While the creation of the tagging resources can be associated with a particular effort, it is a step which only needs to be conducted once.

The adaptation of the *correction algorithm* to other languages has one additional requirement. Since we use WordNet for transforming nominalized actions into verbs, the replacement of WordNet represents a critical issue. For resolving this problem, we propose the following solutions. Either the English WordNet database is replaced with a local WordNet solution or the verb derivation must be implemented using a corpus. For the latter case a stemming algorithm could be used to derive the word stem of the considered noun. Using this stem, the corresponding verb can then be identified in a corpus. As an example, consider the noun *notification*. Using a stemmer, the word stem *notif* can be easily and efficiently computed. Having a stem at hand, it is straightforward to identify verbs in the corpus containing it. As a result, the verb *notify* is correctly identified. Analogously to the aforementioned adaptation steps, this implementation represents a one-time effort with reasonable complexity. Stemmers, as for instance the Porter Stemmer [268], can be freely obtained for various languages.

---

[2] http://spanish.speak7.com/spanish_irregular_verbs.htm
[3] http://www.orbilat.com/Languages/Portuguese/Grammar/
Verbs/index.html
[4] http://www.evertype.com/gram/german-verbs.html

Altogether, it can be stated that the guideline violation detection and correction approach can be effectively adapted to other languages. Since natural language text corpora and stemmers are widely and freely available, the adaptation to other languages is not impeded by complex modifications of the presented algorithms.

4.6   Summary

In this chapter, we addressed the problem of automatically detecting and correcting naming convention violations in process model elements. We built on the parsing algorithms from Chapter 3 and text corpora to create flexible techniques for detecting and correcting process models violating linguistic guidelines. In contrast to previous research, it is not only suitable for enforcing naming conventions but also for the ex-post compliance checking and correction of labels. The evaluation using three business process model collections from practice demonstrates the applicability of the techniques. For the detection of guideline violations we achieved recall values between 90% and 99.5%. With regard to the correction of naming convention violations we observed that about 75% of the action-noun and descriptive labels were properly corrected into verb-object labels in all the three collections. An analysis of the error sources revealed that compound words, adjective-noun ambiguity, and irregular labels are the main sources for erroneous corrections. However, the values for the correction effect of between 48% and 50% also illustrate that the damage due to erroneously corrected labels is kept to a manageable amount. As a result, the presented techniques help to further automate the quality assurance of process models in practice. Due to the greatest possible independence from linguistic tools, this is not restricted to English models, but can also be realized for other languages. As many companies model processes using their local language, this can be considered as a particularly important feature. While the detection and correction of linguistic guideline violations helps to automatically address important quality issues, the modeler still needs to be familiar with process models to understand its semantics. In the next chapter, we investigate how far modelers can be further supported by automatically generating natural language texts from process models.

Chapter 5
Generation of Natural Language Texts from Process Models

Process models are widely used for documenting and redesigning the operations of companies. The audience of these models ranges from well-trained system analysts and developers to casual staff members who are unexperienced in terms of modeling. Hence, most of the latter lack the ability to understand process model in detail. This is a particular problem as this impedes the usage of process models to the desired extent. In this chapter, we investigate in how far the concept of natural language generation can be adapted to process models in order to provide all staff members with a understandable process description. To this end, we define an approach which automatically transforms BPMN process models into understandable natural language texts.

In order to point out the difficulties which are associated with generating natural language from process models, Section 5.1 reflects on the current state of the art of natural language generation systems. Then, in Section 5.2, we introduce our approach for generating text from process models on a conceptual level. Subsequently, in Section 5.3, we demonstrate the applicability of the defined approach for generating accurate and understandable natural language texts. In Section 5.4, we continue with discussing the necessary steps for adapting the technique to languages other than English. Finally, Section 5.5 closes the chapter.

5.1 Generation of Natural Language

Natural Language Generation systems have been around for many years and were applied in many different scenarios. Examples include the generation of weather forecasts [133], the creation of reports on computer systems [160], and the automatic documentation of planning engineering activities [218]. There are also a few applications of text generation for conceptual modeling. The *ModelExplainer* generates natural language descriptions of object models [202] and the *GeNLangUML* system transforms UML class diagrams into text specifications [229]. In order to better understand how far these systems address the specific problems of generating text from process models, we investigate the generation of natural language in more detail. In Section 5.1.1, we introduce the typical architecture of natural language generation systems. Afterwards, in Section 5.1.2, we discuss the generation of natural language from business process models and highlight the associated challenges.

5.1.1 Architecture of Natural Language Generation Systems

In general, there are different techniques available in order to translate process models into natural language text. Simple, also often called non-linguistic, approaches are based on canned text or templates-based systems. In the first case, some input data is directly mapped to a predefined string. For instance, a system translating weather data into natural language text could use the sentence *The weather will be nice today* for expressing a warm and sunny day. Slightly more advanced is the use of templates where at least some information is added to the predefined string. In this case, the template *Today there is a X% probability of rain* could be filled with the according rain probability derived from a data source. However, such approaches are not considered to be truly linguistic techniques as the manipulation is done at the character string level [279].

Linguistic, or *real* natural language generation approaches, use intermediate structures to obtain a deeper representation of the text. Such an intermediate structure usually specifies the main lexemes (abstract representations of words encapsulating inflectional aspects) for each sentence. Moreover, it carries additional information, defining, for instance, the tense or the modus of the verb. As pointed out by Reiter, many natural language generation systems take a three-step pipeline approach including the following stages [280]:

1. *Text Planning*: First, the information is determined, which is communicated in the text. Furthermore, it is specified in which order this information will be conveyed.
2. *Sentence Planning*: Afterwards, specific words are chosen to express the information determined in the preceding phase. If applicable, messages are aggregated and pronouns are introduced in order to obtain variety.
3. *Surface Realization*: Finally, the messages are transformed into grammatically correct sentences.

Natural language generation systems have also been defined in a functional way [62]. Nevertheless, the core of all these architectures is the usage of an intermediate structure for storing messages before they are transformed into natural language sentences. The advantage of this procedure is the significant gain in maintainability and flexibility. In a template-based system, each template must be manually modified if a change in the output text is required. In a linguistic-based approach, the output of the generation system can be altered by changing a parameter of the intermediate structure. For instance, the sentence *The weather will be nice today* can be easily transformed into *The weather is nice today* by adapting the tense feature of the main verb in the intermediate representation. Although templates and canned

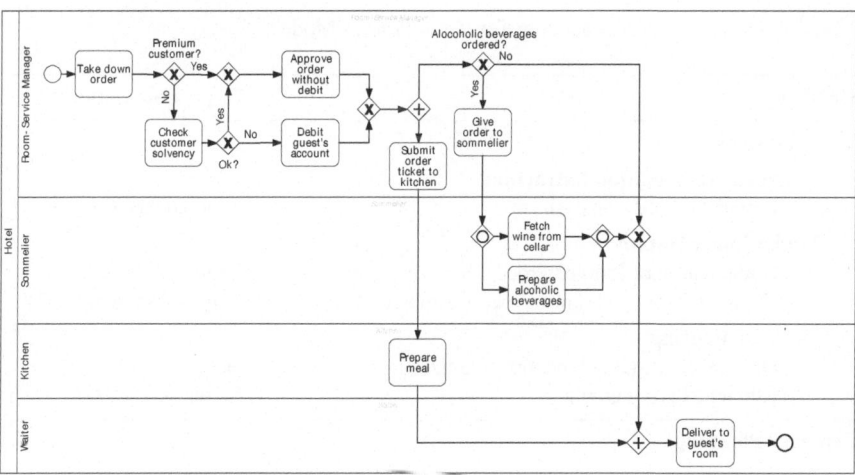

Fig. 5.1 Exemplary BPMN Process

text have been critically discussed, they also have advantages [88]. Therefore, Reiter and Mellish propose a cost-benefit analysis [281]. As a result, many natural language generation systems use hybrid approaches where linguistic techniques are combined with canned text and templates [129, 282, 261].

5.1.2 Challenges for Generating Text from Process Models

There are a number of challenges for the automatic generation of text from process models. To illustrate these challenges, we use the exemplary process model depicted in Figure 5.1. It shows a business process from a hotel represented as a BPMN model. It describes how an order is handled. The process includes four roles and is hence subdivided into four lanes. The process starts when the room-service manager takes down an order. The subsequent steps depend on the status and the solvency of the customer. If the customer has the status *premium* or is considered as solvent, the room-service manager approves the order without debit. Otherwise, the guests account is debited directly . Afterwards, the process is split up into two concurrent streams of action: a meal is prepared in the kitchen and beverages are prepared if required. Finally, the order is delivered to the customer.

In order to develop a proper understanding of the challenges that are associated with generating text from process models, we analyzed the required generation steps and investigated the respective literature on natural language generation systems. The challenges can be assigned to one of four different categories including text planning, sentence planning, surface realization, and flexibility. Table 5.1 provides an overview of the identified challenges (bold font) and the according approaches addressing them (standard font).

Table 5.1 Challenges for Generating Text from Process Models

Challenges	Applicable Concepts
Text Planning	
Linguistic Information Extraction	
Linguistic Label Analysis	Leopold (see Chapter 3)
Model Linearization	
Computation of Refined Process Structure Tree	Vanhatalo et al. [322]
Generalization of Refined Process Structure Tree	Polyvyanyy et al. [265]
Text Structuring	
Optimal Multi-paragraph Text Segmentation	Heinonen [147]
Efficient Text Planning	Meteer [228, 227]
Sentence Planning	
Lexicalization	
Corpus-based Lexical Choice	Bangalore & Owen [31]
Lexical Choice Criteria	Stede [311, 312]
Message Refinement	
Role of Aggregation in Language	Hovy [153]
Role and Definition of Aggregation in NLG	Reape & Mellish [274]
Redundancy Reducing Aggregation in NLG	Dalianis [82]
Framework for Pronominalisation	Kibble & Power [178]
Surface Realization	
Fast and Portable Realizer	Lavoie & Rambow [201]
Integrated Surface Realization	Busemann [60]
Plug-in Syntactic Realization Component	Michael & Robin [106]
Real-time Natural Language Realization for Dialogues	McRoy et al. [220]
Flexibility	
Varying Input	
Generation of Summaries from Multiple News Articles	McKeown & Radev [219]
Generation from Multiple On-line Sources	Radev & McKeown [270]
Output Adaptation	
Generation of Stylistically Varying Texts	Hovy [152]
Multi-lingual Generation	Goldberg et al. [133]
Multi-lingual Generation	Bateman [33]
Generation of Language and Graphics	Wahlster et al. [327]

In the *text planning* phase, we face three main challenges. First, we have to adequately infer the given linguistic information from the process model elements. For instance, the activity *Take down order* must be automatically split up into the action *take down* and the business object *order*. Without this separation, it would be unclear which of the two words defines the verb. As discussed in Chapter 3, this is complicated by the shortness of process model labels and the ambiguity of the English language. The second challenge is the linearization of the process model to a sequence of sentences. The problem in this context is that process models rarely consist of a plain sequence of tasks. Typically, they include non-sequential behaviour represented by concurrent branches and decision points. One solution to this problem is presented by Vanhatalo et al. and Polyvyanyy et al. [265, 322]. They introduce the concept of the Refined Process Structure Tree, which facilitates the linearization of a process model. Nevertheless, as this is not the primary purpose of the tree, we need to adapt the technique in order to successfully employ it for text generation. In this context, it should be noted that the verbalization of concurrency was not addressed by former natural language generation techniques. The third challenge is to decide where techniques of text structuring and formatting such as paragraphs and bullet points should be applied. To adequately address this problem, a lot of research has been conducted in the field of natural language generation (see e.g. [147, 228, 227]). However, these approaches work solely on the text and do not include information from related resources like process models.

The *sentence planning* phase entails the tasks of lexicalization and message refinement. The aspect of lexicalization refers to the mapping from BPMN constructs to specific words. Particularly in the context of natural language generation without natural language input, the choice of words represents a considerable challenge [31, 311, 312]. However, for process models this problem does not occur to the same degree. Due to the extensive natural language input, the lexical choice is reduced to the proper integration of the linguistic information from the process model such that the process is described in an understandable manner. The aspect of message refinement refers to the construction of texts. It includes the aggregation of messages, the introduction of referring expressions as pronouns, and also the insertion of discourse markers such as *afterwards* and *subsequently*. In order to suitably consolidate sentences, the option of aggregation must first be identified and then it has to be decided where it can be applied to improve the text quality. As these problems represent one of the core tasks of natural language generation, they have been extensively discussed in literature. For instance, Hovy investigates the general role of aggregation in language [153]. Reape and Mellish [274] as well as Dalianis [82] present a variety of concrete aggregation approaches. However, these approaches also abstract from the existence of related resources like process models. The introduction of referring expressions requires the automatic recognition of entity types. For instance, the role *kitchen* must be referenced with *it* while the role *waiter* must be referenced with *he* or *she*. The decision on where to apply referring expressions is, for instance, discussed in [178]. The insertion of discourse markers should further increase the readability and variability of the text. Hence, varying markers must be inserted at suitable positions.

In the context of the *surface realization*, the actual generation of a grammatically correct sentence is performed. This requires the determination of a suitable word order, the inflection of words, introduction of function words (e.g., articles), and tasks such as punctuation and capitalization. Up until now, many components for surface realization have been introduced [201, 60, 106, 220, 226]. They are based

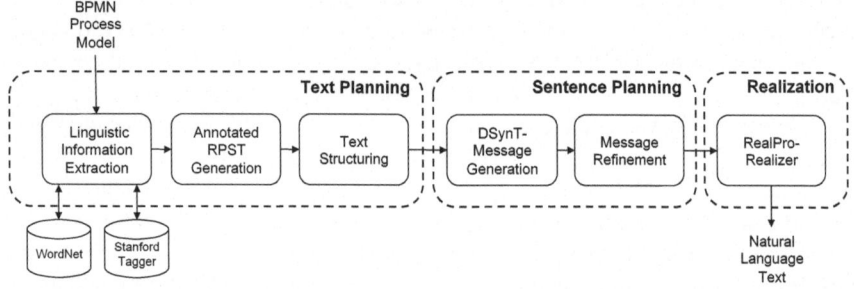

Fig. 5.2 Architecture of the NLG System

on different theoretical concepts such as the Meaning Text Theory [222], functional grammar [175], or the simple frame language [14], and hence ask for different input formats.

Besides the core natural language generation tasks, we consider *flexibility* to be an important feature. As we do not expect the input models to adhere to certain conventions, we have to deal with considerably differing characteristics of the input models. The issue of varying input was also discussed for other natural language generation systems [219, 270]. Although the general problem is similar, these works mainly worked with textual inputs. As natural language only represents one of many dimensions that is subject to variation, we also need to address further aspects. For instance, if a model uses lanes and thus provides a role description, the sentence can be presented in active voice (e.g., *The room-service manager takes down the order*). If it is unknown who performs the considered task, the description must be presented in passive voice (*The order is taken down*). A similar approach was pursued in [152] where stylistically varying texts are generated. Other examples include the generation of multiple languages [133, 33] or the generation of graphics and text [327].

Against the background of the identified challenges and the respective solutions, we define a technique for generating natural language text from process models in the following section.

5.2 Text Generation Approach

This section defines our approach to text generation. First, Section 5.2.1 gives an overview of the general architecture and the comprised components. Subsequently, in the sections 5.2.2 to 5.2.7, we introduce each component in detail.

5.2.1 Overview

The architecture of our text generation approach is building on the traditional NLG pipeline concept [280]. The basic rationale of the approach is to utilize the existing information from the model to generate a text. In order to derive a sequence of sentences, we linearize the model via the creation of a tree structure. In particular, the text generation technique comprises six components (see Figure 5.2):

1. *Linguistic Information Extraction*: Extraction of linguistic components from the process model element labels.
2. *Annotated RPST Generation*: Linearization of process model through the generation of a tree structure. In addition, each node is annotated with the linguistic information from the latter component.
3. *Text Structuring*: Application of text structure techniques such as the insertion of paragraphs and bullet points based on the computed tree structure.
4. *DSynT-Message Generation*: Generation of an intermediate linguistic message structure for each node of the tree. This component represents the core of the generation technique.
5. *Message Refinement*: Refinement of the generated messages through aggregation or the introduction of referring expressions and discourse markers.
6. *RealPro-Realizer*: Transformation of intermediate message structures to grammatically correct sentences.

In the following sections, we introduce and explain each of these components in detail.

5.2.2 Linguistic Information Extraction

The goal of this component is the adequate inference of linguistic information from all labeled process model elements. Consequently, we employ the parsing and annotation techniques defined in Chapter 3 to annotate activities, events, and gateways.

As a result, for instance the activity *Take down order* is adequately decomposed into the action *take down* and the business object *order*. Analogously, events and gateways are analyzed and enriched with the according component annotation. For example, the gateway *Alcoholic Beverages Ordered?* is annotated with the action *order* and the business object *alcoholic beverages*. Note that gateways represent an important source of information in the context of text generation. As they define decision points, they are transformed into conditional sentences describing alternative behaviour in the process. Once the annotation has been conducted for all labeled process model elements, the annotation records are handed over to the next module.

5.2.3 Annotated RPST Generation

The RPST Generation module derives a tree representation from each pool of the input model in order to provide a basis for describing the process step by step. In particular, we compute a Refined Process Structure Tree (RPST), which is a parse tree containing a hierarchy of sub-graphs derived from the original model [265, 322].

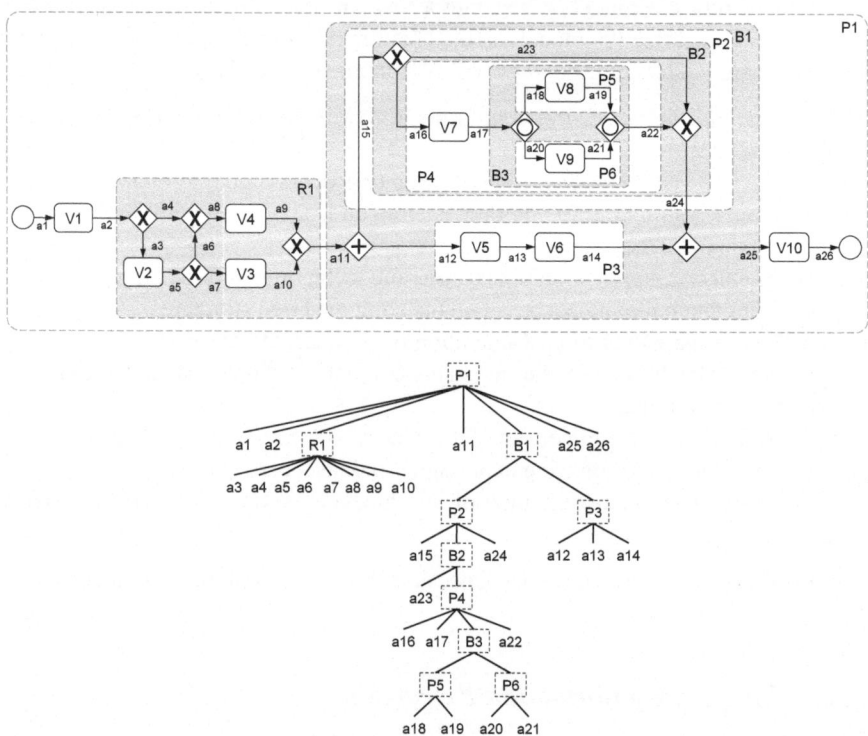

Fig. 5.3 Abstract Version of Figure 5.1 and its RPST

The RPST is based on the observation that every workflow graph can be decomposed into a hierarchy of logically independent sub graphs having a single entry and single exit. Such sub graphs with a single entry and a single exit are referred to as fragments. In an RPST, any two of these fragments are either nested or disjoint. The resulting hierarchy can be shown as a tree where the root is the entire tree and the leaves are fragments with a single arc.

In total, we may encounter four different fragment classes: trivial fragments (T), bonds (B), polygons (P), and rigids (R). Trivial fragments consist of two nodes connected with a single arc. A bond represents a set of fragments sharing two common nodes. In BPMN process models, this generally applies to split and join gateways, including more complex split and join structures such as loops. Polygons capture sequences of other fragments. Hence, any sequence in a process model is reflected by a respective polygon fragment. If a fragment cannot be assigned to one of the latter classes, it is categorized as a rigid. As an example for a rigid, consider the part of the hotel process between the first xor-split and the and-split. Due to the combination of multiple decisions and activities that cannot be represented by trivial, bond, or polygon fragments, this model part is categorized as a rigid.

Figure 5.3 illustrates the previous concepts using an abstracted version of the hotel process and its corresponding RPST. To adapt the original RPST generation algorithm to the specific requirements of text generation, we extend it with three additional features: automatic ordering of the fragments, processing of models with multiple entries and exits, and the annotation of the nodes with the extracted linguistic information.

Since the RPST generation algorithm by [265] *does not order* the fragments with respect to the control flow, we respectively modify the RPST computation. For each level in the RPST, the order can be determined by arranging the fragments according to their appearance in the process model. Hence, the first level starts with the trivial fragment *a1*, connecting the start event and vertex *V1*. Respectively, the trivial fragment *a2*, the rigid *R1*, etc. are following. If the order is not defined, as for instance in case of parallel branches, an objective criterion such as the path length is employed for determining an order that is conducive for text generation purposes. As rigids define behaviour that cannot be represented by sequences of RPST nodes without duplicating nodes, the ordering is not applied to rigids.

To generate RPSTs from process models *with multiple entries and exits*, we extend the algorithm according to the generalization described in [264]. In particular, we augment process models with multiple start events with an additional start node and add an arc from this new node to each of the original start events. Respectively, a model with multiple end events is augmented with an additional end node and an arc from each original end event to the newly introduced end node. At the end of the structuring process, we remove the additionally introduced nodes. As a result, the RPST can also be computed for process models with multiple start and end events.

In addition to these amendments, we also *annotate* the RPST with *the linguistic information* from the extraction phase and with additional meta information. For instance, the vertex *V1* from the trivial fragment *a1* is annotated with the action *take down*, the business object *order*, and the role *room-service manager*. The bond *B1* is annotated with the action *order*, the business object *beverages* and the adjective *alcoholic*. Further, the bond is tagged as an xor-gateway with *Yes/No*-arcs of the type *skip*. The latter aspect is derived from the fact that one branch is directly flowing into the join gateway and hence provides a possibility to skip the activities on the alternative branch.

5.2.4 Text Structuring

The question of how to optimally structure natural texts using paragraphs has been widely discussed in prior research. Many methods employ a similarity metric such as the semantic relatedness between words to compute the lexical cohesion between the sentences of a text [145, 146, 237]. Based on the resulting similarity distribution, a text can be heuristically subdivided into multiple paragraphs. More sophisticated approaches try to use the similarity distribution for identifying the optimal fragment boundaries [147]. However, while the semantic cohesion in standard natural language texts must be completely derived from its semantics, a text generated from a process model can also be structured by building on the features of the model.

Against this background, we introduce two approaches for obtaining a manageable and well-readable text. First, we use bullet points to properly communicate the branches of splits. As a result, the text is partitioned into semantically related paragraphs. Moreover, parallel as well as alternative branches are clearly explicated in the text. In case of nested splits, the bullet points are indented respectively. That enables the reader to easily keep track of nested structures. In addition to bullet points, we also partition the text using multiple paragraphs. A particular problem in this context is that there is no consensus concerning the optimal number of sentences or words per paragraph. Nevertheless, experiments demonstrated that paragraphs containing more than 100 words are already less understandable than paragraphs with fewer words [156]. Building on this insight, we include an editable parameter for defining the size of a paragraph and predefine this parameter with a value of 75 words. Once this threshold is reached, we use a change of the performing role or an intermediate event as indicator for semantic cohesion and respectively introduce a new paragraph.

5.2.5   DSynT-Message Generation

This section introduces the message generation component. It transforms the annotated RPST into a list of intermediate messages. Therefore, it recursively traverses the annotated RPST and derives an intermediate message structure for each RPST node. In the beginning of this section, we introduce the *Deep-Syntactic Tree* as format of the generated messages. Then, we provide a detailed explanation of the transformation of the process model elements. Finally, we discuss how the sub-steps are integrated into the overall transformation approach.

5.2.5.1   Deep-Syntactic Trees

Each message derived from the annotated RPST is stored in a so-called deep-syntactic tree (DSynT). A deep-syntactic tree is a dependency representation, which was introduced in the context of the Meaning Text Theory [172, 222]. It is used to represent the most significant aspects of the syntactic structure of a sentence. The advantage of such trees is the rich yet still manageable representation. Further, there exist several off-the-shelf surface realizers which directly transform deep-syntactic trees into grammatically correct sentences (see e.g. [201, 60, 106, 220]). Hence, we decided to design an algorithm that maps the given RPST into a list of DSynT-based messages.

In a deep-syntactic tree, each node carries a semantically-full lexeme, meaning that words such as conjunctions or auxiliary verbs are excluded. Moreover, each lexeme in a deep-syntactic tree is enriched with grammatical meta information, so-called grammemes. That, for instance, includes the voice and tense of verbs or also the number and definiteness of nouns. The branches of the DSynT define the relationship between two nodes. The required set of relations is rather small. For the

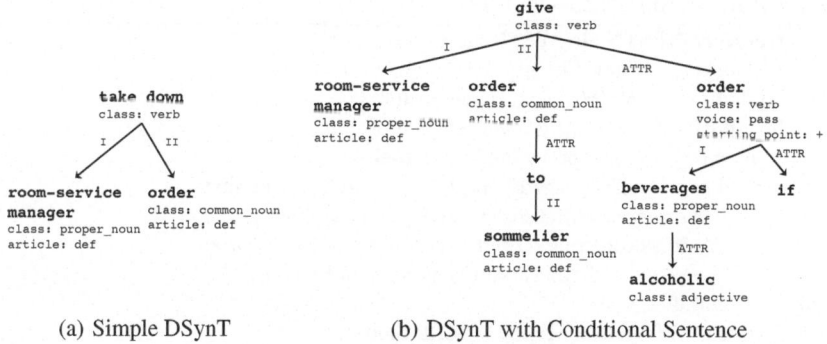

(a) Simple DSynT   (b) DSynT with Conditional Sentence

Fig. 5.4 Two Examples for Deep-Syntactic Trees

purpose of generating text from process models, we employ two actantial[1] relations (denoted with I and II). The first relation is specifying the subject and the second relation determines the object of the referenced verb. In addition, we make use of an attributive relation (ATTR) and a relation for conjoining elements (COORD).

Figure 5.4 illustrates the DSynT concept by showing two example trees. Figure 5.4(a) represents the sentence *The room-service manager takes down the order* and Figure 5.4(b) captures the conditional sentence *If alcoolic beverages are ordered, the room-service manager gives the order to the sommelier*. The two examples illustrate that the root of a deep-syntactic tree is is always formed by the main verb of the sentence and the actantial relations are used to specify subject and object. The ATTR relation is applied in two ways. First, to append adjectives to nouns, and second, to append a conditional sentence to the main sentence. The grammemes of the depicted trees essentially include the *word class* and the *definiteness* of articles. In addition, the lexeme *order* carries the grammeme *starting_point* specifying the position of the conditional clause. As a result, the deep-syntactic trees contain all information that is required for constructing a proper sentence.

5.2.5.2 Traversing the Annotated RPST

Starting point for the transformation of the annotated RPST into a set of intermediate messages is the recursive traversing of the tree. Depending on the type of the considered RPST node, the respective algorithm for the transformation is triggered. Algorithm 14 formalizes this procedure on the highest level of abstraction. The algorithm requires an RPST node as input and returns an ordered list of DSynT messages. Note that the input node may represent the root or any other node of the RPST.

---

[1] An actant is a linguistic term for denoting a noun phrase that is functioning as the agent of the main verb.

Algorithm 14. Annotated RPST Traversing

```
 1: transformRPSTNode(RPSTNode node)
 2: List messages = new List();
 3: Global List passedMessages = new List();
 4: for all RPSTNode child ∈ node.getChildren() do
 5:     if child.getNodeType() = TRIVIAL then
 6:         if child.getEntry().getElementType() = ACTIVITY then
 7:             messages.add(transformActivity(child.getEntry()));
 8:         else if child.getEntry().getElementType() = EVENT then
 9:             messages.add(transformEvent(child.getEntry()));
10:         end if
11:     else if child.getNodeType() = BOND then
12:         messages.add(transformBond(child));
13:     end if
14:     if child.getNodeType() = RIGID then
15:         messages.add(transformRigid(child));
16:     else if child.getNodeType() = POLYGON then
17:         messages.add(transformRPSTNode(child));
18:     end if
19: end for
20: return messages;
```

In the beginning, a list for the DSynT messages and a global list for *passed messages* is created (line 2-3). The latter list serves as a stack for messages that need to be incorporated into the text at a later point in time. It is particularly important for the transformation of bonds. In the following loop, each child node of the current RPST node is analyzed (lines 4-19). If the child is a trivial node, it is further checked whether it is representing an activity or an event. This is done by deriving the data from the entry element of the RPST node because an RPST node always consists of a connection of two vertices, each representing a process model element. Since the exit element is included as an entry element in the subsequent RPST node, this procedure avoids the event that a single process element is considered twice. If the node entry represents an activity, the respective function for transforming activities is triggered (line 7). Otherwise, if the node entry is an event, the event transformation function is executed (line 9). The return value of these functions is a set of DSynT messages which have been created for conveying the semantics of the respective process model element. For the RPST node types *bond* and *rigid*, the algorithm proceeds analogously. If the considered child node represents a bond or a rigid, the respective transformation function is called (lines 12 and 15). Polygon nodes are treated differently. As they represent a sequence of RPST nodes, the algorithm *traverseAnnotatedRPST* is recursively triggered for a polygon. As a result, the comprised nodes are transformed in the underlying iterations. Note that also bonds and rigids contain further RPST nodes. The called transformation functions make equal use of *traverseAnnotatedRPST* to convert the subsumed elements into

DSynT messages. Finally, after all nodes have been transformed into intermediate messages, the list of messages is returned (line 20).

In the following subsections, we discuss the specific steps for the transformation of trivial nodes, bonds, and rigids.

5.2.5.3 Transformation of Trivial RPST Nodes

As trivial nodes are always leaves of the RPST, they either represent activities or events. Thus, every activity and every event is transformed into a single sentence. This is accomplished by properly representing the activity or event as a deep-syntactic tree. Due to the annotation, all required information is readily available. In total, four pieces of information must be properly organized in a DSynT: action, business object, additional information, and the role.

Algorithm 15 illustrates the required steps for activities. It requires an RPST node pointing to an activity as input and returns a deep-syntactic tree representing the resulting sentence.

The algorithm starts with deriving the activity from the RPST node (line 2). As previously discussed, an RPST node always consists of a connection of two vertices, each representing a process model element. In order to avoid that an element is considered twice, we always extract the entry vertex from the given RPST node. After the activity object has been obtained, a new DSynT and a DSynT node for the action is created (lines 3-4). The class of the action node is specified with *verb* and the lemma is determined with the annotated infinitive of the action (lines 5-6). Subsequently, the node is added to the deep-syntactic tree representation (line 7). As the action node represents the root of the tree, the *relation* attribute is not further specified.

If the considered activity contains a business object, a respective node is created. Therefore, the class of the node is determined with *noun* and the relation is specified with type *II*. Then, the business object node is appended to the action node as a child (lines 9-13). As a result, the business object plays the grammatical role of an object. Considering the represented sentence, this means that the business object is positioned after the verb. For the incorporation of the additional fragment, the insertion of two nodes is required. The first captures the preposition introducing the addition. The second node contains the additional fragment itself. In case the considered activity includes an addition, a node of the class *preposition* with the relation type *ATTR* is created (lines 15-20). Then, a node for the addition belonging to the class noun and the relation type *II* is introduced. The incorporation of the nodes into the DSynT is realized by appending the addition node to the preposition node and the preposition node to the action node (lines 26-27). Afterwards, the role insertion is handled.

If a role description is available, a respective node is created (line 30). As the role plays the grammatical role of a subject, the relation is specified with type *I* (line 33). In case no role description is available, the *voice* attribute of the verb is set to *passive* (line 36). As a result, a missing role description causes a passive sentence. To illustrate this approach consider the activity *Prepare Meal*. Knowing that this activity is conducted by the role *kitchen*, we can describe this activity with *The*

Algorithm 15. Activity Transformation

```
 1: transformActivity(RPSTNode node)
 2: Activity a = node.getEntry();
 3: DSynT dsynt = new DSynT();
 4: DSynTNode actionNode = new DSynTNode();
 5: actionNode.setClass('verb');
 6: actionNode.setLemma(a.getAnnotation().getAction());
 7: dsynt.addNode(actionNode);
 8: if a.getAnnotation().getBO().isEmpty() = false then
 9:     DSynTNode boNode = new DSynTNode();
10:     boNode.setClass('noun');
11:     boNode.setLemma(a.getAnnotation().getBO());
12:     boNode.setRelationType('II');
13:     actionNode.addNode(boNode);
14: end if
15: if a.getAnnotation().getAdd().equals(") = false then
16:     DSynTNode prepNode = new DSynTNode();
17:     prepNode.setClass('preposition');
18:     String preposition = a.getAnnotation().getAdd().getPreposition();
19:     prepNode.setLemma(preposition);
20:     prepNode.setRelationType('ATTR');
21:     DSynTNode addNode = new DSynTNode();
22:     addNode.setClass('noun');
23:     String addition = a.getAnnotation().getAdd().getAddition();
24:     prepNode.setLemma(addition);
25:     addNode.setRelationType('II');
26:     prepNode.addNode(addNode);
27:     actionNode.addNode(prepNode);
28: end if
29: if a.getAnnotation().getRole().isEmpty() = false then
30:     DSynTNode roleNode = new DSynTNode();
31:     roleNode.setClass('noun');
32:     roleNode.setLemma(a.getAnnotation().getRole());
33:     roleNode.setRelationType('I');
34:     verbNode.addNode(roleNode);
35: else
36:     actionNode.setVoice('passive');
37: end if
38: if passedMessages.getSize() > 0 then
39:     dsynt = mergeSentences(dsynt, passedFragments);
40: end if
41: return dsynt;
```

---

kitchen prepares the meal. If the role *kitchen* was not available, the passive voice would be used to communicate this activity as *The meal is prepared.*

In case there are passed messages from prior transformation steps such as conditions from splits and joins, these messages are incorporated into the activity (lines

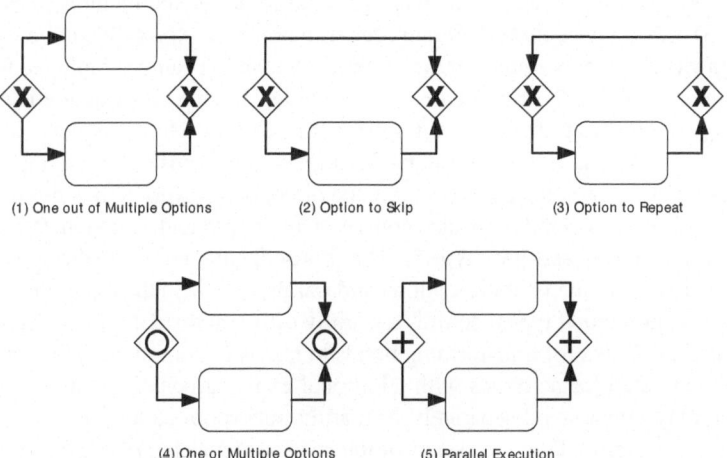

Fig. 5.5 Main Bond Structures in BPMN Process Models

38-40). Finally, the created DSynT object *dsynt* is returned (line 41). Due to complexity, the presented algorithm only discusses the main steps. Exceptional cases and further modifications such as the number of nouns or the specification of articles are not covered. Based on the circumstances, the generation algorithm automatically decides about these features. The details are implemented in a rule system.

Since the transformation steps for events are very similar to the activity transformation, we do not provide a formal description of the event transformation function *transformEvent*. The key difference is that events are enriched with additional meta information. For example, we provide an XML DSynT template for intermediate timer events that communicate that a certain time condition must be met before the process can continue. In a similar way, message, error, and other event types are transformed into natural language text. For attached events, we implemented a special treatment. As they typically lead to an alternative path in the model, they often result in a rigid. In order to communicate attached events in the most intuitive fashion, we create an extra RPST for each attached event and the respective alternative path. By linking this RPST to the source activity, attached events are transformed to text without using the transformation algorithm for rigids.

5.2.5.4 Transformation of Bonds

We previously defined a bond as a set of RPST fragments sharing two common nodes. In addition, we pointed out that this applies to block-structured splits and joins. In order to adequately transform bonds into natural language, it is necessary to investigate which particular bond types we may encounter in process models.

Figure 5.5 gives an overview of the main bond types in BPMN process models. It illustrates that there are five main process model structures that are captured by bonds. Each of them is conveying semantics that need to be addressed slightly differently in terms of natural language generation. Bonds containing an xor-split (type 1-3) may capture three different scenarios. First, an xor-split can be used for indicating a choice between different activities. Second, it can be employed for providing the possibility to skip one or more activities. Such a construction is characterized by an empty arc from the xor-split to the xor-join. Third, an xor-split might be used to implement a loop. Similarly to skips, a loop construction comprises an empty arc. However, in the case of a loop, the direction is inverted. Besides the three xor-based structures, bonds may also consist of an or-split and an or-join (type 4), or of an and-split and an and-join (type 5). They consequently represent the opportunity to choose between one or more options and parallel behaviour. It is quite intuitive that each of these bond types requires a slightly different textual representation.

The essential idea for transforming bonds to text is to complement the sentences that are generated for activities with additional explanations. Such an explanation sentence may either stand separately or may be incorporated into an activity sentence. Table 5.2 provides an overview of the basic sentence templates for each bond type. The table distinguishes between labeled and unlabeled gateways and the scope of the sentence. The concrete choice about one of the options is depending on three parameters:

- *The Existence of a Gateway Label*: If a gateway carries a label (which is generally only the case for xor and or-splits), we use this label to create a sentence that explains the condition of the split. If a considered gateway is unlabeled, we use a set of predefined sentences to explain the semantics. Note that the predefined sentences are stored as DSynTs in external XML files. Hence, the set can be easily complemented or adapted to the specific needs of the user.
- *The Gateway Type*: As an and-split must be communicated differently than an xor-split, we use different sentences for each of the previously introduced bond types. If a gateway is labeled, the gateway annotation is accordingly incorporated. Nevertheless, the way a given label is employed still depends on the bond type. As a result, the generated text for a skip construction varies from the text generated for a general xor-split.
- *The Number of Outgoing Arcs*: As our goal is to communicate the semantics of the model as natural as possible, we also consider the number of outgoing arcs. Rather simple splits consisting of two arcs do not necessarily require additional meta sentences in the text. For example, an xor-split with two outgoing arcs is transformed into the sentence *If <cond.> then <1. branch>, otherwise <2. branch>*. Hence, we differentiate between splits with exactly two outgoing arcs and splits with more than two outgoing arcs. In the first case, we use an integrated sentence template that incorporates the activities. In the latter case, we employ an isolated sentence such as *If <cond.> then one of the following branches is executed* to explain the model semantics. Nevertheless, if the considered gateway does not carry a label, we abstract from the number of outgoing arcs and employ an isolated sentence to convey the behavior of the model.

To illustrate this procedure, consider the bonds *B2* and *B3* from the example process. Bond *B2* contains an xor-gateway with two outgoing arcs and the label

Table 5.2 Sentence Templates for Transforming Bonds

Bond Type $g \in G_\lambda$		Scope	Sentence Template
	yes	split	*If <cond.> then one of the following branches is executed.*
		join	*Once one of the alternative branches was executed ...*
		integ.	*If <cond.> then <1. branch>, otherwise <2. branch>*
	no	split	*One of the following branches is executed.*
		join	*Once one of the alternative branches was executed ...*
		integ.	-
	yes	split	*If <cond.> then ...*
		join	*In any case ...*
		integ.	-
	no	split	*If required ...*
		join	*In any case ...*
		integ.	-
	yes	split	-
		join	*As long as <cond.> the <role> repeats the latter steps and continues with ... Once <cond.> ...*
		integ.	-
	no	split	-
		join	*If required <role> repeats the latter steps and continues with.... Once the loop is finished ...*
		integ.	-
	yes	split	*The process is split into <no.> parallel branches.*
		join	*Once all <no.> branches were executed ...*
		integ.	-
	no	split	*The process is split into <no.> parallel branches.*
		join	*Once all <no.> branches were executed ...*
		integ.	-
	yes	split	*If <cond.> then one or more of the following branches is executed*
		join	*Once all desired branches were executed ...*
		integ.	-
	no	split	*One or more of the following branches is executed*
		join	*Once all desired branches were executed ...*
		integ.	-

Alcoholic Beverages Ordered. Accordingly, we use the annotation of the gateway to derive the sentence fragment *If alcoholic beverages are ordered.* This clause is then passed to the first activity of the *yes*-arc, where the condition and the main clause are combined. As a result, we obtain a DSynT representing the sentence *If alcoholic*

Algorithm 16. Bond Transformation

```
 1: transformBond(RPSTNode node)
 2: List messages = new List();
 3: Gateway g = node.getEntry();
 4: DSynT splitSentence = new DSynT();
 5: DSynT joinSentence = new DSynT();
 6: if | g● |> 2 then
 7:    if g ∈ Gλ then
 8:        splitSentence = deriveFromGatewayLabel(g, 'separate');
 9:    else
10:        splitSentence = loadSplitSentence(g.getType(), 'separate');
11:    end if
12:    joinSentence = loadJoinSentence(g.getType(), 'integrated');
13:    if passedMessages.getSize() > 0 then
14:        splitMessage = mergeSentences(splitMessage, passedFragments);
15:    end if
16:    messages.add(spitSentence);
17:    for all RPSTNode child ∈ node.getChildren() do
18:        messages.add(transformRPSTNode(child));
19:    end for
20:    passedMessages.add(joinSentence);
21: else if | g● |= 2 then
22:    if g ∈ Gλ then
23:        splitSentence = deriveFromGatewayLabel(g, 'integrated');
24:    else
25:        splitSentence = loadSplitSentence(g.getType(), 'separate');
26:    end if
27:    joinSentence = loadJoinSentence(g.getType(), 'integrated');
28:    passedMessages.add(splitSentence);
29:    messages.add(transformRPSTNode(node.getChildren().get(1)));
30:    passedMessages.add(joinSentence);
31:    messages.add(transformRPSTNode(node.getChildren().get(2)));
32: end if
33: return messages;
```

---

beverages are ordered, the room-service manager gives the order to the sommelier. The respective DSynT is depicted in Figure 5.4(b). Similarly, we can accomplish the transformation of the join-gateway. The join-condition clause is analogously passed to the first activity after the bond (*Deliver to Guest's Room*) and incorporated into the sentence. As opposed to bond *B2*, the gateway in bond *B3* does not carry a label. Hence, we use the predefined sentence *one or both of the following paths are executed* to describe the or-split although it only has two outgoing arcs. This procedure is used to handle bonds of different size and type. Within the bond, the recursive transformation algorithm is executed accordingly.

Algorithm 16 formalizes this procedure. In the beginning, a new list for the generated messages is created and the gateway object is extracted from the RPST node (lines 2-3). Then, two new DSynTs for the split and the join sentences are created. If the considered gateway has more than two outgoing arcs, it is handled by lines 7-20. In case the gateway is labeled, the sentence explaining the split is extracted from the gateway (line 8). Otherwise, it is loaded from the external XML files (line 10). In either case, a *separate* sentence is constructed as the bond consists of more than two branches. As the split sentence was created as a separate sentence, it can be directly added to the message list. If there exist passed messages that need to be incorporated, the split sentence is first merged with the passed messages (lines 13-15). A scenario where such a situation occurs is in direct succession of a join gateway by a split gateway. Technically, the combination of two or more messages is trivial. Each DSynT of a passed message is added to the main DSynT using the ATTR or COORD relation. In the following loop, the RPST main transformation algorithm is executed for each child fragment of the bond (lines 17-19). Afterwards, the join sentence is added to the global set of *passedFragments* (line 20). Hence, the sentence is incorporated into the next activity of the process model. The handling of gateways with exactly two outgoing branches is implemented by the lines 21-32. The key difference is that a labeled gateway is transformed into an *integrated* split sentence (line 23) and that the join sentence is passed to the first activity of the second branch (line 30). Finally, the message list is returned (line 33).

5.2.5.5 Transformation of Rigids

As discussed earlier, a Rigid is a part of a process model that captures non block-structured behavior and hence cannot be characterized by the means of nested bonds, polygons, and trivial fragments. Thus, the previously defined transformation techniques are not sufficient for textualizing the behavior of rigids. In order to properly communicate the behavior of rigids, we explain the different execution options to the reader. More specifically, we discuss one particular execution sequence through the rigid from start to end and then explain the possible deviations from this path. To automatically derive such an execution sequence and its deviations, we transform the rigid into a Petri Net. From this Petri Net we then compute a set of *concurrent runs* covering all activities of the original rigid [134, 210]. Figure 5.6 shows an abstract version of the rigid from Figure 5.1 and the corresponding Petri Net. The BPMN to Petri Net transformation can be accomplished using standard transformation algorithms [87, 99]. As we use element identifiers to link transitions and places to the respective BPMN elements, we do not lose any semantics of the BPMN model. After the execution sequences have been computed, we can still associate the places and transitions of the Petri Net with the respective BPMN elements.

Building on the definitions from [134, 210], we designed an algorithm to automatically construct concurrent runs from the derived Petri Net. Therefore, the algorithm computes the minimal spanning tree of the rigid and uses the depth-first search algorithm to extract the runs from the tree [109, p.46-49]. The rationale behind this approach is to start with the root of the spanning tree and to first determine the longest path. This path is determined as the main run. The unvisited branches accordingly represent the deviations and are extracted analogously.

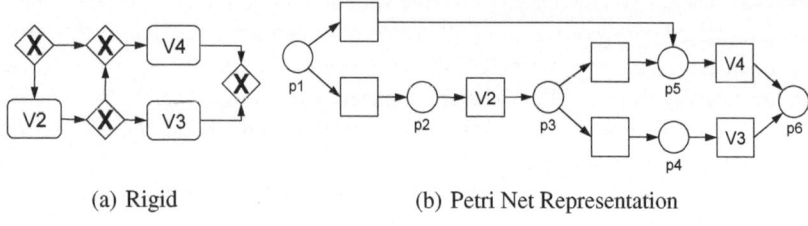

(a) Rigid   (b) Petri Net Representation

Fig. 5.6 Rigid from Fig. 5.1 and the Corresponding Petri Net Representation

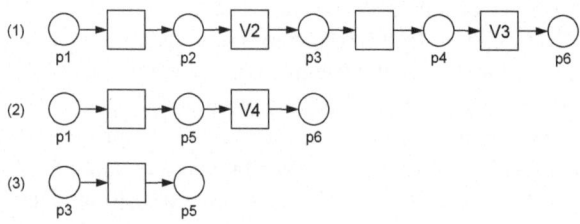

Fig. 5.7 Concurrent Runs Computed from the Petri Net Representation

Figure 5.7 shows the result of the run computation. It illustrates that the considered rigid can be covered using three runs. The first run captures the case that the customer has no premium status and is hence debited directly. The second run represents the case of a premium customer. In that case the order is approved without debit. The third run clarifies that the solvency check may also lead to a positive decision. In this case the execution continues with the place *p5*. These runs demonstrate that concurrent runs are well-suited for properly describing the possible behavior of a rigid. While the first run shows one possible path through the rigid, the remaining runs describe the possible deviations. In particular, the second run describes an alternative after the beginning of the rigid and the third run represents an alternative after the execution of the activity *v2*.

Using the concept of the concurrent run generation, the text generation of a rigid can be accomplished by transforming each run using the previously introduced generation techniques. As every run represents a Petri Net process model, the introduced algorithms can be applied in a straightforward manner. Algorithm 17 formalizes the required steps. It requires an RPST node representing a rigid as input and returns a list of deep-syntactic trees representing the resulting text.

Algorithm 17 starts by defining a list and two meta sentences for describing the behavior of the rigid (lines 2-4). The *rigidIntroSentence* is used for communicating that a rigid captures several execution sequences and how the following text describes its behavior. The *rigidDeviationSentence* is inserted for introducing the list of possible deviations. After defining the required variables, a Petri Net is derived from the given rigid (line 5). Then, a list of concurrent runs is computed from the Petri Net. In order to present the main run separately, the first run is extracted and transformed to text (lines 7-9). As Petri Nets can be easily mapped to the

---
Algorithm 17. Rigid Transformation

 1: **transformRigid**(RPSTNode *rigid*)
 2: List *messages* = **new** List();
 3: DSynT *rigidIntroSentence* = loadRigidIntroductionSentence();
 4: DSynT *rigidDeviationSentence* = loadRigidDeviationSentence();
 5: PetriNet *p* = transformToPetriNet(*rigid*);
 6: List *runs* = generateConcurrentRuns(*p*);
 7: PetriNet *mainRun* = *runs*.get(1);
 8: *messages*.add(*rigidIntroSentence*);
 9: *messages*.add(transformRPSTNode(*mainRun*.getAnnotatedRPST()));
10: *messages*.add(*rigidDeviationSentence*);
11: *runs*.remove(1);
12: **for all** PetriNet *run* ∈ *runs* **do**
13:     *messages*.add(transformRPSTNode(*run*.getAnnotatedRPST()));
14: **end for**
15: **return** *messages*;

---

canonical process definition introduced in Section 1.4, the textualization of Petri Nets can be accomplished without further adaptations of the text generation algorithm. After transforming the main run, the remaining runs are paraphrased accordingly (lines 12-14). Once all runs have been transformed, the list of messages is returned (line 15).

5.2.6 Message Refinement

Within the message refinement component, we take care of message aggregation, referring expression generation, and discourse marker insertion. At this stage, the the complete RPST has been transformed to a list of DSynT-based sentences. The resulting list *messages* serves as input for the refinement component.

The need for *message aggregation* usually arises when the considered process contains long sequences. In such cases, we make use of three aggregation techniques:

- *Role Aggregation*: If two successive activities are performed by the same role, the messages are merged to a single sentence. Instead of generating the two sentences *The waiter serves the customer* and *The waiter issues the invoice*, we merge the sentences to *The waiter serves the customer and issues the invoice*.
- *Business Object Aggregation*: Neighboring activities sharing a common business object are aggregated in a similar fashion. For example, the two sentences *The bill is created* and *The bill is sent* are aggregated to *The bill is created and sent*.
- *Action Aggregation*: Analogously to activities sharing a common business object, we use identical actions two merge sentences. For instance, the sentences *The manager is informed* and the *The customer is informed* are consolidated to *The manager and the customer are informed*.

Note that aggregation may also include more than two activities. The minimum and maximum number of aggregations can be flexibly configured. The overall goal

---

Algorithm 18. Sentence Aggregation

 1: **aggregateSentences**(List *messages*, int *min*, int *max*, String *scope*)
 2: List *refinedMessages* = **new** List();
 3: List *candidates* = **new** List();
 4: **for int** *i* = 2 **to** *messages*.getSize() **do**
 5:     **if** *messages*.get(*i*).get(*scope*) = *messages*.get(*i*-1).get(*scope*) **then**
 6:         *candidates*.add(*messages*.get(i-1));
 7:         **if** *candidates*.getSize() = *max*-1 **then**
 8:             *candidates*.add(*messages*.get(i));
 9:             DSynT *newMessage* = mergeSentences(*candidates*);
10:             *refinedMessages*.add(*newMessage*);
11:             *candidates*.clear();
12:         **end if**
13:     **else**
14:         **if** *candidates*.getSize() ≥ *min* **then**
15:             DSynT *newMessage* = mergeSentences(*candidates*);
16:             *refinedMessages*.add(*newMessage*);
17:             *candidates*.clear();
18:         **else**
19:             *refinedMessages*.add(*messages*.get(i));
20:         **end if**
21:     **end if**
22: **end for**
23: **return** *refinedMessages*;

---

is to generate text that is as natural as possible. Algorithm 18 defines the detailed aggregation steps. The algorithm requires four input parameters: the list *messages* from the RPST transformation, the minimum number of sentence aggregations in a row, the maximum number of sentence aggregations in a row, and the aggregation scope (role, business object, or action). As a result, the algorithm returns the refined list of DSynTs. In the beginning of the algorithm, two lists are introduced (lines 2-3). The list *refinedMessages* contains the messages after the refinement and the list *candidates* is used for storing the current aggregation candidates. In the subsequent loop, each DSynT from the list *messages* is investigated (lines 4-22). If two neighbouring sentences match with regard to the defined aggregation scope, the preceding DSynT is added to the candidate list (line 6). In case the candidate size has already reached the maximum threshold minus one, the current sentence is added to the candidate list and the sentence constructed from these candidates is added to the list of refined messages (lines 8-10). Afterwards, the candidate list is cleared (line 11). If the compared sentences do not contain the same aggregation object, it is checked whether the candidate list contains sentences from previous iterations. If the number of candidates is greater or equal to the minimum threshold, a new sentence is constructed from the candidates and added to the list of refined messages (lines 14-17). Otherwise, the current sentence is added to the refined list without modifications (line 19). Finally, the list with the refined messages is returned (line 23).

Algorithm 19. Referring Expression Insertion

```
 1: insertReferringExpressions(List messages, boolean male)
 2: for int i = 2 to messages.getSize() do
 3:    if messages.get(i).getRole() = messages.get(i-1).getRole() then
 4:       String role = messages.get(i).getRole();
 5:       if WordNet.getAllHypernyms(role).contains('person') ∧ male = true then
 6:          messages.get(i).setRole('he');
 7:       else if WordNet.getAllHypernyms(role).contains('person') ∧ male = false then
 8:          messages.get(i).setRole('she');
 9:       else
10:          messages.get(i).setRole('it');
11:       end if
12:    end if
13: end for
14: return messages;
```

If there are still adjacent messages with the same role after the aggregation, the role description in the second message is replaced with a *referring expression*. We use WordNet for replacing a role with a suitable personal pronoun. More specifically, we infer all hypernyms of the word associated with the considered role. As a result, we obtain a set of more abstract words which semantically include the role description. If we, for instance, look up the role *waiter*, we can identify the hypernym *person* indicating that this role should be replaced with *he* or *she*. By contrast, the set of hypernyms of *kitchen* only contains words like *artifact* or *physical entity* and no link to a human being. Hence, the role *kitchen* is referenced with *it*.

Algorithm 19 formalizes the respective steps. It requires two input parameters: the list of messages from the previous refinement algorithm and a boolean variable *male* defining the gender of the referring expression. As a result, it returns the modified message list. The algorithm iteratively checks all neighboring sentences for identical roles (line 3). If two sentences with the same role are detected, the role of the current sentence is updated with an adequate expression. The decision about the referring expression is based on the input variable *male* and the set of all hypernyms derived from the WordNet dictionary. If the set of the role hypernyms contains the word *person*, the referring expression is determined with *he* if *male* is true (lines 5-6) and with *she* otherwise (lines 7-8). If the role hypernyms do not contain the word *person*, the referring expression is determined with *it* (lines 9-10). Once all sentences have been investigated, the message list is returned (line 14).

For the *discourse marker introduction*, we identify messages appearing in a strict sequence. Using an extendible set of connectors such as *then*, *afterwards*, and *subsequently*, we randomly insert a suitable word. In this way, we obtain a well-readable text with sufficient variety. As the technical implementation of the discourse marker introduction is trivial, we do not provide a detailed algorithm.

Algorithm 20. Surface Realization

1: **realizeText**(List *messages*, Realizer *realizer*)
2: String *surfaceText* = **new** String();
3: **for all** DSynT *message* ∈ *messages* **do**
4:     String *sentence* = *realizer*.transform(*message*);
5:     *surfaceText*.append(*sentence*);
6: **end for**
7: **return** *surfaceText*;

5.2.7 Surface Realization

As already pointed out earlier, the complexity of the surface realization task led to the development of publicly available realizers such as TG/2 [60] or RealPro [201]. Considering aspects as the manageability of the intermediate structure, license costs, generation speed, and Java compatibility, we decided to utilize the DSynT-based realizer RealPro from CoGenTex. RealPro requires a deep-syntactic tree as input and returns a grammatically correct sentence.

Algorithm 20 formalizes the realization procedure. The algorithm requires the list *messages* containing the DSynT-based sentences as input. Moreover, the algorithm requires an instance from the employed surface realizer. As a result, the final natural language text is returned. In the beginning of the algorithm, a string variable for the surface text is defined (line 2). In the subsequent loop, each DSynT from the list *message* is passed to the realizer (line 4). The resulting text-based sentence is then added to the surface text variable (line 5). After all sentences have been transformed, the final text is returned (line 7).

5.3 Evaluation

To demonstrate the capability of the presented technique for generating natural language texts from process models, we conduct an evaluation with real-world data. The overall goal of the evaluation is to learn how the generated texts compare to textual descriptions that were created by humans. Section 5.3.2 presents the general setup of the evaluation experiment and the employed metrics. Section 5.3.2 introduces the test collection we utilize. Then, in Section 5.3.3, we investigate the technique from a run time performance perspective. Subsequently, Section 5.3.4 presents the results from the text generation and comparison. Finally, Section 5.3.5 provides a detailed discussion of the comparison.

5.3.1 Setup

In the context of the evaluation, we aim at learning how the generated texts compare to texts that were created by humans. In particular, we consider two dimensions: text structure and text content.

The *text structure* dimension is concerned with syntactic characteristics of the texts indicating their complexity. Since syntactic complexity imposes a higher cognitive demand on the reader, it is often considered as an important factor decreasing the understandability of texts [171, 273]. Nevertheless, up until now there is no consensus regarding metrics that are best suited for assessing the syntactic complexity [211]. The first approaches that tried to automatically assess the quality and complexity of texts date back to the sixties to the works of Page [253, 254]. He employed simple text features such as word count or word length to evaluate text quality. Today, more sophisticated techniques are available, taking into account that humans typically have a more holistic view on a text [58, 199, 22]. For the purpose of this evaluation, we adapt the sentence complexity metrics proposed by Lu [211]. As they include different characteristics indicating the syntactic complexity of sentences, they are well-suited for comparing the complexity of texts. In order to also consider the relationship between text and model structure, we further add a metric capturing the number of sentences per node. Altogether, we employ the following metrics:

- *Mean Number of Sentences (S)*: Average number of sentences per text.
- *Words per Sentence Ratio (W/S)*: Average number of words per sentence.
- *Clauses per Sentence Ratio (C/S)*: Average number of clauses per sentence.
- *T-Units per Sentence Ratio (T/S)*: Average number of t-units per sentence. A t-unit is a main clause that contains an attached or embedded subordinate clause or any non-clausal structure [154].
- *Complex T-Units per Sentence Ratio (CT/S)*: Average number of complex t-units per sentence. A t-unit is categorized as complex if it contains a dependent clause [63].
- *Average Sentences per Node Ratio (S/N)*: Average number of sentences used for describing a node of the process model.

The *text content* dimension refers to the extent the text reflects the semantics of the model. In general, we identified that the sentences of the generated as well as the manually created texts can be subdivided into three types: sentences describing the model content (i.e., the nodes of the model), sentences solely discussing the control flow, and sentences providing additional context information that is not captured by the model. Hence, we operationalize the text content dimension using the following metrics:

- *Activity Coverage (AC)*: Share of activities that are discussed in the text.
- *Content Sentences (CS)*: Share of sentences explaining the model content, i.e., the semantics of the model nodes.
- *Meta Sentences (MS)*: Share of sentences that only discuss the control flow of the model.
- *Information Sentences (IS)*: Share of sentences that provide additional context information that is not captured by the model.

5.3.2 Test Collection Demographics

For the evaluation, we employ the BPMN test collection used in [124], which varies with regard to several dimensions such as model source, size, complexity, and the employed element set.[2] Hence, it is well-suited for achieving a high external validity of the results. In addition, each model is complemented with a natural language text. Thus, the collection contains the necessary material for a comparison of the generated and manually created texts. Table 5.3 summarizes the main characteristics of the test collection aggregated by the comprised sources. Note that the column headings refer to the symbols we introduced in Section 1.4. In addition, M denotes the number of models, P the number of Pools, L the number of Lanes, and NS the number of different BPMN symbols used. In total, the test collection consists of ten different sources:

1. *Humboldt University of Berlin (HUB)*: The models from HU-Berlin represent BPMN exercises which are used in BPMN tutorials. The models and the texts were translated from German to English.
2. *Technical University of Berlin (TUB)*: The models from the TU-Berlin were created in the context of a research project and are discussed in [150, 149].
3. *Queensland University of Technology (QUT)*: Similar to the models from HU-Berlin, the models from the QUT represent BPMN exercises with according solutions.
4. *Eindhoven University of Technology (TUE)*: The BPMN model from TU-Eindhoven was also created in the context of a research project. The details are discussed in [278].
5. *Vendor Tutorials (VT)*: The vendor tutorial models stem from the websites or online help documentations of the BPM tool vendors *Active VOS* and *BizAgi*.
6. *inbuit AG (IAG)*: The models from the inubit AG represent modeling tutorials that are used in the context of client and employee trainings. All included texts and models were translated from German to English.
7. *BPM Practitioners (BPMP)*: This model represents an exercise that was provided by a BPM consultant. It is used in BPMN modeling tutorials.
8. *BPMN Practice Handbook (PHB)*: These models represent exercises from the BPMN Practice Handbook [122]. Both models and texts were translated from German to English.
9. *BPMN M&R Guide (MRG)*: As the models from the BPMN Practice Handbook, these models represent exercises from the BPMN M&R Guide [336].
10. *FNA - Metrology Processes (FNA)*: This sample includes models from the Federal Network Agency of Germany. The models were initially provided as UML Sequence diagrams. Hence, they were transformed to BPMN as documented in [124]. In addition, text and models were translated from German to English.

---

[2] We removed one model from the sample as it did not fulfil the soundness criteria required for computing an execution sequence.

Table 5.3 Overview of Test Data Set Characteristics by Source (Average Values)

ID	Source	Type	M	|N|	|A|	|E|	|G|	|F|	|P|	|L|	NS
1	HUB	Academic	4	20.8	9.0	5.3	6.5	22.8	1.3	2.5	10
2	TUB	Academic	2	54.5	22.5	21.5	10.5	55.5	3.5	3.5	11
3	QUT	Academic	8	10.6	6.1	2.5	2.0	10.5	1.0	1.6	8
4	TUE	Academic	1	30.0	18.0	4.0	8.0	33.0	1.0	5.0	7
5	VT	Industry	3	10.0	5.3	3.3	1.3	9.7	1.0	2.3	8
6	IAG	Industry	4	17.8	9.0	5.0	3.8	18.3	1.3	4.0	9
7	BPMP	Industry	1	8.0	4.0	3.0	1.0	8.0	1.0	2.0	4
8	PHB	Text Book	3	10.3	5.0	3.3	2.0	10.0	1.0	1.7	6
9	MRG	Text Book	6	18.3	7.0	8.2	3.2	18.2	1.3	1.8	12
10	FNA	Public Sector	14	20.1	8.0	9.0	3.1	18.9	2.3	2.3	8
	Total		**46**	**18.2**	**8.1**	**6.7**	**3.5**	**18.1**	**1.6**	**2.3**	**22**

The data from Table 5.3 illustrates that the models from the different sources vary in many regards. While the models stemming from exercises and tutorials are rather small, some models from the research projects contain more than 50 nodes. Particularly the number of gateways and arcs emphasize that the majority of the models are not simple sequences of tasks, but frequently contain splits and joins. Further, the number of pools and lanes highlight that the models also include different degrees of interaction. The models from TU-Eindhoven and the inubit AG include, on average, four or more lanes. The models from the TU-Berlin and the FNA frequently make use of multiple pools. Concerning the number of BPMN symbols, we observe differences between 4 and and 12 different BPMN symbols for models from a single source. In total, the models cover 22 different BPMN symbols including various event and gateway types, attached events, and subprocesses. Against the background of this data, we consider the test sample to be suitable for illustrating the general capability of the technique to successfully generate natural language texts.

5.3.3 Performance Results

The main application scenario for the presented text generation technique is to provide domain experts with a complementary text. Hence, the generation is not necessarily time critical. However, if the generation is included in a modeling tool, for instance to provide an alternative view on the model, the computation must be adequately fast. We tested the text generation on a MacBook Pro with a 2.26 GHz Intel Core Duo processor and 4 GB RAM, running on Mac OS X 10.6.8 and Java Virtual Machine 1.5. To exclude distortions due to one-off setup times, we ran the generation twice and considered the second run only.

Table 5.4 Average Generation Time for Each Model by Source

ID	Source	Avg (s)	Min (s)	Max (s)
1	HUB	4.91	4.02	5.94
2	TUB	9.45	8.38	10.53
3	QUT	5.01	3.85	8.41
4	TUE	4.77	4.77	4.77
5	VT	5.07	3.78	6.32
6	IAG	4.99	4.07	6.93
7	BPMP	4.19	4.19	4.19
8	PHB	4.97	3.88	6.91
9	MRG	5.33	4.87	6.26
10	FNA	6.47	3.84	8.02
	Total	**5.66**	**3.78**	**10.53**

Table 5.4 summarizes the average, minimum, and maximum execution times of the text generation technique for each source. The numbers show that an average generation run consumes 5.66 seconds. Large deviations from this value can be only observed for extremely large or extremely small models. Thus, the longest generation run was measured for the largest model of the collection containing over 50 nodes and 4 pools. Considering the details, it becomes apparent that especially the number of pools increases the generation time. This can be explained by the fact that a model with multiple pools is split up into several individual models and that the generation is triggered for each pool separately. Nevertheless, the models from the TU Berlin illustrate that also large models are converted into text between 8 and 10 seconds. As the generation technique is not required to instantly present a result to the user, we consider this as reasonable performance.

5.3.4 Text Generation Results

From the evaluation experiment we learned that the presented technique is capable of generating grammatically correct texts, which appropriately describe the respective process models. As an example consider the following text, which was generated by our technique and represents the process model from Figure 5.1. It illustrates the handling of labeled and unlabled gateways, nested structures, and rigids.

The process begins, when the Room-Service Manager takes down an order. Subsequently, the process contains a part which allows for different execution paths. One option from start to end is the following:
  – The Room-Service Manager checks the customer solvency. If it is not ok, the Room-Service Manager debits the guest's account.
In addition, the part allows for a number of deviations:

- *In case of a premium customer the Room-Service Manager approves the order without debit.*
- *After checking the customer solvency the Room-Service Manager may also approve the order without debit.*

Then, the process is split into 2 parallel branches:
- *If it is necessary, the Room-Service Manager gives the order to the sommelier. In case alcoholic beverages were ordered, one or more of the following paths is executed:*
  - *The Sommelier prepares the alcoholic beverages.*
  - *The Sommelier fetches the wine from the cellar.*
- *The Room-Service Manager submits the order ticket to the kitchen. Then, the Kitchen prepares the meal.*

Once both branches were executed, the Waiter delivers to the guest's room. Afterwards, the process is finished.

Table 5.5 summarizes the overall evaluation results for the structural dimension. A general observation is that the generated sentences are shorter than the manually created sentences. While the sentences from the original texts contain an average of 15.5 words, the generated sentences only include an average of 8.3 words. However, the shortness does not imply that the generated texts use less words to communicate the content. In fact, the shortness in terms of word count is compensated by a higher number of sentences. Still, the complexity metrics clauses per sentence ratio (C/S), t-units per sentence ratio (T/S), and complex t-units per sentence ratio (CT/S) indicate that the generated sentences are less complex with regard to the syntactic dimension. Particularly the number of clauses per complex t-units is, on average, much smaller for the generated sentences.

Table 5.5 Comparison of the Structural Dimension of Original and Generated Texts

		Original Texts					**Generated Texts**				
ID Source		**S**	**W/S**	**C/S**	**T/S**	**CT/S**	**S/N**	**S**	**W/S**	**C/S**	**T/S**	**CT/S**	**S/N**
1	HUB	10.3	15.6	1.5	1.0	0.5	0.5	17.5	8.5	1.3	1.0	0.3	0.8
2	TUB	34.0	20.0	1.8	1.0	0.6	0.6	42.2	8.9	1.2	0.9	0.1	1.0
3	QUT	7.1	16.2	1.5	1.1	0.5	0.6	11.0	7.5	1.2	1.0	0.2	0.8
4	TUE	40.0	16.7	1.3	0.9	0.4	1.3	24.0	8.9	1.3	1.0	0.3	0.8
5	VT	7.0	16.6	2.0	0.8	0.7	0.7	9.0	8.7	1.1	1.0	0.1	0.9
6	IAG	11.5	16.3	1.5	1.2	0.6	0.7	15.5	8.5	1.4	1.0	0.3	0.9
7	BPMP	7.0	8.1	1.1	1.0	0.1	0.9	8.0	10.0	1.3	0.9	0.2	1.0
8	PHB	4.7	15.1	1.6	1.6	0.4	0.5	8.0	8.4	1.4	1.0	0.4	0.8
9	MRG	7.0	19.3	1.8	1.0 ·	0.5	0.4	18.3	9.7	1.4	1.0	0.3	1.0
10	FNA	6.4	12.8	1.2	0.9	0.3	0.3	19.2	7.7	1.1	0.9	0.1	1.0
	Total	**9.0**	**15.5**	**1.5**	**1.0**	**0.5**	**0.5**	**16.8**	**8.3**	**1.2**	**0.9**	**0.2**	**0.9**

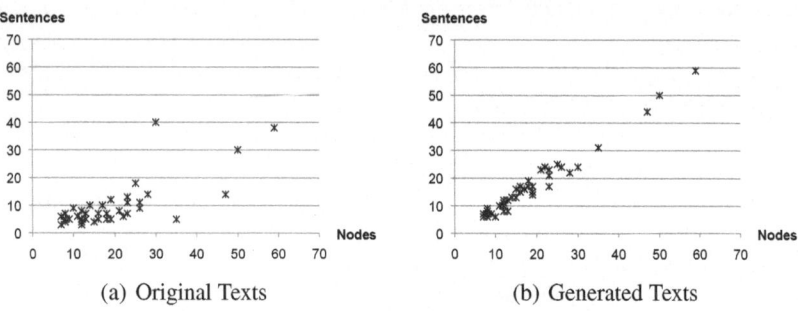

(a) Original Texts   (b) Generated Texts

Fig. 5.8 Node-Sentence Comparison of Original and Generated Texts

Considering the individual values from the employed sources, reveals that these general observations do not equally apply to all collections. As the original texts were created by humans, they are subject to a certain degree of variation. For instance, the original text for the TUE model contains 40 sentences while the generated text only consists of 24. We also observe significant deviations for the complexity of the manually created texts. As example, consider the complex t-units per sentence ratio for the BPMP model (0.1) and the Vendor Tutorial models (0.7). Likewise, the sentence to node ratio illustrates great differences. Among the set of original texts we observe differences between 0.3 and 1.3 sentences per node. Among the generated texts, we face a rather stable value of 0.9. Figure 5.8 further illustrates the relationship between the number of nodes and the number of sentences. For the original texts, it shows a rather weak linear relationship with some obvious exceptions. By contrast, it shows a clear linear relationship for the set of generated texts. This emphasizes that the results of the text generation is much more stable than the results produced by humans.

Table 5.6 shows the results for the content dimension. The data illustrates that the generated texts cover all activities that are included in the models. Considering the design of the generation algorithm, this is actually a predictable result. As we traverse the RPST and convert the model node by node, it is technically not possible to miss an activity. Although the manually created texts are also very close to a coverage of 100%, in total three activities are not discussed in the considered texts. While these cases do not significantly affect the ability of the reader to understand the models, it reflects the general risk that humans may miss activities when describing a model. A further observation in this context is that the manually created texts occasionally use other words to describe activities. For example, instead of using the word *message* as provided in the model activity, an original text used the word *notification*. While this has the positive effect of introducing more variety, it may also confuse model readers who need to identify the correspondence between sentence and activity.

Considering the type distribution of the sentences, we observe more substantial differences. First, the generated texts do not contain information sentences providing additional context information. By contrast, the manually created texts include

Table 5.6 Comparison of the Content Dimension of Original and Generated Texts

		Original Texts				Generated Texts			
ID	**Source**	**AC**	**CS**	**MS**	**IS**	**AC**	**CS**	**MS**	**IS**
1	HUB	97%	81%	4%	15%	100%	84%	16%	0%
2	TUB	100%	99%	0%	1%	100%	87%	13%	0%
3	QUT	100%	96%	0%	4%	100%	95%	5%	0%
4	TUE	94%	55%	3%	43%	100%	92%	8%	0%
5	VT	100%	94%	0%	6%	100%	88%	12%	0%
6	IAG	100%	91%	0%	14%	100%	90%	10%	0%
7	BPMP	100%	100%	0%	0%	100%	88%	13%	0%
8	PHB	100%	89%	0%	11%	100%	100%	0%	0%
9	MRG	98%	94%	1%	5%	100%	85%	15%	0%
10	FNA	100%	100%	0%	0%	100%	77%	23%	0%
	Total	**99%**	**91%**	**1%**	**8%**	**100%**	**85%**	**15%**	**0%**

an average of 8% information sentences. Typical examples for such information sentence are *A small company manufactures customized bicycles* or *The Evanstonian is an upscale independent hotel.* They help to understand the context of the model, but are not necessary for understanding the model semantics. Similar to the activity coverage, this result is not surprising. Since the generation algorithm solely builds on the information from the model, all generated sentences are either content or meta sentences. The second difference with regard to the sentence types is the share of meta sentences. While the generated texts often explicitly discuss control flow aspects such as splits, joins, and rigids, the manually created sentences do not discuss these aspects in isolation. They rather use short fragments *like in parallel* or conditional sentences to explain the control flow on a higher abstraction level. Although the explicit discussion of such control flow aspects may reduce the natural impression of generated texts, it can help readers to fully understand the model semantics.

5.3.5 Discussion of Results

Although the comparison reveals several differences among generated and manually created texts, it is not possible to make general conclusions about the superiority of either approach. Nonetheless, there are three dimensions that help to point out the differences between the approaches: the stability of the structural text characteristics, the semantic coverage, and the cost for creation and adaptation.

The evaluation demonstrated that the generated texts are very *stable* with respect to structural characteristics. In particular, we learned that the generated sentences are comparably short and simple. However, as this is the direct result of the parametrization of the algorithm, the complexity of the output can be adapted to the specific requirements of the users. If readers perceive the generated sentences as artificially short, the configuration of the aggregation component can be accordingly adjusted. In case readers face understandability problems due to long sentences, the aggregation can be turned off. Analogously, the segmentation of the text using bullet points or paragraphs can be adapted. In general, it is important to note that the structural characteristics of the generated text are configurable and hence not subject to notable variations. In comparison to manually created texts, this represents an important advantage. As illustrated by the varying complexity among the texts of the test sample, the complexity of manually created texts is hard to predict. In order to guarantee for a stable level of complexity among manually created texts, it would be necessary to sufficiently train the text writers.

With respect to the *semantic coverage*, the evaluation illustrated that the generated texts reliably cover all activities of the model. As the purpose of textual descriptions is to increase the model understanding, this is an important feature. The evaluation data showed that the manual creation of texts might be associated with a coverage below 100%. This may either originate from unintentionally leaving out an activity due to the complexity of the model or from the conscious decision of a model writer to skip a certain step. Abstracting from the particular reason, we may conclude that the manual creation of a text is always subject to incompleteness in terms of semantic coverage. Due to the algorithm design, the generated texts do not suffer from this problem. Besides the activity coverage, we also learned that the generated sentences are semantically much closer to the model. This applies to content sentences as well as to meta sentences describing the control flow. As the presented technique builds on the information from the model, additional context information is only provided by manually created texts. Nevertheless, as context sentences are much more general than sentences describing the model, they are also not subject to frequent changes. Hence, we consider the manual complementation of context sentences as a reasonable approach.

Concerning the *costs of creating or adapting* textual descriptions, it is quite apparent that the automatic generation is not associated with additional costs. They can be created with a single click. By contrast, a manual creation of a textual description is, depending on the size of the model, associated with considerable effort. Having in mind that large corporations maintain collections with up to thousands of process models [289], the manual creation does not appear to be a reasonable solution. It is also important to note that process models are typically subject to changes. Hence, the describing texts must be adapted accordingly. While the generated texts can be updated by repeating the generation run, the manual adaptation might be a cumbersome task. Especially if the changes in the model are not well documented, the user must first identify the delta between the model and the text in order to subsequently update the text.

Altogether, we can state that the introduced technique successfully generated texts that are, in many regards, close to those created by humans. The generated results are, however, much more stable than the manually created models. Important characteristics such as sentence complexity, text size, and also the full coverage of all activities in the text are a direct result of the algorithm design and not subject to variation. While the manual creation of texts might be associated with considerable effort, the automatic generation is accomplished with a single click. In view of these facts, the benefits and practical usefulness of the technique have been clearly demonstrated.

5.4 Adaptation to Other Languages

Although the general concept of the text generation technique is not language-specific, the adaptation to languages other than English requires the replacement of three resources: the parsing and annotation component, the predefined DSynT templates, and the surface realizer.

As the generation technique builds on the linguistic information from the input process model, the replacement of the *parsing and annotation component* is an essential task. Without the proper inference of action, business object, and addition, it is not possible to generate a text with the introduced technique. As we already discussed the details of adapting the parsing and annotation technique in Chapter 3, we do not revisit them here.

In addition to the parsing and annotation component, it is required to replace the *predefined DSynT-templates*. As these templates significantly contribute to the verbalization of events, bonds, and rigids, the proper adaptation is an important prerequisite. As an example, consider the fragment *The process begins when*, which is used to communicate a start event. In a German implementation of the generation technique we use the fragment *Der Prozess beginnt wenn* and in a Portuguese implementation we use the fragment *O processo começa quando*. In total, we defined about 50 different fragments. However, the templates can be translated with reasonable effort as they represent short and rather simple text fragments. In addition, it should be kept in mind that this represents a one time effort.

As a last step, the surface realization component of the generation approach needs to be replaced with a component that is capable of realizing sentences of the target language. Hence, one option is to replace the English realization component with an off-the-shelf realizer of the target language. Although such tools have been developed for various languages including German [75], French [306], and Portuguese [247], their availability is often restricted. The second solution is to replace the English realizer with a self-developed solution. In general, the development of a full-fledged realizer represents a tremendous effort that requires profound linguistic knowledge. By contrast, the development of a realizer for generating texts from process models is significantly less complex. The reason for this is that the sentences generated by the introduced technique do not cover the full grammatical scope of the target language. As example, consider the following sentence that was generated from the activity *Check customer solvency* and its associated role *Room-Service Manager*:

The Room-Service Manager checks the customer solvency.

In fact, this sentence consists of a simple sequence of the role, the verb in the third person singular, and the business object. In order to transform the information from the activity and the role into this sentence it is only required to conjugate the verb and to insert definite articles for the role and the business object. Using a verb table as introduced in Chapter 4, the verb conjugation can be easily accomplished. The insertion of articles can be implemented using a rule system. In the same manner, transformation rules for conditional and passive sentences can be defined. As the number of required sentence structures is known beforehand, it is not necessary to cover all features and grammatical details of the target language. Thus, the implementation of a German adaptation of the realization component was conducted in three work days.

Altogether, it can be stated that the adaptation of the text generation technique may require additional implementation effort. Considering the overall benefits of the text generation, the time effort can be considered as reasonable. Once the text generation technique is available, text can be generated and updated with a single click.

5.5 Summary

In this chapter, we addressed the problem of automatically transforming process models into natural language text. Building on a literature review on natural language generation, we identified several challenges that are associated with generating natural language from process models. Examples include the automatic extraction of the linguistic information from the model elements, the linearization of concurrent and alternative branches, and also various linguistic challenges such as text structuring or message refinement. In order to adequately address these aspects, we introduced a pipeline architecture with six components. We used the parsing and annotation technique from Chapter 3 and the computation of a Refined Process Structure Tree to successfully transform BPMN process models to textual descriptions. The evaluation of the technique using a set of 46 process models from different sources demonstrated the applicability of the presented technique for generating texts from process models. The comparison of the generated and the manually created texts showed that the generated texts convey the model semantics in more compact and also syntactically less complex manner. Due to the design of the technique, the generated texts are also closer to the model and explicitly describe the model content and control flow. Altogether, the evaluation demonstrated that the presented technique is capable of generating appropriate texts that fully explain the model semantics. The fact that the generation is accomplished within a few seconds and without any manual effort, further emphasizes the usefulness of the technique. In the next chapter, we investigate how far process models can be used to infer information that is only implicitly captured. More specifically, we define a technique for automatically inferring service candidates from process models.

Chapter 6
Service Derivation from Process Models

Service-oriented Architecture has been discussed for roughly a decade as a concept to increase the agility of a company in providing goods and services to external partners and organizing internal operations. Consequently, a plethora of approaches to service derivation have been defined in the past. A core problem is that many of these approaches lack methodological detail, and that none of them considers the consequent support using automatic analysis techniques. Hence, they do not scale up to the size of a whole company.

In this chapter, we address the problem of manual work in the phases of service derivation. We consider the situation where an extensive set of hundreds of process models is available, which is often the case for medium-sized and big companies [289]. We present an approach for the automatic derivation of service candidates, augmented with a set of metrics giving first clues about priorities. In Section 6.1, we give an overview of existing service derivation approaches and highlight the necessity of automation in this context. Afterwards, in Section 6.2, we present the service derivation approach on a conceptual level. Then, Section 6.3 discusses the results of testing our prototypical implementation on three large process model collections from practice. Finally, Section 6.4 summarizes the chapter.

6.1 Derivation of Service Candidates

In the context of Service Oriented Architectures, a service can be understood as an action that is performed by an entity on behalf of another one, such that the capability of performing this action represents an asset [252]. The focus on services is supposed to improve business and IT alignment, as it establishes principles like abstraction, autonomy, and reuse [188]. For identifying such services, various approaches have been proposed in prior research. Many of them explicitly differentiate between business and software services. This distinction is brought forth from different perspectives. A business service can be understood as a *specific set of actions that are performed by an organization* [112], while a software service describes a part of an application system that is utilized by several entities independently [188].

Table 6.1 Overview of Service Identification Approaches

Main Input	Approach	Automation	Type
Conceptual Models			
Process Models	Azevedo et al. [25]	None	BS + SWS
Process Models	Bianchini et al. [44]	Partial	SWS
Process Models & Applications	Erradi et al. [108]	None	SWS
Process & Organizational Models	Jamshidi et al. [164]	None	SWS
Process Models	Kleinert et al. [184]	Partial	BS + SWS
Process Models	Klose et al. [185]	None	BS + SWS
Process Models & Enterprise Model	Kohlmann & Alt [189]	None	SWS
Process Architecture	Dwivedi & Kulkarni [103]	Partial	SWS
Process Models	Sewing et al. [299]	None	BS + SWS
Process Models	Yousef [339]	Partial	SWS
Process Models	Zimmermann et al. [344]	None	SWS
Object Models	Jain et al. [162]	Partial	SWS
Goal-Scenario Models	Kim et al. [179]	None	BS + SWS
Use Case Models	Kim & Doh [180]	Partial	SWS
Feature Model	Lee et al. [204]	Partial	SWS
Data Flow Diagram	Yun et al. [341]	None	SWS
Application Data			
Legacy Code	Aversano et al. [24]	Partial	SWS
Legacy Code	Chen et al. [66]	Partial	SWS
Legacy Code	Sneed [309]	Partial	SWS
Legacy Code	Zhang et al. [342]	Partial	SWS
Legacy Code	Zhang & Yang [343]	Partial	SWS
Relational Database Applications	Baghdadi [27]	Partial	SWS
User Interface Designs	Mani et al. [215]	Partial	SWS
General Requirements & Capabilities			
Stakeholder Requirements	Adamopoulos et al. [15]	None	SWS
Stakeholder Requirements	Chang & Kim [64]	None	SWS
Business Capabilities	Arsanjani et al. [21]	None	BS + SWS
Business Entities	Flaxer & Nigam [113]	None	BS + SWS

The concept of a business service puts more emphasis on the economic perspective, as the software service is more related to information technology. This divide is also apparent in many of the methodological contributions on service derivation. Typically, the derivation of business services tends to take more of a top-down approach, and the software service derivation is rather bottom-up [41, 107, 272, 139].

Table 6.1 gives an overview of existing service derivation approaches. It shows the main input type, the degree of automation, and whether the approach is targeting software services (SWS) or business services (BS). Altogether, we differentiate between three main input types for service identification techniques: conceptual models, application data, and general requirements and capabilities.

In general, service identification techniques building on *conceptual models* pursue the strategy of clustering the comprised elements in order to obtain a set of service candidates. Depending on the type of the conceptual model, different techniques are employed. One of the most frequently used artifacts in this context is the process model. Against the background of the multitude of automatic process model analysis techniques, it is surprising that many of the identification techniques building on process models suggest a manual analysis (see [25, 164, 185, 189, 344, 299, 108]). Typically, they propose different heuristics on how to derive service candidates from process model activities. For instance, Azevedo et al. [25] suggest the grouping of activities based on the model structure. By contrast, Klose et al. [185] define an evaluation template for considering each activity in detail. Although many techniques build on the manual analysis, there are also techniques providing automatic support. For instance, Yousef et al. [339] use an ontology to generate a service model from a set of process models. Similarly, Bianchini et al. [44] employ the lexical database WordNet and a reference ontology to identify component services. Kleinert et al. take a different perspective by employing a RPST to identify process regions that represent suitable service candidates. Dwivedi and Kulkarni [103] introduce heuristics that also consider the hierarchical relationships among processes. Even though these approaches make use of automated techniques, the scope of the automation is limited to a particular set of steps. As a result, they still require a considerable amount of manual work.

In addition to the numerous identification techniques focusing on process models, there are also approaches building on other conceptual models. For instance, Lee et al. [204] derive services from feature models by grouping features according to their binding time. In a similar way, Jain et al. [162] employ a spanning tree to group the classes of object models for identifying web service candidates. An alternative approach is taken by Kin and Doh [180]. They define a rule-based approach to derive service interfaces from use-case diagrams. Like many process model based approaches, the latter techniques only partially support the identification using algorithms or tools. Hence, they all require manual work. A further shortcoming is the lack of a detailed discussion of those technical solutions that are provided. For example, Kin and Doh [180] do not explicitly discuss how they analyze the natural language in the considered use-case diagrams. Hence, it is difficult to build on the results of their research. Approaches without any automation are introduced by Yun et al. [341] and Kim et al. [179]. Yun et al. propose guidelines to extract flow relations from data flow diagrams. The consolidated flow relations are then used for defining services. Likewise, Kim et al. present guidelines for deriving services from goal models.

Service identification techniques building on *application data* typically have a high degree of automation. One of the most prominent strategies in this context is the automated analysis and service derivation from source code [24, 66, 309, 342, 343]. Although user interaction is required at different stages, all source code based approaches provide support in terms of selection or grouping algorithms. Besides the multitude of service identification approaches utilizing source code, there are also other strategies. For instance, Baghdadi [27] analyzes the schemas of relational database applications to define web services. In a quite similar vein, Mani et al. [215] investigate the user interfaces of applications to derive requirements for information services.

In addition to the various approaches building on a particular input artifact such as process models or source code, there are also many service identification methods that build on rather *general requirements or capabilities*. These approaches are usually more generic in nature and provide guidelines to identify relevant services. For instance, Adamopoulos [15] as well as Chang and Kim [64] propose to use a general analysis of service requirements as starting point for service identification. Similarly, Arsanjani et al. [21] propose a three-step approach for deriving service candidates from different business capabilities. Flaxer and Nigam [113] are a bit more specific by asking for the analysis of business entities in order to identify business components and services in the next step. What such analysis-driven approaches have in common is that they lack technological support. Usually, the entire identification process must be conducted manually.

Altogether, the review of existing approaches reveals that there exists a plethora of different service identification approaches building on different inputs. Particularly for process models many methods have been defined. The problem is, however, that many of them do not provide enough methodological details. Among others, it remains unclear how these approaches deal with the linguistic information that is captured by process model activities. Although, for instance, Bianchini et al. [44] employ WordNet for analyzing activities, it remains unclear whether they explicitly address the semantic components such as action or business object.

In order to fully reflect on automation of existing service derivation approaches, consider the process of service derivation as depicted in Figure 6.1. It contains four phases: preparation, identification, detailing, and prioritization. The derivation of services usually starts with a *preparation phase*. In this phase, an information base for the service analysis is established. This information base may include different types of business documents such as enterprise architectures, organizational structures, or business processes. Notably, all investigated service identification techniques building on process models ask for manual work during this phase. Particularly those who provide automatic support at later stages, require the user to align the language of activities or to manually annotate activities with information such as input and output [44, 184, 339]. The subsequent *identification phase* is concerned with identifying capabilities. In the case of process models, capabilities can be closely related to actions. If required, the available processes have to be further decomposed in order to arrive at a suitable level of detail. In this phase, some approaches support the user with automated techniques for grouping [339, 184] or for computing suggestions [44]. Manual feedback is, however, still required to continue with the service derivation process. In the following *detailing phase*, the relationships and interactions between services are identified. This includes the detection of overlaps with existing services and the proper incorporation of new services into the existing SOA landscape. For accomplishing this task, almost all process model based identification techniques rely on the user. Only Bianchini et al. [44] provide partially automated support by introducing metrics that indicate the relationships

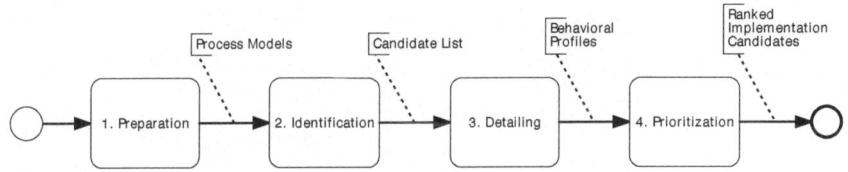

Fig. 6.1 The Four Phases of Service Derivation (adapted from [188])

among the identified service candidates. Finally, the *prioritization phase* is utilized to decide which services should be considered for implementation with which priority. Among the considered service identification approaches, there was no technique that supported the user in automatically prioritizing the identified candidates. Hence, this phase must be manually conducted by the user.

Considering the degree of automation that is provided for this four-phase process, it becomes apparent that none of the previously discussed approaches considers the potential of fully automating these steps. In general, a considerable amount of manual work is required to derive a set of services. Particularly the preparation and the prioritization phase include manual effort. As a consequence, these approaches do not scale up to large organizations when a service-oriented architecture is embraced as a company-wide concept. In fact, many of the previously introduced approaches do not consider the situation where large process model repositories are available. However, as recent research revealed [289], this is a realistic scenario.

Against the background of these findings, we define an approach that addresses the identified weaknesses of existing service derivation approaches. More specifically, we aim at introducing an approach that addresses the problem of the proper handling of linguistic information, automation, and scalability. Our goal is to take a set of process models as input and to automate the steps from preparation to prioritization. As a result, the manual work in the context of service identification is reduced to the final selection of appropriate services from a ranked list of proposals.

6.2 Automatic Service Derivation and Detailing

This section discusses our approach for the automatic identification and detailing of service candidates from process models. Section 6.2.1 starts by giving an overview of the presented service identification technique. Subsequently, Sections 6.2.2 through 6.2.4 introduce the details of the comprised phases.

6.2.1 Overview

The goal of our service identification technique is to automate all phases of the previously introduced service identification process. In order to accomplish this,

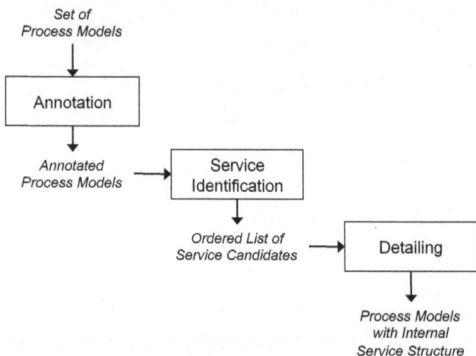

Fig. 6.2 Overview of Service Derivation Technique

we build on a set of process models P. In particular, we build on the set of all activities A_P that are included in this process model collection and the natural language these activities contain. The main rationale behind this approach is that the sophisticated usage of natural language provides us with the possibility to automate important key tasks such as grouping or prioritizing that are associated with the service identification process. Figure 6.2 illustrates our three-phase service derivation approach. In the first phase, we parse all activities contained in A_P and annotate them with their according action and business object. As a consequence, we obtain a set of annotated process models. In the second phase, we employ different strategies to identify a list of service candidates from the annotated process models. Finally, we use behavioral profiles for a detailing of the services. From this detailing, we obtain a set of process models reflecting the internal structure of the identified service candidates. The following sections introduce each of these phases in detail.

6.2.2 Annotation of Process Model Activities

The goal of this phase is the annotation of activity labels with action and business object. In order to accomplish this, we make use of the parsing and annotation technique defined in Chapter 3. As a result, an activity such as *Notify Customer* is automatically decomposed into the action *notify* and the business object *customer*. In this context, it is of particular importance that we abstract from labeling styles and only consider the annotation record. As an example, consider the activity label *Customer Notification* which has exactly the same annotation record as *Notify Customer*. After the automatic annotation, such differences with respect to the labeling styles are neutralized and semantically identical activities can be associated with the same service candidate.

Algorithm 21. Atomic Service Identification

1: **computeAtomicServices**(Set A_P)
2: List *candidates* = **new** List();
3: **for all** Activity $a \in A_P$ **do**
4:      F_A = countFrequency(a, A_P);
5:      **if** $F_A \geq 2 \wedge$ *candidates*.contains(a) = **false then**
6:          a.setFrequency(F_A);
7:          *candidates*.add(a);
8:      **end if**
9: **end for**
10: *candidates*.orderByFrequency();

6.2.3 Identification of Service Candidates

At this stage, the action and business object from all activity labels of the considered process model collection are adequately determined. Building on the annotation information, we introduce four different approaches to identify service candidates. The overall strategy of providing four different techniques is twofold. First, it is useful to exploit the different linguistic aspects that are provided by activity labels. Focusing on the combination of action and business object, yields a different result than focusing on the business objects only. Second, the approaches allow to address the appropriate level of granularity. Each of the presented techniques increases the aggregation scope such that the first technique identifies the most fine-granular services and the fourth technique generate the most course-grained services. The following subsections introduce each approach in detail.

6.2.3.1 Atomic Service Identification

The atomic service identification strategy focuses on single activities and is based on the notion that reoccurring activities are likely to represent relevant service candidates. This approach is in line with the viewpoint of [158] that each activity in a process model can be considered as a potential service. Consequently, the frequency of a particular activity throughout the model collection determines its potential of being a suitable service candidate. In order to capture these considerations, we introduce the activity frequency metric F_A, which determines the number of similar activities in a process model collection for a given activity. The similarity between two activities is based on the congruence between their actions and business objects. Thus, activities following different labeling styles are considered as semantically identical.

The details of the atomic service identification approach are illustrated in Algorithm 21. In order to identify service candidates for a whole process model collection, we compute F_A for each activity in the collection P (lines 3-4). Therefore, we iterate over the set of all activities and determine the total frequency for each activity. If the frequency F_A of an activity is equal or greater than two and the activity has not been considered in a previous iteration, the activity is added to the candidate list (lines 5-7). After all activities were analyzed, the candidates are ordered according to their frequency (line 10). As a consequence, we obtain a list of candidates ordered by their potential of being suitable service candidates.

6.2.3.2 Composite Service Identification

The Composite Service Identification approach aims at identifying composite service candidates based on business object groups. Hence, it abstracts from single activities and focuses on activity groups having the same business object. For each business object grouping, we introduce the frequency F_{BO} that determines the relevance of that group based on the occurrence of the business object among all activities of the model collection.

Algorithm 22 provides an algorithmic description for identifying composite service candidates. First, we iterate over the set of all activities and extract business object and action from each activity (lines 4-5). In case the list of composite candidates does not already contain the considered business object, its frequency is determined (line 7). If the frequency of a considered business object is equal or greater than two, the frequency and the action is stored in the business object variable (lines 9-10). Then, the business object is added to the candidate list (line 11). If the object is already included, the algorithm checks whether the action is part of the action list of the business object (line 13). If not, the action is added accordingly (line 14). Once all activities were inspected, the candidate list is cleaned from business object groups with a single action (lines 17-21). This is reasonable as such candidates do not represent proper composite services. After ordering the remaining business object groups according to their frequencies (line 22), we obtain a list of composite service candidates ordered by their relevance.

6.2.3.3 Refined Composite Service Identification

The refined composite service identification approach aims at consolidating semantically similar behavior within composite services. The rationale behind this approach is that many process models from practice use synonymous terms for expressing the same semantics [260]. For instance, a composite service with the business object *process* and the actions *handle* and *manage* may also be considered as a single trivial service since *handle* and *manage* are synonyms. Following this line of argumentation, we introduce the metric F_{SemBO} capturing the number of business objects with semantically distinct action groups.

Algorithm 23 gives a formal description of the refined composite service derivation. Essentially, the steps of the algorithm correspond to those of Algorithm 22. The key difference is how actions are treated when they are added to an existing business object group (lines 13-24). Instead of adding every action to the business object list, a non-contained action is first investigated in more detail. In particular, the current action is compared with every action from the business object list (lines 15-20). Using WordNet, each action pair is checked for synonymy (line 16). If two actions are synonymous, they are used to form an action group (line 17). In case the

---

Algorithm 22. Composite Service Identification

 1: **computeCompositeServices**(Set A_P)
 2: List *compCandidates* = **new** List();
 3: **for each** Activity $a \in A_P$ **do**
 4:         *bo* = *a*.getBusinessObjectFromAnnotation();
 5:         *action* = *a*.getActionFromAnnotation();
 6:         **if** *compCandidates*.contain(*bo*) = **false then**
 7:                 F_{BO} = countFrequency(*bo*,A_P);
 8:                 **if** $F_{BO} \geq 2$ **then**
 9:                         *bo*.setFrequency(F_{BO});
10:                         *bo*.addAction(*action*);
11:                         *compCandidates*.add(*bo*);
12:                 **end if**
13:         **else if** *compCandidates*.get(*bo*).containsAction(*action*) = **false then**
14:                 *compCandidates*.get(*bo*).addAction(*action*);
15:         **end if**
16: **end for**
17: **for each** Object $bo \in compCandidates$ **do**
18:         **if** *bo*.getActions().getSize() = 1 **then**
19:                 *compCandidates*.remove(*bo*);
20:         **end if**
21: **end for**
22: *compCandidates*.orderByFrequency();

---

considered action does not represent a synonym for any of the comprised actions, it is added to the list (line 22). Afterwards, the algorithm continues as Algorithm 22. Once all activities were inspected, the candidate list is cleaned from groups with a single action or a single action group (lines 26-30). Finally, the remaining groups are ordered according to their frequencies (line 31).

6.2.3.4 Inheritance Hierarchy Identification

The inheritance hierarchy identification approach is based on the considerations of the composite service identification strategy. However, it extends this approach by taking hierarchical relationships between the business objects into account. This is motivated by the design principle of service cohesion [255] that refers to the degree of relatedness between the operations of a service. Assuming that activities with related business objects may also lead to related services, we aim for identifying business object hierarchies. In order to identify relationships between business objects, we decompose the business object terms. As an example, consider the business object *purchase order*. Apparently, the word *purchase* is a specification of the main word *order* at the end. Hence, a hierarchy can be constructed by relating different parts of the business objects. For computing the relevance of such a hierarchy

---

Algorithm 23. Refined Composite Service Identification

1: **computeRefinedCompositeServices**(Set A_P)
2: List *compCandidates* = **new** List();
3: **for each** Activity $a \in A_P$ **do**
4:      bo = a.getBusinessObjectFromAnnotation();
5:      *action* = a.getActionFromAnnotation();
6:      **if** *compCandidates*.contain(bo) = **false then**
7:          F_{SemBO} = countFrequency(bo,A_P);
8:          **if** $F_{SemBO} \geq 2$ **then**
9:              bo.setFrequency(F_{BO});
10:              bo.addAction(*action*);
11:              *compCandidates*.add(bo);
12:          **end if**
13:      **else if** *compCandidates*.get(bo).containsAction(*action*) = **false then**
14:          **boolean** *isSynonymous* = **false**;
15:          **for each** Action *boAction* $\in$ *bo*.getActions() **do**
16:              **if** WordNet.areSynonyms(*boAction*,*action*) = **true then**
17:                  *compCandidates*.get(bo).formActionGroup(*boAction*,*action*);
18:                  *isSynonymous* = **true**;
19:              **end if**
20:          **end for**
21:          **if** *isSynonymous* = **false then**
22:              *compCandidates*.get(bo).addAction(*action*);
23:          **end if**
24:      **end if**
25: **end for**
26: **for each** Object $bo \in$ *compCandidates* **do**
27:      **if** bo.getActions().getSize() = 1 **then**
28:          *compCandidates*.remove(bo);
29:      **end if**
30: **end for**
31: *compCandidates*.orderByFrequency();

---

group, we introduce the metric F_{IH}, which is based on the occurrence of the main word among all business objects. The identified hierarchy groups can then be used for constructing according composite services which explicitly respect the notion of service cohesion.

Algorithm 24 illustrates the details of this approach. The basis of the hierarchy consideration are business objects which contain more than one word (line 5). If such a business object is identified, we determine the frequency of its main word among all activities (line 6). In case the frequency of the main word is equal or greater than two and no respective hierarchy tree exists, a new tree with the main word as a root node is created (lines 8-11). Afterwards, all possible business object parts are computed (lines 12-14). This is accomplished by iteratively complementing the first word of the business object until we finally obtain the original business

---

Algorithm 24. Inheritance Hierarchy Identification

```
 1: computeHierarchyServices(Set A_P)
 2:   TreeList hierarchies = new TreeList();
 3:   for each Activity a ∈ A_P do
 4:       bo = a.getBusinessObjectFromAnnotation();
 5:       if bo.getWordCount() > 1 then
 6:           mainWord = bo.words[bo.getWordCount()];
 7:           F_IH = countFrequency(mainWord,A_P);
 8:           if F_IH ≥ 2 ∧ hierarchies.containsTree(mainWord) = false then
 9:               mainWord.setFrequency(F_IH);
10:               hierarchies.createNewTree(mainWord);
11:           end if
12:           for i= 1 to bo.getWordCount()) do
13:               term = bo.words[1] + ... + bo.words[i];
14:               F_IH = countFrequency(term,A_P);
15:               if F_IH ≥ 2 then
16:                   hierarchies.getTree(mainWord).addNode(term, i);
17:               end if
18:           end for
19:       end if
20:   end for
21:   hierarchies.orderByFrequency();
```

---

object. Each business object part having a frequency greater or equal than two is inserted as a node on the according hierarchy level (lines 16-18). Finally, the hierarchy trees are sorted according to the frequency of the main word (line 21).

6.2.4 Detailing of Service Candidates

Service detailing refers to the definition of the structure and behavior of a service, or a set of services. To this end, we adopt an approach for mining action patterns. Action patterns define recurring behavior [308]. The conceptual foundation for action patterns are so-called behavioral profiles. Our approach takes a collection of process models as a starting point for deriving action patterns of a specific business object. From these patterns, we can use synthesis techniques in order to arrive at a process model that details the lifecycle of a service candidate. Therefore, this section defines the notion of a behavioral profile, explains how action patterns can be identified, and how a process model showing the service lifecycle can be found.

Behavioral Profiles. With our approach, we aim to identify service candidates that are utilized in various processes in a company. In order to detail such a service, we have to extract its behavioral constraints from different process models, and consolidate them in an appropriate way. So-called *behavioral profiles* capture such constraints on the level of pairs of activities. A behavioral profile builds on trace semantics for a process model, namely the weak order relation [334]. It contains all pairs (x, y) if there is a trace in which x occurs before y. For a process model p, we write $x \succ_p y$. The behavioral profile then defines a partition over the cartesian product of activities, such that a pair (x, y) is in one of the following relations:

- strict order relation $\rightsquigarrow_p$, if $x \succ_p y$ and $y \not\succ_p x$;
- exclusiveness relation $+_p$, if $x \not\succ_p y$ and $y \not\succ_p x$;
- interleaving order relation $\|_p$, if $x \succ_p y$ and $y \succ_p x$.

Based on this behavioral profile, we can define the behavioral constraints of a service candidate.

Action Patterns. Once we have derived the behavioral profile relations from a set of process models, we can determine the support and confidence of action patterns. This works similar to association rule mining. For each pair of activities that co-occur in one of the process models, we map them to their behavioral profile relation. Accordingly, a behavioral action pattern can be defined as a rule R with a minimum support and confidence value [308] such that:

- R is a rule $X \Rightarrow Y$, where $X, Y \subset V \times \{\rightsquigarrow, \rightsquigarrow^{-1}, +, \|\} \times V$, such that X and Y are pairs of actions for which behavioral relations are specified;
- *minsup* is the value of the required minimal support;
- *minconf* is the value of the required minimal confidence.

Such a pattern typically captures the relationship between actions, i.e., verbs mentioned in the activity labels. We can define object-sensitive action patterns if we only consider actions of the same business object. In our context, such object-sensitive action patterns provide the basis for detailing the lifecycle of a service candidate.

Synthesis of Service Lifecycle. The remaining challenge is to define a process model that matches the behavioral relationships of the service candidate. A corresponding synthesis technique has been defined in [307]. The idea is to identify the consistent set of behavioral relations. From these relations, we can construct a process model. The strict order relation defines the skeleton of a corresponding process model. Activities that are not in an order relation are organized in nested xor- or and-blocks depending on whether they are exclusive or interleaving. The notion of profile consistency guarantees that such a nesting exists [307].

6.3 Evaluation

To demonstrate the capability of the introduced technique for deriving useful service candidates, we conduct an evaluation with real-world process models. Section 6.3.1 presents the test collection of our experiment. Then, Section 6.3.2 investigates the performance of the service derivation technique. As we aim at automatically processing large process model collections from practice, we consider a good performance as important criterion. Subsequently, Section 6.3.3 discusses the results from the service identification.

6.3.1 Test Collection Demographics

For the evaluation of the service candidate derivation technique, we consider it as essential to build on model collections from industry. Although the technique can be applied to any given set of process models, particularly industry collections can provide us with insights on the practical usefulness of the identified candidates. Following this line of argumentation, we employ three process model collections from practice: The SAP and the Claims Handling collection from Chapter 3 and 4, and a process model collection from a large telecommunication service provider. The telecommunication collection (TC) contains 3,338 process models covering diverse aspects of the organization. Due to its extensive size, it is well-suited for complementing the test collection. By using such a large collection, we achieve two important goals. First, the size allows us to demonstrate the scalability of the technique. Second, a comparison among the different collections illustrates the effect of the collection size on the number and quality of the identified services. Table 6.2 summarizes the main features of the employed model collections.

6.3.2 Performance Results

A typical application scenario for automatic service derivation is, for instance, an initiative that aims at consolidating and bundling software functionality. However, as such an initiative is not likely to be conducted regularly, the derivation of service candidates is a rather non-time-critical task. Nevertheless, we consider computation time to be an important factor, especially to demonstrate the scalability of the technique with respect to large process model collections. We tested the text generation on a MacBook Pro with a 2.26 GHz Intel Core Duo processor and 4 GB RAM, running on Mac OS X 10.6.8 and Java Virtual Machine 1.5. To exclude distortions

Table 6.2 Details about Used Model Collections

	SAP	CH	TC
Number of Models	604	328	3,338
No. of Activities	2,433	4,414	17,687
Average No. of Activities per Model	4.03	13.45	4.61
Average No. of Words per Label	3.50	5.59	4.01
Minimum No. of Words per Label	1	1	1
Maximum No. of Words per Label	12	19	24
Notation	EPC	EPC	BPMN

Table 6.3 Performance Results

Collection	Scope	Annotation	AS	CS	RCS	IHS	Total
SAP	Total Time (ms)	26,180	380	499	9,475	572	37,106
	Time per Activity (avg. ms)	10.97	0.16	0.21	3.89	0.24	15.47
CH	Total Time (ms)	42,068	493	587	2,442	551	46,141
	Time per Activity (avg. ms)	9.53	0.11	0.13	0.55	0.12	10.44
TC	Total Time (ms)	220,988	1,301	1,203	172,473	1,018	396,983
	Time per Activity (avg. ms)	9.67	0.06	0.05	7.55	0.04	17.37

due to one-off setup times, we ran the derivation twice and considered the second run only. Table 6.3 summarizes the computation times for the annotation, the atomic service derivation (AS), the composite service derivation (CS), the refined composite service derivation (RCS), and the inheritance hierarchy service derivation (IHS). In addition, it shows total processing time including annotation and all service identification techniques.

The computation time results show that the actual derivation of the services is very fast. Apart from the refined composite services, the computation time per activity is less than one millisecond. The reason for the higher computation time for the refined composite services is given by the expensive synonymy comparison among the actions via WordNet. However, even for the large and complex TC collection, the computation time per activity is less than 8 milliseconds. The major share of the total computation time is consumed by the annotation. For the CH collection, the annotation represents 90% of the total running time. Still, the computation of all service candidates including annotation is conducted within seven minutes for the extensively large TC collection. Against the background that the service derivation is not a time critical task, we consider the computation time to be appropriate.

In addition to the computation time for service derivation, we also investigated the performance time of the service detailing. The average time for the detailing of a business object group consumed 893 milliseconds for the SAP collection, 1,464 milliseconds for the CH collection, and 17,287 milliseconds for the TC collection. Considering the fact that detailing is typically only conducted for individual service candidates, these run times represent a satisfying performance.

6.3.3   Service Derivation Results

This section discusses the results from the service derivation and detailing. First, Sections 6.3.3.1 through 6.3.3.4 present the results from the service derivation. Then, Section 6.3.3.5 gives an example for the detailing of an identified service candidate.

6.3.3.1 Atomic Service Results

For obtaining atomic service candidates, we computed the metric F_A for each activity in the investigated process model collections. The quantitative results are summarized in Table 6.4. The table shows the number of identified service candidates for different F_A values and the corresponding share of the identified services with respect to the size of the model collections. The numbers illustrate that there are, in general, many activities that occur more than once. Among all investigated process model collections at least 19% of the activities occur twice or more. Considering the development of $F_A \geq 2$ to $F_A \geq 50$, we can also see that the number of service candidates decreases rapidly. Still, the number of activities occurring 10 times or more amounts to 0.5% for the SAP collection to 1.6% for the TC collection. Depending on the complexity of the underlying task, such frequent activities may represent suitable service candidates.

Table 6.5 presents the top five atomic service candidates for each model collection. The results illustrate that the identified service candidates give a good impression of the overall scope of the model collections. This actually emphasizes the relevance of the identified services with respect to the modeled domain. As an example, consider the SAP collection, which focuses on goods processing and the associated financial aspects. The top five service candidates for the SAP collection accordingly include related services such as *Process Goods Issue* or *Billing*. For the CH and the TC collections, we observe a similar tendency. As these collections are primarily concerned with the interaction with customers, we observe top candidates like *Contact Customer* or *Inform Customer*.

Although the identified candidates represent important activities within the process model collections, it is still necessary to decide whether an identified candidate is suitable for being established as a service. In addition, we must decide whether a candidate can be established as a business or as a software service. For instance, *Process Goods Issue*, *Planning*, and *Contact Customer* are more likely to represent business services as they do not represent activities that are likely to be automated. However, as they are conducted quite frequently, it might be beneficial to consider their standardization and encapsulation as a business service. Candidates that have the potential for automation are, for instance, given by *Billing*, *Create Transaction*, and *Inform Customer*. Hence, they represent good candidates for software services. For example, the billing of a customer could be supported by an application that

Table 6.4 Number of Identified Atomic Services

Collection	F_A					$F_A/$Size				
	≥ 2	≥ 5	≥ 10	≥ 20	≥ 50	≥ 2	≥ 5	≥ 10	≥ 25	≥ 50
SAP	464	88	12	0	0	19.1%	3.6%	0.5%	0.0%	0.0%
CH	965	207	37	7	1	21.9%	4.7%	0.8%	0.2%	0.0%
TC	7,575	1,119	361	106	14	33.2%	4.9%	1.6%	0.5%	0.1%

Table 6.5 Results for Atomic Service Identification

Collection	Rank	Candidate	F_A
	1	Process Goods Issue	20
	2	Calculate Overhead	17
SAP	3	Billing	13
	4	Planning	13
	5	Difference Processing	13
	1	Contact Customer	69
	2	Create Transaction	63
CH	3	Cancel Assessment	28
	4	Decline Assessment	28
	5	Determine Third Party	27
	1	Inform Customer	586
	2	Request	187
TC	3	Identify Customer	150
	4	Cancel Order	90
	5	Manage Customer Satisfaction	83

Table 6.6 Number of Identified Composite Services

	F_{BO}					$F_{BO}/Size$				
Collection	≥ 2	≥ 5	≥ 10	≥ 20	≥ 50	≥ 2	≥ 5	≥ 10	≥ 25	≥ 50
SAP	51	27	13	1	0	2.1%	1.1%	0.5%	0.0%	0.0%
CH	54	45	28	11	3	1.2%	1.0 %	0.6%	0.2%	0.1%
TC	711	547	305	118	49	3.1%	2.4%	1.3%	0.5%	0.2%

requires a set of input data and automatically generates an according invoice. Similarly, the creation of a transaction or the notification of a customer can be supported by software services.

6.3.3.2 Composite Service Results

Based on the consideration of the metric F_{BO}, we use the model collections to identify business object groups. Table 6.6 summarizes the quantitative results. It shows that the business object grouping significantly reduces the total number of identified services. However, the identified services do not represent simple activities but groups consisting of two or more different actions. The number of identified composite services with F_{BO} greater or equal than two ranges from 1.0% for the SAP collection to 3.1% for the TC collection.

Table 6.7 Results for Composite Service Identification

Collection	Rank	Object	Top Actions	F_{BO}	NoA
	1	Order	Execute, Settle, Archive	48	14
	2	Time Sheet	Report, Permit, Process	23	5
SAP	3	Invoice	Release, Verify, Process	23	7
	4	Budget	Release, Plan, Update	23	10
	5	Posting	Perform, Release, Direct	19	3
	1	Customer	Contact, Inform, Determine	209	12
	2	Claim	Determine, Review, Finalize	87	14
CH	3	Assessment	Decline, Cancel, Submit	76	9
	4	Transaction	Create, Stop	63	2
	5	Quote	Update, Authorize, Check	35	14
	1	Order	Cancel, Deliver, Complete	789	83
	2	Customer	Inform, Identify, Create	753	80
TC	3	Case	Create, Dispatch, Accept	383	61
	4	Request	Log, Send, Handle	241	58
	5	Offer	Implement, Confirm, Validate	182	30

Table 6.8 Number of Identified Refined Composite Services

Collection	F_{SemBO}					$F_{SemBO}/Size$				
	≥ 2	≥ 5	≥ 10	≥ 20	≥ 50	≥ 2	≥ 5	≥ 10	≥ 25	≥ 50
SAP	50	27	13	1	0	2.1%	1.1%	0.5%	0.0%	0.0%
CH	48	40	25	9	3	1.1%	0.9%	0.6%	0.2%	0.1%
TC	685	527	299	117	48	3.0%	2.3%	1.3%	0.5%	0.2%

Table 6.7 shows the top five ranked business object groups for each model collection. In addition to the rank and the respective value of F_{BO}, the table also provides the most frequent actions and the total number of unique actions (NoA) that are applied on the business objects. The results illustrate that the composite services include business objects that are not part of the trivial service list. As examples, consider *budget*, *claim*, and *case*. This emphasizes the importance of considering business object groups as candidates since important business objects might also be outnumbered by single activities. The potential of business object groups for representing relevant service candidates is illustrated by the comprised actions. Thinking of the life cycle of a business object like *order*, it becomes apparent that *execute*, *settle*, and *archive* are core tasks in this context. As the composite service derivation automatically derives this information, the user can efficiently evaluate all tasks related to a business object and establish a composite service.

Table 6.9 Results for Refined Composite Service Identification

Collection	Rank	Object	Top Synonym Cluster	F$_{SemBO}$	NoA	NoS
SAP	1	Order	-	48	14	0
	2	Time Sheet	-	23	5	0
	3	Invoice	-	23	7	0
	4	Budget	-	23	10	0
	5	Posting	-	19	3	0
CH	1	Customer	{Notify, Advise}	209	10	1
	2	Claim	-	87	14	0
	3	Assessment	-	76	9	0
	4	Transaction	-	63	2	0
	5	Quote	{Check, Verify}	35	14	1
TC	1	Order	{Delete, Cancel}, {Handle, Manage}	789	65	7
	2	Customer	{Help, Assist}, {Charge, Bill},	753	67	16
	3	Case	{Handle, Manage}	383	50	3
	4	Request	{Evaluate, Assess}, {Refuse, Reject, Deny}	241	58	10
	5	Offer	{Select, Choose}, {Conform, Adjust}	182	26	5

6.3.3.3   Refined Composite Service Results

The importance of the consideration of refined services is depending on the degree of synonymy within the considered process model collections. The more synonymous actions are included, the bigger the effect of the synonym clustering. Besides the internal consolidation, we may also observe an overall reduction of the composite service candidates. As we only consider candidates with at least two different actions, the synonym clustering may result in the exclusion of a candidate since the included actions are grouped to a single synonym cluster. Table 6.8 summarizes the quantitative results of the refined composite service derivation. It illustrates that the synonym clustering has a rather moderate effect. For F_{SemBO} greater or equal than two, we observe an average reduction of the candidates of 0.1% percentage points. However, in order to assess the internal consolidation effect of the synonym clustering, we need to take a look at the actions of the candidates.

Table 6.9 shows the top five candidates for the refined composite service identification. While the identified services are identical to those of the composite service identification, we observe some differences with respect to the internal structure. From a quantitative perspective the internal consolidation can be derived from the number of actions (NoA). Particularly for the TC collection, the total number of unique actions decreased considerably. More generally, the synonym cluster examples illustrate the value of the synonym perspective. As an example, consider the actions *handle* and *manage* for the business object *case* or the actions *help* and *assist* for the business object *customer*. For the business object *request*, we even identified a cluster with three elements: *refuse*, *reject*, and *deny*. These examples illustrate that the refined composite services can provide the user with valuable information when aiming at establishing composite services. Although not all clusters necessarily refer to the same semantics, the automatic identification helps the user to quickly identify semantically similar behavior.

6.3.3.4 Inheritance Hierarchy Service Results

To extract a business object hierarchy, we derived the different parts for each business object and computed their frequencies. In this way, for instance, the business object *Service Product Order* was first reduced to *Product Order* and then to *Order*. Whenever a part term was identified twice, a new node in the business object hierarchy was created. Taking the given example, only a new node for *Order* is introduced as the term *Product Order* only appeared once among all activities of the model collection. By computing the metric F_{IH} for each main word, we obtain a ranked list of business object hierarchies. Table 6.10 gives an overview of the quantitative results. In comparison to composite services, the numbers show that the consideration of the inheritance hierarchy causes a shift with respect to the number of identified candidates. While the number of candidates with a low occurrence ($F_{IH} \geq 2$) is decreasing, the number of candidates with a higher occurrence ($F_{IH} \geq 10$) is increasing. This highlights that the concentration on the main word of the business objects is a valuable strategy for identifying semantically-related candidates consisting of multiple activities.

Table 6.11 gives an overview of the top-ranked candidates for each collection. It includes the main word, a set of sub node examples, the frequency F_{IH}, and the total number of distinct sub nodes (NoN). The results show that there are some dominant business objects that were already included in the candidate lists of the other services identification techniques. Examples include the objects *order*, *claim*, and *case*. Apparently, those objects are of central importance for the operations of the investigated processes. However, we also observe that highly-ranked business objects from the other approaches are no longer included. For example, the business object *customer* or *invoice* are no longer among the top-ranked service candidates. This emphasizes the importance of different perspectives. As business objects like *document* are almost exclusively used in a more specific context (e.g., billing document or customer document), they do not achieve high values in the context of the previously discussed techniques. Nevertheless, as documents may also have important commonalities that may be encapsulated by a service, the inheritance hierarchy is an important perspective for service derivation.

Table 6.10 Number of Identified Inheritance Hierarchy Services

Collection	F_{IH}					$F_{IH}/$Size				
	≥ 2	≥ 5	≥ 10	≥ 20	≥ 50	≥ 2	≥ 5	≥ 10	≥ 25	≥ 50
SAP	43	38	25	8	2	1.8%	1.6%	1.0%	0.3%	0.1%
TC	72	72	57	30	8	1.6%	1.6%	1.3%	0.7%	0.2%
CH	612	557	423	242	133	2.7%	2.4%	1.9%	1.1%	0.6%

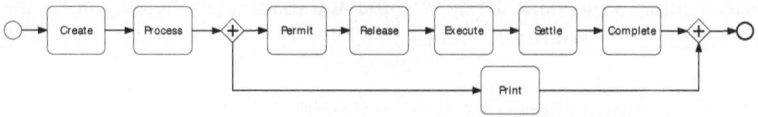

Fig. 6.3 The Process Model for the Composite Service *order*

Table 6.11 Results for Inheritance Hierarchy Service Identification

Collection	Rank	Object	Top Nodes	F_{IH}	NoN
	1	Order	Business Order, Sales Order, Service Order	112	18
	2	Data	Plan Data, Transaction Data, Time Sheet Data	51	10
SAP	3	Sheet	Time Sheet, Balance Sheet	27	7
	4	Document	Measurement Doc., Billing Doc., Customer Doc.,	27	4
	5	Cost	Plan Cost, Process Cost, Shipment Cost	27	6
	1	Details	Loss Details, Claim Details, Report Details	227	81
	2	Claim	Flood Claim, BAU Claim, X-Ref Claim	119	10
CH	3	Status	Job Status, Investigation Status, Policy Status	116	19
	4	Assessment	Onsite Asmt., Specialist Asmt., Recovery Asmt.	95	8
	5	Quote	Vendor Quote, Winning Quote, Sublet Quote	73	13
	1	Order	Purchase Order, HW Order, Status Order	1,243	155
	2	Request	Customer Req., Porting Req., Change Req.	806	164
TC	3	Details	Customer Details, Contact Details, Order Details	633	145
	4	Information	Customer Inf., Device Inf., Bundle Inf.	597	130
	5	Case	Customer Case, Dispute Case, Business Case	562	63

6.3.3.5   Detailing of a Service Candidate

To demonstrate the derivation of the internal service structure, we use the top-ranked business object *order* from the SAP collection.

In order to determine the internal structure of such a composite service, we compute the behavioral profile for the comprised activities. Table 6.12 shows the corresponding behavioral profile for the composite service *order*. Recalling that the behavioral relation of a strict order results in a sequence and the interleaving relation in a parallel path, this profile illustrates that there exists a well-defined order in which the activities must be executed. Apart from the activity *print*, which can be performed at any time after the activity *process*, the order is strict. The synthesis of this profile yields the process model depicted in Figure 6.3.

The generated process model is the result of synthesizing the information from 18 different process models from the SAP collection. Although, in total, 23 process models contain the business object *order*, only 18 of them include two or more activities with this business object. As it is not possible to compute a behavioral relation

Table 6.12 The Behavioral Profile for the Composite Service *order*

	create	process	print	release	execute	permit	settle	complete
create		⤳	⤳	⤳	⤳	⤳	⤳	⤳
process			⤳	⤳	⤳	⤳	⤳	⤳
print				∥	∥	∥	∥	∥
release					⤳	⤳$^{-1}$	⤳	⤳
execute						⤳$^{-1}$	⤳	⤳
permit							⤳	⤳
settle								⤳

from a single activity, we excluded these models from the life cycle computation. The associated processing time of the detailing amounts to 978 milliseconds. Considering that *order* is the most frequent business object, this illustrates the practical applicability of the life cycle computation.

From a general perspective, this example illustrates that the information from a process model collection can also help to support the internal design. By configuring the minimal support *minsup* and the minimal confidence *minconf*, the automatically generated internal structure can be adapted to the needs of the user, i.e., less frequent activities can be excluded or included. Although this structure may not represent the final implementation of the service, it represents valuable information, which can be presented to the user in a fully automated fashion.

6.3.3.6 Discussion of Results

The results from the evaluation demonstrated that we can successfully generate useful service candidates. In comparison to previously defined service identification techniques, we can emphasize three important differences: degree of automation, sophisticated usage of linguistic information, and different service perspectives.

The presented approach *fully automates* the four phases of service identification from preparation to prioritization of the candidates. The most important difference to previous service identification techniques can be found in the preparation and the prioritization phase. By building on the linguistic parsing and annotation technique from Chapter 3, we are able to automatically identify heterogeneous labeling structures and thus to relieve users from the manual preparation. In the prioritization phase, we support users by ranking the derived service candidates. Although the final selection is still left to the user, the automation significantly reduces the manual effort. The application of the technique on three large process model collections, one including more than 17,000 activities, demonstrates the potential of the automation. Up to the final selection, no manual work is required. Hence, the technique can be scaled up to extremely large process model collections.

As opposed to existing techniques, we *sophistically analyze the natural language* of process model activities. Thus, we are able to use action and business object to obtain different service candidates and to compute the internal structure of a service.

Moreover, the detailed consideration of the natural language allows us to group semantically similar behavior. In general, the linguistic analysis represents an important delta as it facilitates the automated yet reliable and useful clustering of model behavior. While some approaches suggested similar strategies, none of them provided support for automatically implementing them.

As a consequence of the possibility to individually consider actions and business objects, the presented approach includes different service perspectives. The benefits of having different perspectives are, for instance, reflected by the commonalities among the different service lists. We observed that some business objects such as *order* are included in the top five list of all identification techniques, while other candidates can be only found in the list of a single technique. On the one hand that highlights the importance of these candidates, on the other hand that emphasizes the benefits of taking different perspectives as additional candidates are also provided by each technique. Another benefit of the different perspectives is the coverage of different levels of granularity. While atomic services represent fine granular services, inheritance hierarchy services represent rather course-grained services. Depending on the needs of the user, this represents an important feature.

Altogether, the presented technique can be considered as an important step towards the fully automated derivation of service candidates.

6.4 Summary

In this chapter, we addressed the problem of manual work in the identification of services from process models. Using a literature review, we identified that current approaches lack the adequate handling of linguistic information and automatic support. The approach presented in this chapter addresses these problems by providing the possibility to automatically derive a list of ranked service candidates from business process models. In particular, it generates a ranked list of atomic services, composite services, refined composite services, and inheritance hierarchy services. An evaluation with three large process model collections from industry demonstrated that the approach can successfully generate useful service candidates. Further, it illustrates the benefits of the delta to previously defined techniques. The sophisticated analysis of natural language facilitates the usage of action and business object to generate different service candidate lists. In addition, it enables the computation of an internal service structure. The automation provides users with the possibility to apply the technique on huge process model collections. As a result, services can also be derived from extensively large collections with hardly any manual effort.

Chapter 7
Conclusion

In this chapter, we summarize and discuss the results of this book. First, Section 7.1 summarizes the main findings. Afterwards, Section 7.2 discusses the implications of these findings before Section 7.1 gives an outlook on future research.

7.1 Summary of Results

In this book, we presented a novel approach facilitating the precise and reliable analysis of natural language in process models. Further, we introduced a set of innovative techniques that leverage the natural language analysis to automatically support companies in maintaining large process model collections. More specifically, we can summarize the results as follows.

- *Conceptualization of the Role of Natural Language in Process Models*: We demonstrate that there is currently no common understanding of the role of natural language in process models. While some authors consider natural language as a syntactic aspect, others discuss it as a pragmatic issue. In Chapter 1, we address this inconsistency by illustrating the relationship between modeling and natural language. We clarify that both consist of a syntactic and a semantic dimension and hence the overall semantics of a process model is constituted by combining the semantics of natural language and modeling language.
- *Taxonomy of Process Model Element Styles*: In process models from practice, we often observe that element labels follow different grammatical structures. In Chapter 3, we demonstrate that there still exist reoccurring patterns, so-called labeling styles. Based on an extensive analysis of process model collections from practice, we present a taxonomy of labeling styles for activities, events, and gateways. An explorative analysis of German and Portuguese process model collections highlighted that these labeling styles cannot only be found in English models, but also in models of other languages.
- *Annotation of Process Model Element Labels*: The effective linguistic analysis and annotation of process models is impeded by the shortness and ambiguity of the comprised element labels. Due to these characteristics, it is cumbersome to

detect the various labeling structures and to precisely determine the label components such as action or business object. Prior research circumvented this problem by employing different heuristics to infer the important terms from process model labels. However, such approaches ignore the syntactic structure of process model labels and are not capable of annotating labels with their semantic components. In Chapter 3, we provide a solution to this problem by presenting a technique for automatically recognizing the labeling style and subsequently annotating the label with action, business object, and addition. The technique is building on the previously defined labeling style taxonomy and shows a good performance in the context of an evaluation with process model collections from industry.

- *Detection and Correction of Linguistic Guideline Violations*: Process model guidelines are an important strategy to assure the consistency of process models that are created by different modelers. However, not all conventions are intuitively understood by casual modelers. Hence, many modeling tools provide automatic support. While many formal model properties can be checked in an automated fashion, there is a notable gap for detecting linguistic violations. In Chapter 4, we address this problem by introducing a corpus-based technique for automatically detecting and correcting linguistic guideline violations in process models. An evaluation with industry process model collections illustrates the high reliability of the violation detection and also demonstrates the usefulness of automatically correcting detected violations among process model activities.

- *Generation of Natural Language Texts from Process Models*: Although process models are widely used for documenting and redesigning the operations of companies, often only a small group of employees is capable of understanding them in detail. This becomes a particular problem when domain experts are not able to provide feedback as they are not familiar with the concept of a process model. In Chapter 5, we address this issue by presenting a technique for automatically generating natural language texts from BPMN process models. The technique builds on the combination of natural language analysis and the generation of an RPST. The evaluation of the technique shows that the technique reliably generates appropriate texts. The comparison against a set of manually created texts illustrates that the generated texts are much more stable with respect to characteristics as sentence complexity, text size, and the full coverage of activities. As the text generation is fully automatic, the user can generate or update a text with a single click.

- *Derivation of Service Candidates from Process Models*: Process models comprise important information on the operations of companies. Hence, they are often used as a basis for identifying service candidates. However, service identification techniques from prior research only partially support users with automated techniques. Thus, such methods cannot be applied on large process model collections. Moreover, existing techniques do not make adequate use of the linguistic information of process models. In Chapter 6, we close this research gap by introducing a technique for automatically deriving a list of ranked service candidates from process models. The technique leverages the linguistic analysis of process model activities to explicitly address the semantic label components such as action and business object. An evaluation with three large process model collections from practice illustrates the usefulness of the derived candidates and that the technique can reduce the service identification process to the final selection of services from a ranked list.

7.2 Implications

The results of this book have several implications for the field of business process modeling and for conceptual modeling in general. In the following, we discuss the major implications for the linguistic analysis in conceptual models, for the quality of business process models, for the matching of business process models, for the modeling of business processes, for the range and impact of business process models, and for the alignment of business and IT.

- *Linguistic Analysis in Conceptual Models*: The techniques and the results we presented in this book highlight the importance and the potential of the linguistic analysis of process models. The precise annotation of process model elements with their semantic components paves the way for a completely new set of opportunities. In fact, this does not only apply to process models, but also to other conceptual models. For instance, the problem of naming is also discussed for use case diagrams [71], feature diagrams [205], and goal models [287]. As the text labels in these models follow similar grammatical structures, also other conceptual models can benefit from the presented linguistic analysis techniques. This may include the checking of naming conventions as well as the definition of other techniques building on the linguistic analysis.
- *Quality of Business Process Models*: The analysis of modeling behavior in the context of this book revealed that the naming of process model elements represents an important quality issue. Many modelers do not comply with standard conventions such as the verb-object style for activities. Using the introduced violation detection approach, process model collections can be automatically checked for linguistic violations. In this way, the technique complements other automated quality assurance techniques that are concerned with formal model properties such as soundness. As an outcome, we shift the boundary of process model quality issues that can be checked automatically from formal model properties to linguistic aspects.
- *Matching of Business Process Model*: Techniques for automatically comparing and aligning process models, so-called matchers, represent an important requisite for many activities such as process model compatibility analysis or the identification of clones within a process model repository. Up until now, matching techniques either solely concentrated on structural aspects or used heuristics to make use of the natural language of process models [333, 94]. The parsing and annotation technique from this book creates a wide range of new opportunities for process model matchers. For instance, it enables the precise comparison of actions and business objects. As a result, a matcher could easily determine that the two activities *Reject Applicant* and *Accept Applicant* do not represent a matching

candidate as *reject* and *accept* are listed as antonyms in WordNet. Without the annotation of the semantic components, such aspects related to natural language could not be addressed.

- *Modeling of Business Processes*: Today, many modeling tools provide comprehensive support in terms of quality checks. As a result, modeling errors can often be avoided right from the start. In a similar vein, the violation detection technique can indicate linguistic problems during the modeling process. If applicable, the modeler can also ask for an automatic correction of the detected violation. As a consequence, these techniques can help modelers avoid errors and reflect on their style of modeling. Altogether, these techniques may ease the task of process modeling since problem detection as well as correction can be integrated in a modeling tool.
- *Range and Impact of Business Process Models*: The range and the impact of process models are currently limited to those that are capable of understanding the models and the details they provide. The text generation technique presented in this book has the potential of significantly reducing this limitation. First, the generated texts support employees in understanding the details of process models even if they are not familiar with process modeling. Second, the text generation may also train employees in reading and interpreting process models. As long as text and model are presented together, readers can see and learn about the connection between model text. As a result, their overall familiarity with process models can be expected to increase in the long term.
- *Alignment of Business and IT*: Numerous approaches from prior research demonstrated that process model collections represent a suitable source for service identification. Using the automatic service identification technique from this book, we cannot only support organizations in automatically identifying services, but also in improving the alignment between business and IT. As the ranked service candidates give a good impression on the relative importance of a business operation, they can also provide companies with first clues on where IT support is needed and where it could be reduced.

7.3 Future Research

There are several points for future research that have not been addressed within this book. Our main focus was the syntactic dimension of natural language in process models and how it can be recognized and utilized in different contexts. However, considering the different phases of the business process management life cycle, there are several other application scenarios of natural language analysis:

In the *process identification phase*, parsers can be employed to automatically analyze natural language documents in order to discover frequently executed activities, critical decisions, and interrelations among processes. Such a preprocessing step has the potential of significantly reducing the manual word load and providing first insights about the key activities and processes of an organization.

Natural language can support the *process discovery phase* in different ways. First, natural language processing tools can be employed to automatically evaluate interviews with domain experts and other natural language documents such as reports and e-mails. As a result, activities or even entire process models can be automatically synthesized. First approaches pursuing this goal have been proposed by Gonçalves et al [136] and by Friedrich et al. [124]. Although these techniques cannot deal with multiple input sources and rather unstructured text like interviews, these approaches demonstrate the general feasibility and the value of this endeavour. Another application scenario of natural language processing in the process discovery phase is the enrichment of process mining techniques. Although process mining algorithms are typically not concerned with language processing, the analyzed event logs often include natural language information such as event names. Hence, the introduced label annotation technique can, for instance, be used to associate event logs with process model activities for the purpose of conformance checking.

In the *process analysis phase*, natural language analysis can be applied in two scenarios. First, the introduced techniques can be employed to discover weaknesses of the process such as redundant activities or media disruptions. Also control flow verification techniques can benefit from natural language analysis. By building on the annotation of action and business object, preconditions of activities can be automatically evaluated or compared against an ontology. In addition, unlikely behaviour could be spotted. As example, consider an and-split leading to the activities *Reject Request* and *Approve Request*. With the help of WordNet, a technique can identify that *reject* and *approve* are antonyms and are hence not very likely to occur with the same business object in the same process instance. A second application scenario is the identification of weaknesses of the process model. In this book, we extensively discussed how to identify and resolve syntactical problems. Nevertheless, there are also semantic issues that decrease the understandability of process models. One of the most important points is the identification and resolution of synonyms and homonyms. If process models use different words for the same concept (e.g., bill and invoice) or the same word for different concepts (e.g., application for a *computer application* and for a *job application*), this may considerably confuse model readers.

The role of natural language during the *redesign phase* is comparable to the process discovery phase. Using the automated analysis of process documentations, potential improvement strategies can be detected. For instance, by comparing different cases, it can be derived which circumstances lead to the non-successful completion of a process. This information can then serve as an input for concrete redesign strategies.

In the *implementation phase*, natural language analysis can particularly support the realization of workflow-based processes. For instance, natural language processing techniques can be used to automatically generate the workflow input forms. By parsing the data objects of the process model with the introduced techniques, the required information can be automatically derived from the process model.

Natural language techniques may also support the *process monitoring and controlling phase*. For instance, natural language analysis can complement current process mining techniques for evaluating process compliance. As a result, the behavior of employees can not only be derived from event logs, but also from natural language text sources such as e-mails and system data entries.

The sketched application scenarios illustrate that the potential use of natural language in business process management is in no way limited to process models. However, process models still represent the central artifact in the business process management life cycle. Consequently, the techniques presented in this book represent an important step forward. They provide the foundations for sophistically working with natural language in process models and also give an idea of the potential and the possibilities that arise from it.

References

1. Proceedings of the European Conference on Information Systems (ECIS). Association for Information Systems (2012)
2. Proceedings of the International Conference on Information Systems. Association for Information Systems (2012)
3. van der Aalst, W.M.P.: The application of Petri nets to workflow management. The Journal of Circuits, Systems and Computers 8(1), 21–66 (1998)
4. van der Aalst, W.M.P.: Formalization and verification of event-driven process chains. Information and Software Technology 41(10), 639–650 (1999)
5. van der Aalst, W.M.P.: Formalization and verification of event-driven process chains. Information and Software Technology 41(10), 639–650 (1999)
6. van der Aalst, W.M.P.: Workflow Verification: Finding Control-Flow Errors Using Petri-Net-Based Techniques. In: van der Aalst, W.M.P., Desel, J., Oberweis, A. (eds.) BPM 2000. LNCS, vol. 1806, pp. 161–183. Springer, Heidelberg (2000)
7. van der Aalst, W.M.P., Dreiling, A., Gottschalk, F., Rosemann, M., Jansen-Vullers, M.: Configurable process models as a basis for reference modeling. In: Bussler, C.J., Haller, A. (eds.) BPM 2005. LNCS, vol. 3812, pp. 512–518. Springer, Heidelberg (2006)
8. van der Aalst, W.M.P., Hirnschall, A., Verbeek, H.M.W.: An Alternative Way to Analyze Workflow Graphs. In: Pidduck, A.B., Mylopoulos, J., Woo, C.C., Ozsu, M.T. (eds.) CAiSE 2002. LNCS, vol. 2348, pp. 535–552. Springer, Heidelberg (2002)
9. van der Aalst, W.M.P., Kumar, A.: XML-Based Schema Definition for Support of Interorganizational Workflow. Information Systems Research 14(1), 23–46 (2003)
10. van der Aalst, W.M.P., ter Hofstede, A.H.M.: Workflow patterns: On the expressive power of (petri-net-based) workflow languages. In: Proceedings of the 4th Workshop on the Practical Use of Coloured Petri Nets and CPN Tools, pp. 1–20 (2002)
11. van der Aalst, W.M.P., ter Hofstede, A.H.M., Kiepuszewski, B., Barros, A.P.: Workflow patterns. Distributed Parallel Databases 14(1), 5–51 (2003)
12. van der Aalst, W.M.P., ter Hofstede, A.H.M., Weske, M.: Business process management: A survey. In: van der Aalst, W.M.P., ter Hofstede, A.H.M., Weske, M. (eds.) BPM 2003. LNCS, vol. 2678, pp. 1–12. Springer, Heidelberg (2003)
13. van der Aalst, W.M.P., van Hee, K.: Workflow Management: Models, Methods, and Systems. The MIT Press (2002)
14. Abrett, G., Burstein, M., Deutsch, S.: Tarl: Tactical action representation language, an environment for building goal directed knowledge based simulations. Tech. Rep. 7062, BBN (1989)

15. Adamopoulos, D., Pavlou, G., Papandreou, C.: Advanced service creation using distributed object technology. IEEE Communications Magazine 40(3), 146–154 (2002)
16. Afonso, S., Bick, E., Haber, R., Santos, D.: Floresta sintá(c)tica: A treebank for portuguese. In: Proceedings of the 3rd International Conference on Language Resources and Evaluation (2002)
17. Allweyer, T.: BPMN 2.0 - Business Process Model and Notation, 2nd edn. Books on De-mand GMBH, Norderstedt (2009)
18. Analysts, G.I.: Business process management (bpm) - a global strategic business report. Tech. rep. (2012)
19. de, A.R., Goncalves, J.C., Santoro, F.M., Baiao, F.A.: Business process mining from group stories. In: International Conference on Computer Supported Cooperative Work in Design, pp. 161–166 (2009)
20. Aronoff, M., Rees-Miller, J.: The Handbook of Linguistics. Blackwell Handbooks in Linguistics. Wiley (2008)
21. Arsanjani, A., Allam, A.: Service-oriented modeling and architecture for realization of an soa. In: Proceedings of the IEEE International Conference on Services Computing. IEEE Computer Society, Washington, DC (2006)
22. Attali, Y., Burstein, J., Attali, Y., Burstein, J., Russell, M., Hoffmann, D.T., Attali, Y., Burstein, J.: The automated essay scoring with e-rater v.2. Journal of Technology, Learning, and Assessment (2006)
23. Austin, J.L.: How to do things with words. Harvard University Press (1975)
24. Aversano, L., Cerulo, L., Palumbo, C.: Mining candidate web services from legacy code. In: 10th International Symposium on Web Site Evolution, pp. 37–40 (2008)
25. Azevedo, L.G., Santoro, F., Baião, F., Souza, J., Revoredo, K., Pereira, V., Herlain, I.: A method for service identification from business process models in a soa approach. In: Halpin, T., Krogstie, J., Nurcan, S., Proper, E., Schmidt, R., Soffer, P., Ukor, R. (eds.) BPMDS 2009 and EMMSAD 2009. LNBIP, vol. 29, pp. 99–112. Springer, Heidelberg (2009)
26. Baeza-Yates, R.A., Ribeiro-Neto, B.: Modern Information Retrieval. ACM Press / Addison-Wesley (1999)
27. Baghdadi, Y.: Reverse engineering relational databases to identify and specify basic web services with respect to service oriented computing. Information Systems Frontiers 8(5), 395–410 (2006)
28. Bajwa, I.S., Choudhary, M.A.: From Natural Language Software Specifications to UML Class Models. In: Zhang, R., Zhang, J., Zhang, Z., Filipe, J., Cordeiro, J. (eds.) ICEIS 2011. LNBIP, vol. 102, pp. 224–237. Springer, Heidelberg (2012)
29. Baker, C.F., Fillmore, C.J., Lowe, J.B.: The berkeley framenet project. In: Proceedings of the 17th International Conference on Computational Linguistics, COLING 1998, pp. 86–90. Association for Computational Linguistics, Stroudsburg (1998)
30. Baker, P.: Using Corpora in Discourse Analysis. Continuum Discourse Series. Bloomsbury (2006)
31. Bangalore, S., Rambow, O.: Corpus-based lexical choice in natural language generation. In: Proceedings of the 38th Annual Meeting on Association for Computational Linguistics, ACL 2000, pp. 464–471. Association for Computational Linguistics, Stroudsburg (2000)
32. Barros, A., Gal, A., Kindler, E. (eds.): BPM 2012. LNCS, vol. 7481. Springer, Heidelberg (2012)
33. Bateman, J.A.: Enabling technology for multilingual natural language generation: the kpml development environment. Natural Language Engineering 3(1), 15–55 (1997)

34. Battista, G.D., Eades, P., Tamassia, R., Tollis, I.G.: Graph Drawing: Algorithms for the Visualization of Graphs, 1st edn. Prentice Hall PTR (1998)
35. Becker, J., Bergener, P., Breuker, D., Räckers, M.: An empirical assessment of the usefulness of weakness patterns in business process redesign. In: Proceedings of the 20th European Conference on Information Systems, Barcelona, Spain (2012)
36. Becker, J., Breuker, D., Delfmann, P., Dietrich, H.A., Steinhorst, M.: Identifying business process activity mappings by optimizing behavioral similarity. In: Proceedings of the 18th Americas Conference on Information Systems, Seattle, USA (2012)
37. Becker, J., Delfmann, P., Herwig, S., Lis, Ł., Stein, A.: Formalizing linguistic conventions for conceptual models. In: Laender, A.H.F., Castano, S., Dayal, U., Casati, F., de Oliveira, J.P.M. (eds.) ER 2009. LNCS, vol. 5829, pp. 70–83. Springer, Heidelberg (2009)
38. Becker, J., Delfmann, P., Herwig, S., Lis, L., Stein, A.: Towards Increased Comparability of Conceptual Models - Enforcing Naming Conventions through Domain Thesauri and Linguistic Grammars. In: ECIS 2009 (2009)
39. Becker, J., Rosemann, M., Schütte, R.: Grundsätze ordnungsmäßiger modellierung. Wirtschaftsinformatik 37(5), 435–445 (1995)
40. Becker, J., Rosemann, M., von Uthmann, C.: Guidelines of Business Process Modeling. In: van der Aalst, W.M.P., Desel, J., Oberweis, A. (eds.) BPM 2000. LNCS, vol. 1806, pp. 30–49. Springer, Heidelberg (2000)
41. Bell, M.: Service-oriented modeling. Service Analysis, Design and Architecture. John Wiley and Sons, Hoboken (2008)
42. Bertino, E., Ferrari, E., Atluri, V.: The Specification and Enforcement of Authorization Constraints in Workflow Management Systems. ACM Transactions on Information and System Security 2(1), 65–104 (1999)
43. Bézivin, J., Gerbé, O.: Towards a precise definition of the omg/mda framework. In: Proceedings of the 16th IEEE International Conference on Automated Software Engineering, p. 273. IEEE Computer Society, Washington, DC (2001)
44. Bianchini, D., Cappiello, C., De Antonellis, V., Pernici, B.: P2S: A methodology to enable inter-organizational process design through web services. In: van Eck, P., Gordijn, J., Wieringa, R. (eds.) CAiSE 2009. LNCS, vol. 5565, pp. 334–348. Springer, Heidelberg (2009)
45. Bickel, B., Nichols, J.: Inflectional synthesis of the verb. In: The World Atlas of Language Structures, pp. 94–97. Oxford University Press (2005)
46. Bieswanger, M., Becker, A.: Introduction to English Linguistics. UTB für Wissenschaft: Uni-Taschenbücher. Francke (2010)
47. Bod, R., Hay, J., Jannedy, S.: Probabilistic Linguistics. Bradford Books. Mit Press (2003)
48. Bögl, A., Schrefl, M., Pomberger, G., Weber, N.: Semantic annotation of epc models in engineering domains to facilitate an automated identification of common modelling practices. In: Filipe, J., Cordeiro, J. (eds.) ICEIS 2008. LNBIP, vol. 19, pp. 155–171. Springer, Heidelberg (2009)
49. Bolloju, N., Schneider, C., Sugumaran, V.: A knowledge-based system for improving the consistency between object models and use case narratives. Expert Systems with Applications 39(10), 9398–9410 (2012)
50. Booth, T.L.: Probabilistic representation of formal languages. In: Proceedings of the 10th Annual Symposium on Switching and Automata Theory, SWAT 1969, pp. 74–81. IEEE Computer Society (1969)
51. Brants, S., Dipper, S., Hansen, S., Lezius, W., Smith, G.: The TIGER treebank. In: Proceedings of the Workshop on Treebanks and Linguistic Theories (2002)

52. Breuker, D., Pfeiffer, D., Becker, J.: Reducing the variations in intra- and interorganizational business process modeling - an empirical evaluation. In: Proceedings of the Internationale Tagung Wirtschaftsinformatik (2009)

53. vom Brocke, J., Rosemann, M.: Handbook on Business Process Management 1: Introduction, Methods, and Information Systems, 1st edn. Springer Publishing Company, Incorporated (2010)

54. Brown, A.W.: Model driven architecture: Principles and practice. Software and Systems Modeling 3(4), 314–327 (2004)

55. Brown, P.F., Cocke, J., Della Pietra, S.A., Della Pietra, V.J., Jelinek, F., Lafferty, J.D., Mercer, R.L., Roossin, P.S.: A Statistical Approach to Machine Translation. Computational Linguistics 16(2), 79–85 (1990)

56. Brown, R., Recker, J., West, S.: Using virtual worlds for collaborative business process modeling. Business Process Management Journal 17(3), 546–564 (2011)

57. Bühler, K.: Theory of Language: The Representational Function of Language. Foundations of Semiotics. J. Benjamins Publishing Company (1990 (1934))

58. Burstein, J.: The e-rater scoring engine: Automated essay scoring with natural language processing. In: Shermis, M.D., Burstein, J. (eds.) Automated Essay Scoring: A Cross-Disciplinary Perspective, pp. 113–122. Lawrence Erlbaum Associates (2003)

59. Burton-Jones, A., Wand, Y., Weber, R.: Guidelines for empirical evaluations of conceptual modeling grammars. Journal of the Association for Information Systems 10(6) (2009)

60. Busemann, S.: Best-first surface realization (1996)

61. Cabré, M., Sager, J.: Terminology: Theory, Methods, and Applications. Terminology and Lexicography Research and Practice. J. Benjamins Publishing Company (1999)

62. Cahill, L., et al.: In search of a reference architecture for nlg systems, pp. 77–85 (1999)

63. Casanave, C.P.: Language development in students' journals. Journal of Second Language Writing 3(3), 179–201 (1994)

64. Chang, S.H., Kim, S.D.: A systematic approach to service-oriented analysis and design. In: Münch, J., Abrahamsson, P. (eds.) PROFES 2007. LNCS, vol. 4589, pp. 374–388. Springer, Heidelberg (2007)

65. Charniak, E., Johnson, M.: Coarse-to-fine n-best parsing and maxent discriminative reranking. In: Proceedings of the 43rd Annual Meeting on Association for Computational Linguistics, ACL 2005, pp. 173–180. Association for Computational Linguistics (2005)

66. Chen, F., Zhang, Z., Li, J., Kang, J., Yang, H.: Service identification via ontology mapping. In: 2012 IEEE 36th Annual Computer Software and Applications Conference, vol. 1, pp. 486–491 (2009)

67. Chen, P.P.S.: The entity-relationship model–toward a unified view of data. ACM Transactions on Database Systems 1(1), 9–36 (1976)

68. Chomsky, N.: Syntactic Structures. Mouton classic. Mouton De Gruyter (2002), http://books.google.de/books?id=SNeHkMXHcd8C

69. Church, K.W.: A stochastic parts program and noun phrase parser for unrestricted text. In: Proceedings of the 2nd Conference on Applied Natural Language Processing, ANLC 1988, pp. 136–143. Association for Computational Linguistics, Stroudsburg (1988)

70. Clark, A., Fox, C., Lappin, S.: The Handbook of Computational Linguistics and Natural Language Processing. Blackwell Handbooks in Linguistics. Wiley (2010)

71. Cockburn, A.: Writing effective use cases, vol. 1. Addison-Wesley, Boston (2001)

72. Collins, M.: Head-driven statistical models for natural language parsing. Computational Linguistics 29(4), 589–637 (2003)

73. Comrie, B.: Language Universals and Linguistic Typology, 2nd edn. University of Chicago (1989)
74. Cook, G., Widdowson, H.: Applied Linguistics. Oxford Introduction to Language Study ELT. OUP Oxford (2003)
75. Corston-oliver, S., Gamon, M., Ringger, E., Moore, R.: An overview of amalgam: A machine-learned generation module. In: Proceedings of the International Natural Language Generation Conference, pp. 33–40 (2002)
76. Coulmas, F.: Sociolinguistics: The Study of Speakers' Choices. Cambridge University Press (2005)
77. Crampton, J., Khambhammettu, H.: Delegation and Satisfiability in Workflow Systems. In: SACMAT 2008, pp. 31–40. ACM, New York (2008)
78. Cummings, L.: Pragmatics: A Multidisciplinary Perspective. Edinburgh University Press (2005)
79. Curran, T., Keller, G., Ladd, A.: Sap R/3 Business Blueprint: Understanding the Business Process Reference Model. Enterprise Resource Planning Series. Prentice Hall (1998)
80. Cutting, D., Kupiec, J., Pedersen, J., Sibun, P.: A practical part-of-speech tagger. In: Proceedings of the 3rd Conference on Applied Natural Language Processing, ANLC 1992, pp. 133–140. Association for Computational Linguistics, Stroudsburg (1992)
81. Dalianis, H.: A method for validating a conceptual model by natural language discourse generation. In: Loucopoulos, P. (ed.) CAiSE 1992. LNCS, vol. 593, pp. 425–444. Springer, Heidelberg (1992)
82. Dalianis, H.: Aggregation in natural language generation. Computational Intelligence 15(4), 384–414 (1999)
83. Davenport, T.: Process Innovation: Reengineering Work Through Information Technology. Harvard Business School Press (1993)
84. Davenport, T.H., Short, J.E.: The new industrial engineering: Information technology and business process redesign. Sloan Management Review 31(4), 11–27 (1990)
85. Davies, M.: Word Frequency Data from the Corpus of Contemporary American English (COCA) (2011), http://www.wordfrequency.info
86. Davis, R., Brabänder, E.: ARIS Design Platform: Getting Started with BPM, 1st edn. Springer (2007)
87. Decker, G., Dijkman, R., Dumas, M., García-Bañuelos, L.: Transforming BPMN diagrams into YAWL nets. In: Dumas, M., Reichert, M., Shan, M.-C. (eds.) BPM 2008. LNCS, vol. 5240, pp. 386–389. Springer, Heidelberg (2008)
88. van Deemter, K., Krahmer, E., Theune, M.: Real versus Template-Based Natural Language Generation: A False Opposition? Computational Linguistics 31(1), 15–24 (2005)
89. Deeptimahanti, D.K., Babar, M.A.: An automated tool for generating uml models from natural language requirements. In: Proceedings of the IEEE/ACM International Conference on Automated Software Engineering, ASE 2009, pp. 680–682. IEEE Computer Society, Washington, DC (2009)
90. Deeptimahanti, D.K., Sanyal, R.: Semi-automatic generation of uml models from natural language requirements. In: Proceedings of the 4th India Software Engineering Conference, ISEC 2011, pp. 165–174. ACM, New York (2011)
91. Deissenboeck, F., Pizka, M.: Concise and consistent naming. Software Quality Control 14(3), 261–282 (2006)
92. Delfmann, P., Herwig, S., Lis, L., Stein, A.: Supporting Distributed Conceptual Modelling through Naming Conventions - A Tool-based Linguistic Approach. Enterprise Modelling and Information Systems Architectures 4(2), 3–19 (2009)

93. DeRose, S.J.: Grammatical category disambiguation by statistical optimization. Computational Linguistics 14(1), 31–39 (1988)
94. Dijkman, R.: Diagnosing differences between business process models. In: Dumas, M., Reichert, M., Shan, M.-C. (eds.) BPM 2008. LNCS, vol. 5240, pp. 261–277. Springer, Heidelberg (2008)
95. Dijkman, R.M., Dumas, M., van Dongen, B.F., Käärik, R., Mendling, J.: Similarity of Business Process Models: Metrics and Evaluation. Information Systems 36(2), 498–516 (2011)
96. Dijkman, R., Dumas, M., García-Bañuelos, L.: Graph matching algorithms for business process model similarity search. In: Dayal, U., Eder, J., Koehler, J., Reijers, H.A. (eds.) BPM 2009. LNCS, vol. 5701, pp. 48–63. Springer, Heidelberg (2009)
97. Dijkman, R.M., Dumas, M., Garcia-Banuelos, L., Kaarik, R.: Aligning Business Process Models. In: Proceedings of the 2009 IEEE International Enterprise Distributed Object Computing Conference, pp. 45–53. IEEE (2009)
98. Dijkman, R.M., Dumas, M., Ouyang, C.: Formal semantics and analysis of bpmn process models using petri nets. Tech. rep., Queensland University of Technology (2007)
99. Dijkman, R.M., Dumas, M., Ouyang, C.: Semantics and analysis of business process models in bpmn. Information and Software Technology 50(12), 1281–1294 (2008)
100. Dik, S.: The Theory of Functional Grammar. Functional grammar series. Foris Publications (1989)
101. Duby, C.K., Meyers, S., Reiss, S.P.: Ccel: A metalanguage for c++. Tech. rep., Providence, RI, USA (1992)
102. Dumas, M., Rosa, M., Mendling, J., Reijers, H.: Fundamentals of Business Process Management. Springer, Heidelberg (2013)
103. Dwivedi, V., Kulkarni, N.: A model driven service identification approach for process centric systems. In: Proceedings of the IEEE Congress on Services Part II, SERVICES-2 2008, pp. 65–72. IEEE Computer Society, Washington, DC (2008)
104. Effinger, P., Jogsch, N., Seiz, S.: On a study of layout aesthetics for business process models using BPMN. In: Mendling, J., Weidlich, M., Weske, M. (eds.) BPMN 2010. LNBIP, vol. 67, pp. 31–45. Springer, Heidelberg (2010)
105. Ehrig, M., Koschmider, A., Oberweis, A.: Measuring similarity between semantic business process models. In: Proceedings of the 4th Asia-Pacific Conference on Conceptual Modelling, vol. 67, pp. 71–80. Australian Computer Science Communications (2007)
106. Elhadad, M., Robin, J.: Surge: a comprehensive plug-in syntactic realization component for text generation. Tech. rep. (1998)
107. Erl, T.: Service-Oriented Architecture: Concepts, Technology, and Design. Prentice Hall PTR, Upper Saddle River (2005)
108. Erradi, A., Kulkarni, N., Maheshwari, P.: Service design process for reusable services: Financial services case study. In: Krämer, B.J., Lin, K.-J., Narasimhan, P. (eds.) ICSOC 2007. LNCS, vol. 4749, pp. 606–617. Springer, Heidelberg (2007)
109. Even, S., Even, G.: Graph Algorithms. Computer software engineering series. Cambridge University Press (2011)
110. Fahland, D., Favre, C., Koehler, J., Lohmann, N., Völzer, H., Wolf, K.: Analysis on Demand: Instantaneous Soundness Checking of Industrial Business Process Models. Data & Knowledge Engineering 70(5), 448–466 (2011)
111. Ferrario, R., Guarino, N., Janiesch, C., Kiemes, T., Oberle, D., Probst, F.: Towards an ontological foundation of services science: The general service model. In: Wirtschaftsinformatik (2011)
112. Feuerlicht, G.: Design of service interfaces for e-business applications using data normalization techniques. Information Systems and E-Business Management 3(4), 363–376 (2005)

113. Flaxer, D., Nigam, A.: Realizing business components, business operations and business services. In: Proceedings of the E-Commerce Technology for Dynamic E-Business, IEEE International Conference, CEC-EAST 2004, pp. 328–332. IEEE Computer Society, Washington, DC (2004)

114. Fliedl, G., Kop, C., Mayr, H.C., Salbrechter, A., Vöhringer, J., Weber, G., Winkler, C.: Deriving static and dynamic concepts from software requirements using sophisticated tagging. Data & Knowledge Engineering 61(3), 433–448 (2007)

115. Fliedl, G., Kop, C., Mayr, H.C., Salbrechter, A., Vöhringer, J., Weber, G., Winkler, C.: Deriving Static and Dynamic Concepts from Software Requirements using Sophisticated Tagging. Data & Knowledge Engineering 61(3), 433–448 (2007)

116. Ford, H.: My Life and Work - An Autobiography of Henry Ford. Nuvision Publications (2007)

117. France, R., Rumpe, B.: Model-driven development of complex software: A research roadmap. In: Proceedings of the Future of Software Engineering, FOSE 2007, pp. 37–54. IEEE Computer Society, Washington, DC (2007)

118. Di Francescomarino, C., Tonella, P.: Supporting ontology-based semantic annotation of business processes with automated suggestions. In: Halpin, T., Krogstie, J., Nurcan, S., Proper, E., Schmidt, R., Soffer, P., Ukor, R. (eds.) BPMDS 2009 and EMMSAD 2009. LNBIP, vol. 29, pp. 211–223. Springer, Heidelberg (2009)

119. Francis, W.N., Kucera, H.: Brown corpus manual. Tech. rep., Department of Linguistics, Brown University, Providence, Rhode Island, US (1979)

120. Frederiks, P., van der Weide, T.: Information modeling: The process and the required competencies of its participants. Data & Knowledge Engineering 58(1), 4–20 (2006)

121. Frege, G.: On sense and reference. Philosophical Review 57, 209–230 (1892)

122. Freund, J., Rücker, B.: Praxishandbuch BPMN 2.0, 3rd edn. Carl Hanser Verlag GmbH & CO. KG (2012)

123. Friedman, C., Alderson, P., Austin, J., Cimino, J., Johnson, S.: A General Natural-language Text Processor for Clinical Radiology. Journal of the American Medical Informatics Association 1(2), 161–174 (1994)

124. Friedrich, F.: Automated generation of business process models from natural language input. Master's thesis, Humboldt Universität zu Berlin (2010)

125. Friedrich, F., Mendling, J., Puhlmann, F.: Process Model Generation from Natural Language Text. In: Mouratidis, H., Rolland, C. (eds.) CAiSE 2011. LNCS, vol. 6741, pp. 482–496. Springer, Heidelberg (2011)

126. Fromkin, V., Rodman, R., Hyams, N.: An Introduction to Language. Wadsworth, Cengage Learning (2011)

127. Fromkin, V.A., Hayes, B., Curtiss, S.: An Introduction to Linguistic Theory. Blackwell Publishers (2001)

128. Gacitua-Decar, V., Pahl, C.: Automatic business process pattern matching for enterprise services design. In: IEEE Congress on Services Part II, pp. 111–118 (2009)

129. Galley, M., Fosler-Lussier, E., Potamianos, A.: Hybrid natural language generation for spoken dialogue systems (2001)

130. Gangopadhyay, A.: Conceptual modeling from natural language functional specifications. Artificial Intelligence in Engineering 15(2), 207–218 (2001)

131. Ghose, A.K., Koliadis, G., Chueng, A.: Rapid Business Process Discovery (R-BPD). In: Parent, C., Schewe, K.-D., Storey, V.C., Thalheim, B. (eds.) ER 2007. LNCS, vol. 4801, pp. 391–406. Springer, Heidelberg (2007)

132. Ghose, A.K., Koliadis, G., Chueng, A.: Process Discovery from Model and Text Artefacts. In: Proceedings of the IEEE Congress on Services, pp. 167–174. IEEE Computer Society (2007)

133. Goldberg, E., Driedger, N., Kittredge, R.: Using natural-language processing to produce weather forecasts. IEEE Expert 9(2), 45–53 (1994)

134. Goltz, U., Reisig, W.: The non-sequential behaviour of petri nets. Information and Control 57(2-3), 125–147 (1983)

135. Gomez, F., Segami, C., Delaune, C.: A system for the semiautomatic generation of e-r models from natural language specifications. Data & Knowledge Engineering 29(1), 57–81 (1999)

136. Gonçalves, J.C., Santoro, F.M., Baião, F.A.: Let me tell you a story – on how to build process models. Journal of Universal Computer Science 17, 276–295 (2011)

137. Greene, B., Rubin, G.: Automated grammatical tagging of english. Tech. rep., Department of Linguistics, Brown University (1971)

138. Gruhn, V., Laue, R.: Detecting Common Errors in Event-Driven Process Chains by Label Analysis. Enterprise Modelling and Information Systems Architectures 6(1), 3–15 (2011)

139. Gu, Q., Lago, P.: Service identification methods: A systematic literature review. In: Di Nitto, E., Yahyapour, R. (eds.) ServiceWave 2010. LNCS, vol. 6481, pp. 37–50. Springer, Heidelberg (2010)

140. Halliday, M.A.K.: An Introduction to Functional Grammar. Arnold Publishers (1994)

141. Hammer, M., Champy, J.: Reengineering the Corporation: A Manifesto for Business Revolution. HarperBusiness (1993)

142. Hamp, B., Feldweg, H.: Germanet - a lexical-semantic net for german. In: Proceedings of ACL Workshop Automatic Information Extraction and Building of Lexical Semantic Resources for NLP Applications, pp. 9–15 (1997)

143. Harel, D., Rumpe, B.: Modeling languages: Syntax, semantics and all that stuff, part i: The basic stuff. Tech. rep (2000)

144. Harris, Z.S.: String Analysis of Sentence Structure. Mouton, The Hague (1962)

145. Hearst, M.A.: Multi-paragraph segmentation of expository text. In: Proceedings of the 32nd Annual Meeting on Association for Computational Linguistics, ACL 1994, pp. 9–16. Association for Computational Linguistics, Stroudsburg (1994)

146. Hearst, M.A.: Texttiling: segmenting text into multi-paragraph subtopic passages. Computational Linguistics 23(1), 33–64 (1997)

147. Heinonen, O.: Optimal multi-paragraph text segmentation by dynamic programming. In: Proceedings of the 36th Annual Meeting of the Association for Computational Linguistics and 17th International Conference on Computational Linguistics, ACL 1998, vol. 2, pp. 1484–1486. Association for Computational Linguistics, Stroudsburg (1998)

148. Höfferer, P.: Achieving business process model interoperability using metamodels and ontologies. In: Proceedings of the 15th European Conference on Information Systems, pp. 1620–1631 (2007)

149. Holschke, O.: Granularität als kognitiver Faktor in der adaptiven Wiederverwendung von Geschäftsprozessmodellen. Ph.D. thesis, Technische Universität Berlin (2010)

150. Holschke, O.: Impact of granularity on adjustment behavior in adaptive reuse of business process models. In: Hull, R., Mendling, J., Tai, S. (eds.) BPM 2010. LNCS, vol. 6336, pp. 112–127. Springer, Heidelberg (2010)

151. Hoppenbrouwers, S., Proper, H., van der Weide, T.: Fundamental understanding of the act of modelling. Tech. rep., Radboud University Nijmegen (2005)

152. Hovy, E.H.: Pragmatics and natural language generation. Artificial Intelligence 43, 153–197 (1990)

153. Hovy, E.H.: Aggregation in natural language generation. In: Proceedings of the 4th European Workshop on Natural Language Generation, pp. 28–30 (1993)

154. Hunt, K.W.: Do sentences in the second language grow like those in the first? TESOL Quarterly 4, 195–202 (1970)
155. Hutchins, W.J.: Machine Translation: Past, Present, Future. John Wiley & Sons, Inc., New York (1986)
156. Hynes, G.E., Bexley, J.B.: Understandability of banks' annual reports. In: Proceedings of the 69th Association for Business Communication Annual Convention (2003)
157. Ide, N., Macleod, C.: The american national corpus: A standardized resource for american english. In: Proceedings of Corpus Linguistics, pp. 831–836 (2001)
158. Inaganti, S., Behara, G.K.: Service identification: Bpm and soa handshake. BPTrends (2007)
159. Indurkhya, N., Damerau, F.: Handbook of Natural Language Processing. Chapman & Hall/CRC machine learning & pattern recognition series. Chapman & Hall/CRC (2010)
160. Iordanskaja, L., Kittredge, R., Polguère, A.: Lexical selection and prarphrase in a meaning-text generation model. In: Natural Language Generation in Artificial Intelligence and Computational Linguistics, pp. 293–312 (1991)
161. Jackson, P., Moulinier, I.: Natural Language Processing for Online Applications. Text Retrieval, Extraction and Categorization. In: Natural Language Processing, vol. 5. John Benjamins (2002)
162. Jain, H.K., Zhao, H., Chinta, N.R.: A spanning tree based approach to identifying web services. In: Zhang, L.J. (ed.) ICWS, pp. 272–277. CSREA Press (2003)
163. Jakobson, R.: Closing statements: Linguistics and poetics. In: Sebeok, T.A. (ed.) Style in Language, New York, pp. 350–377 (1960)
164. Jamshidi, P., Sharifi, M., Mansour, S.: To establish enterprise service model from enterprise business model. In: Proceedings of the IEEE International Conference on Services Computing, SCC 2008, pp. 93–100. IEEE Computer Society, Washington, DC (2008)
165. Janton, P., Tonkin, H.: Esperanto: Language, Literature, and Community. State University of New York Press (1993)
166. Jelinek, F.: Statistical Methods for Speech Recognition. The MIT Press (1998)
167. Johnson, D.: Toward a theory of relationally based grammar. Outstanding dissertations in linguistics. Garland Pub. (1979)
168. Joshi, A.K.: Natural language processing. Science 253(5025), 1242–1249 (1991)
169. Joshi, A.K., Kosaraju, S.R., Yamada, H.: String adjunct grammars. In: Proceedings of the 10th Annual Symposium on Switching and Automata Theory, SWAT 1969, pp. 245–262. IEEE Computer Society, Washington, DC (1969)
170. Jurafsky, D., Martin, J.H.: Speech and Language Processing: An Introduction to Natural Language Processing, Computational Linguistics and Speech Recognition, 2nd edn. Prentice Hall (2008)
171. Just, M.A., Carpenter, P.A.: A capacity theory of comprehension: individual differences in working memory. Psychological Review 99(1), 122–149 (1992)
172. Kahane, S.: What is a natural language and how to describe it? Meaning-text approaches in contrast with generative approaches. In: Gelbukh, A. (ed.) CICLing 2001. LNCS, vol. 2004, pp. 1–17. Springer, Heidelberg (2001)
173. Karagiannis, D., Kühn, H.: Metamodelling platforms. In: Bauknecht, K., Tjoa, A.M., Quirchmayr, G. (eds.) EC-Web 2002. LNCS, vol. 2455, p. 182. Springer, Heidelberg (2002)
174. Karlsson, F., Voutilainen, A., Heikkilä, J., Anttila, A. (eds.): Constraint Grammar: A Language-Independent System for Parsing Unrestricted Text. Mouton de Gruyter, Berlin (1995)
175. Kay., M.: Functional grammar. In: Proceedings of the 5th Annual Meeting of the Berkeley Linguistic Society (1979)

176. Keller, G., Teufel, T.: SAP(R) R/3 Process Oriented Implementation: Iterative Process Prototyping. Addison-Wesley (1998)

177. Kettunen, K., Sadeniemi, M., Lindh-Knuutila, T., Honkela, T.: Analysis of EU languages through text compression. In: Salakoski, T., Ginter, F., Pyysalo, S., Pahikkala, T. (eds.) FinTAL 2006. LNCS (LNAI), vol. 4139, pp. 99–109. Springer, Heidelberg (2006)

178. Kibble, R., Power, R.: An integrated framework for text planning and pronominalisation. In: Natural Language Generation, pp. 77–84. ACL (2000)

179. Kim, S., Kim, M., Park, S.: Service identification using goal and scenario in service oriented architecture. In: Asia-Pacific Software Engineering Conference, pp. 419–426. IEEE Computer Society, Los Alamitos (2008)

180. Kim, Y., Doh, K.-G.: The service modeling process based on use case refactoring. In: Abramowicz, W. (ed.) BIS 2007. LNCS, vol. 4439, pp. 108–120. Springer, Heidelberg (2007)

181. Klein, D., Manning, C.D.: Accurate Unlexicalized Parsing. In: 41st Meeting of the Association for Computational Linguistics, pp. 423–430 (2003)

182. Klein, D., Manning, C.D.: Fast Exact Inference with a Factored Model for Natural Language Parsing. In: NIPS 2003, vol. 15. MIT Press (2003)

183. Klein, S., Simmons, R.F.: A computational approach to grammatical coding of english words. Journal of the ACM 10(3), 334–347 (1963)

184. Kleinert, T., Balzert, S., Fettke, P., Loos, P.: Systematic identification of service-blueprints for service-processes - A method and exemplary application. In: La Rosa, M., Soffer, P. (eds.) BPM 2012 Workshops. LNBIP, vol. 132, pp. 598–610. Springer, Heidelberg (2013)

185. Klose, K., Knackstedt, R., Beverungen, D.: Identification of Services - A Stakeholder-Based Approach to SOA Development and its Application in the Area of Production Planning. University of St. Gallen (2007)

186. Knackstedt, R., Kuropka, D., Müller, O.: An ontology-based service discovery approach for the provisioning of product-service bundles. In: Proceedings of the European Conference on Information Systems (2008)

187. Knauss, E., Lubke, D.: Using the friction between business processes and use cases in soa requirements. In: Annual International Conference on Computer Software and Applications, pp. 601–606. IEEE Computer Society (2008)

188. Kohlborn, T., Korthaus, A., Chan, T., Rosemann, M.: Identification and analysis of business and software services - a consolidated approach. IEEE Transactions on Services Computing 2(1), 50–64 (2009)

189. Kohlmann, F., Alt, R.: Business-driven service modelling - a methodological approach from the finance industry. In: Proceedings of the 1st International Working Conference on Business Process and Services Computing, pp. 180–193 (2007)

190. Kortmann, B.: English Linguistics: Essentials. Cornelsen (2005)

191. Koschmider, A., Blanchard, E.: User assistance for business process model decomposition. In: Proceedings of the 1st IEEE International Conference on Research Challenges in Information Science, pp. 445–454 (2007)

192. Koschmider, A., Hornung, T., Oberweis, A.: Recommendation-based editor for business process modeling. Data & Knowledge Engineering 70(6), 483–503 (2011)

193. Koschmider, A., Song, M., Reijers, H.A.: Social software for business process modeling. Journal of Information Technology 25(3), 308–322 (2010)

194. Krogstie, J., Lindland, O.I., Sindre, G.: Defining quality aspects for conceptual models. In: Proceedings of the International Working Conference on Information System Concepts: Towards a Consolidation of Views, pp. 216–231. Chapman & Hall, Ltd. (1995)

195. Krogstie, J., Sindre, G., Jorgensen, H.: Process models representing knowledge for action: a revised quality framework. European Journal of Information Systems 15(1), 91–102 (2006)
196. Kumar, E.: Natural Language Processing. I.K. International Publishing House (2011)
197. La Rosa, M., Reijers, H.A., van der Aalst, W.M.P., Dijkman, R.M., Mendling, J., Dumas, M., García-Bañuelos, L.: Apromore: An advanced process model repository. Expert Syst. Appl. 38(6), 7029–7040 (2011)
198. Lahtinen, S., Peltonen, J.: Adding speech recognition support to uml tools. Journal of Visual Languages and Computing 16(1-2), 85–118 (2005)
199. Landauer, T., Laham, D., Foltz, P.: Automated scoring and annotation of essays with the intelligent essay assessortm. In: Shermis, M.D., Burstein, J. (eds.) Automated Essay Scoring: A Cross-Disciplinary Perspective. Lawrence Erlbaum (2003)
200. Langner, P., Schneider, C., Wehler, J.: Prozeßmodellierung mit ereignisgesteuerten Prozeßketten (EPKs) und Petri-Netzen. Wirtschaftsinformatik 39(5), 479–489 (1997)
201. Lavoie, B., Rambow, O.: A fast and portable realizer for text generation systems. In: Applied Natural Language Processing, pp. 265–268. ACL (1997)
202. Lavoie, B., Rambow, O., Reiter, E.: The modelexplainer. In: Proceedings of the 8th International Workshop on Natural Language Generation, pp. 9–12 (1996)
203. Lawrie, D., Morrell, C., Feild, H., Binkley, D.: What's in a name? a study of identifiers. In: Proceedings of the 14th IEEE International Conference on Program Comprehension, ICPC 2006, pp. 3–12. IEEE Computer Society, Washington, DC (2006)
204. Lee, J., Muthig, D., Naab, M.: An approach for developing service oriented product lines. In: Proceedings of the 12th International Software Product Line Conference, SPLC 2008, pp. 275–284. IEEE Computer Society, Washington, DC (2008)
205. Lee, K., Kang, K.C., Lee, J.: Concepts and guidelines of feature modeling for product line software engineering. In: Gacek, C. (ed.) ICSR 2002. LNCS, vol. 2319, pp. 62–77. Springer, Heidelberg (2002)
206. Levenshtein, V.: Binary codes capable of correcting deletions, insertions, and reversals. Cybernetics and Control Theory 10(8), 707–710 (1966)
207. Levin, B.: English Verb Classes and Alternations: A Preliminary Investigation. University of Chicago Press (1993)
208. Lindland, O.I., Sindre, G., Solvberg, A.: Understanding quality in conceptual modeling. IEEE Software 11(2), 42–49 (1994)
209. Lipka, L.: English lexicology: lexical structure, word semantics and word-formation. Narr, Tübingen (2002)
210. Lomazova, I.: On occurrence net semantics for petri nets with contacts. In: Chlebus, B., Czaja, L. (eds.) FCT 1997. LNCS, vol. 1279, pp. 317–328. Springer, Heidelberg (1997)
211. Lu, X.: Automatic analysis of syntactic complexity in second language writing. International Journal of Corpus Linguistics 15(4), 474–496 (2010)
212. Ludewig, J.: Models in software engineering - an introduction. Software and Systems Modeling 2(1), 5–14 (2003)
213. Lyons, J.: Semantics, vol. 1. Cambridge University Press (1977)
214. Malone, T., Crowston, K., Herman, G. (eds.): Organizing Business Knowledge: The MIT Process Handbook. The MIT Press (2003)
215. Mani, S., Sinha, V., Sukaviriya, N., Ramachandra, T.: Using user interface design to enhance service identification. In: IEEE International Conference on Web Services, pp. 78–87 (2008)
216. Manning, C., Schütze, H.: Foundations of Statistical Natural Language Processing. Mit Press (1999)
217. McGregor, W.: Linguistics: An Introduction. Bloomsbury (2009)

218. McKeown, K., Kukich, K., Shaw, J.: Practical issues in automatic documentation generation. In: Applied Natural Language Processing, pp. 7–14. ACL (1994)
219. McKeown, K., Radev, D.R.: Generating summaries of multiple news articles. In: Proceedings of the 18th Annual International ACM SIGIR Conference on Research and Development in Information Retrieval, SIGIR 1995, pp. 74–82. ACM, New York (1995)
220. Mcroy, S.W., Channarukul, S., Ali, S.S.: Text realization for dialog. In: Proceedings of the International Conference on Intelligent Technologies (2000)
221. McWhorter, J.: The world's simplest grammars are creole grammars. Linguistic Typology 5, 125–166 (2001)
222. Mel'cuk, I., Polguère, A.: A formal lexicon in the meaning-text theory (or how to do lexica with words). Computational Linguistics 13(3-4), 261–275 (1987)
223. Mendling, J.: Metrics for Process Models: Empirical Foundations of Verification, Error Prediction, and Guidelines for Correctness. LNBIP, vol. 6. Springer, Heidelberg (1974)
224. Mendling, J., Reijers, H.A., van der Aalst, W.M.P.: Seven Process Modeling Guidelines (7PMG). Information and Software Technology 52(2), 127–136 (2010)
225. Mendling, J., Reijers, H.A., Recker, J.: Activity Labeling in Process Modeling: Empirical Insights and Recommendations. Information Systems 35(4), 467–482 (2010)
226. Meteer, M.: Portable natural language generation using spokesman. In: Proceedings of the 3rd Conference on Applied Natural Language Processing, ANLC 1992, pp. 237–238. Association for Computational Linguistics, Stroudsburg (1992)
227. Meteer, M.W.: Bridging the generation gap between text planning and linguistic realization. Computational Intelligence 7(4), 296–304 (1991)
228. Meteer, M.W.: Expressibility and the Problem of Efficient Text Planning. St. Martin's Press, Inc., New York (1992)
229. Meziane, F., Athanasakis, N., Ananiadou, S.: Generating natural language specifications from uml class diagrams. Requirements Engineering 13, 1–18 (2008)
230. Microsystems, I.S.: Code Conventions for the Java Programming Language (1997)
231. Miles, L.: Techniques of Value Analysis and Engineering. McGraw-Hill (1961)
232. Miller, G., Fellbaum, C.: WordNet: An Electronic Lexical Database. MIT Press, Cambridge (1998)
233. Miller, G.A.: WordNet: a Lexical Database for English. Communications of the ACM 38(11), 39–41 (1995)
234. Montes, A., Pacheco, H., Estrada, H., Pastor, Ó.: Conceptual model generation from requirements model: A natural language processing approach. In: Kapetanios, E., Sugumaran, V., Spiliopoulou, M. (eds.) NLDB 2008. LNCS, vol. 5039, pp. 325–326. Springer, Heidelberg (2008)
235. Moody, D.L., Sindre, G., Brasethvik, T., Sølvberg, A.: Evaluating the quality of information models: empirical testing of a conceptual model quality framework. In: Proceedings of the 25th International Conference on Software Engineering, pp. 295–305 (2003)
236. More, P., Phalnikar, R.: Generating uml diagrams from natural language specifications. International Journal of Applied Information Systems 1(8), 19–23 (2012)
237. Morris, J., Hirst, G.: Lexical cohesion computed by thesaural relations as an indicator of the structure of text. Computational Linguistics 17(1), 21–48 (1991)
238. zur Muehlen, M., Recker, J.: How Much Language Is Enough? Theoretical and Practical Use of the Business Process Modeling Notation. In: Bellahsène, Z., Léonard, M. (eds.) CAiSE 2008. LNCS, vol. 5074, pp. 465–479. Springer, Heidelberg (2008)
239. zur Muehlen, M., Rosemann, M.: Multi-paradigm process management. In: Proceedings of the 5th Workshop on Business Process Modeling, Development, and Support, pp. 169–175 (2004)

240. Myers, S.: Zero-derivation and inflection. In: MIT Working Papers in Linguistics, vol. 7, pp. 53–69 (1984)
241. Navigli, R.: Word sense disambiguation: a survey. ACM Computing Surveys 41(2), 1–69 (2009)
242. Neisser, U.: From direct perception to conceptual structure. In: Concepts and Conceptual Development: Ecological and Intellectual Factors in Categorization, pp. 11–24. Cambridge University Press (1987)
243. Nijssen, G., Halpin, T.: Conceptual schema and relational database design: a fact oriented approach. Prentice Hall (1989)
244. Nordsieck, F.: Grundlagen der Organisationslehre. Poeschel (1934)
245. Norman, D.: Some observations on mental models, pp. 7–14 (1983)
246. Noth, W.: Handbook of Semiotics. Advances in Semiotics. Indiana University Press (1995)
247. de Novais, E.M., Tadeu, T.D., Paraboni, I.: Text generation for brazilian portuguese: the surface realization task. In: Proceedings of the Workshop on Computational Approaches to Languages of the Americas, YIWCALA 2010, pp. 125–131. Association for Computational Linguistics, Stroudsburg (2010)
248. Object Management Group: Business Process Model and Notation (BPMN) (2011)
249. Object Management Group: Unified modeling language (uml), version 2.0. Tech. rep. (2012)
250. O'Dwyer, B.: Modern English Structures, second edition: Form, Function, and Position. Broadview Press (2006)
251. Omar, N., Hassan, R., Arshad, H., Sahran, S.: Automation of database design through semantic analysis. In: Proceedings of the 7th WSEAS International Conference on Computational Intelligence, Man-Machine Systems and Cybernetics, CIMMACS 2008, pp. 71–76. World Scientific and Engineering Academy and Society (WSEAS), Stevens Point (2008)
252. O'Sullivan, J., Edmond, D., ter Hofstede, A.H.M.: What's in a service? Distributed and Parallel Databases 12(2/3), 117–133 (2002)
253. Page, E.: The imminence of grading essays by computer. The Phi Delta Kappan 47(5), 238–243 (1966)
254. Page, E.B.: Statistical and linguistic strategies in the computer grading of essays. In: Proceedings of the Conference on Computational Linguistics, COLING 1967, pp. 1–13. Association for Computational Linguistics, Stroudsburg (1967)
255. Papazoglou, M.P., Heuvel, W.V.D.: Service oriented design and development methodology. International Journal of Web Engineering and Technology 2, 412–442 (2006)
256. Peters, N., Weidlich, M.: Automatic Generation of Glossaries for Process Modelling Support. Enterprise Modelling and Information Systems Architectures 6(1), 30–46 (2011)
257. Petri, C.A.: Kommunikation mit Automaten. Ph.D. thesis, Universität Hamburg (1962)
258. Petrov, S., Barrett, L., Thibaux, R., Klein, D.: Learning accurate, compact, and interpretable tree annotation. In: Proceedings of the 21st International Conference on Computational Linguistics and the 44th Annual Meeting of the Association for Computational Linguistics, ACL-44, pp. 433–440. Association for Computational Linguistics (2006)
259. Pinggera, J., Soffer, P., Zugal, S., Weber, B., Weidlich, M., Fahland, D., Reijers, H.A., Mendling, J.: Modeling styles in business process modeling. In: Bider, I., Halpin, T., Krogstie, J., Nurcan, S., Proper, E., Schmidt, R., Soffer, P., Wrycza, S. (eds.) BPMDS 2012 and EMMSAD 2012. LNBIP, vol. 113, pp. 151–166. Springer, Heidelberg (2012)

260. Pittke, F., Leopold, H., Mendling, J.: Spotting terminology deficiencies in process model repositories. In: Nurcan, S., Proper, H.A., Soffer, P., Krogstie, J., Schmidt, R., Halpin, T., Bider, I. (eds.) BPMDS 2013 and EMMSAD 2013. LNBIP, vol. 147, pp. 292–307. Springer, Heidelberg (2013)

261. Piwek, P.: A flexible pragmatics-driven language generator for animated agents. In: Proceedings of the EACL, pp. 151–154 (2003)

262. Pollard, C., Sag, I.: Head-Driven Phrase Structure Grammar. Chicago University Press, Chicago (1994)

263. Polyvyanyy, A., García-Bañuelos, L., Dumas, M.: Structuring acyclic process models. In: Hull, R., Mendling, J., Tai, S. (eds.) BPM 2010. LNCS, vol. 6336, pp. 276–293. Springer, Heidelberg (2010)

264. Polyvyanyy, A., García-Bañuelos, L., Dumas, M.: Structuring acyclic process models. Information Systems 37(6), 518–538 (2012)

265. Polyvyanyy, A., Vanhatalo, J., Völzer, H.: Simplified computation and generalization of the refined process structure tree. In: Bravetti, M. (ed.) WS-FM 2010. LNCS, vol. 6551, pp. 25–41. Springer, Heidelberg (2011)

266. Popper, K.: All Life Is Problem Solving. Routledge (1999)

267. Porter, M.E.: Competitive advantage: Creating and sustaining superior performance. Free Press, New York (1985)

268. Porter, M.F.: An algorithm for suffix stripping. In: Readings in Information Retrieval, pp. 313–316. Morgan Kaufmann Publishers Inc, San Francisco (1997)

269. Rabiner, L., Juang, B.H.: Fundamentals of Speech Recognition. Prentice Hall (1993)

270. Radev, D.R., McKeown, K.R.: Generating natural language summaries from multiple on-line sources. Computational Linguistics 24(3), 470–500 (1998)

271. Ralyté, J., Franch, X., Brinkkemper, S., Wrycza, S. (eds.): CAiSE 2012. LNCS, vol. 7328. Springer, Heidelberg (2012)

272. Ramollari, E., Dranidis, D., Simons, A.J.H.: A survey of service oriented development methodologies. In: Proceedings of the 2nd European Young Researchers Workshop on Service Oriented Computing (2007)

273. Rayner, K., Pollatsek, A.: The Psychology of Reading. Prentice-Hall international editions. Prentice-Hall (1989)

274. Reape, M., Mellish, C.: Just what is aggregation anyway? (2010)

275. Recker, J.: Towards an understanding of process model quality. methodological considerations. In: Ljungberg, J., Andersson, M. (eds.) Proceedings of the 14th European Conference on Information Systems, pp. 434–445 (2006)

276. Recker, J.: Evaluations of Process Modeling Grammars - Ontological, Qualitative and Quantitative Analyses Using the Example of BPMN. LNBIP, vol. 71. Springer, Heidelberg (2011)

277. Recker, J., Mendling, J.: On the Translation between BPMN and BPEL: Conceptual Mismatch between Process Modeling Languages. In: Latour, T., Petit, M. (eds.) CAiSE Workshops, pp. 521–532 (2006)

278. Reijers, H.A., Limam, S., van der Aalst, W.M.P.: Product- based workflow design. Journal of Management Information Systems 20(1), 229–262 (2003)

279. Reiter, E.: Nlg vs. templates. In: Proceedings of the 5th European Workshop on Natural Language Generation, pp. 95–106 (1995)

280. Reiter, E., Dale, R.: Building applied natural language generation systems. Natural Language Engineering 3, 57–87 (1997)

281. Reiter, E., Mellish, C.: Optimizing the costs and benefits of natural language generation. In: IJCAI, pp. 1164–1171 (1993)

282. Reiter, E., Mellish, C., Levine, J., Bridge, S.: Automatic generation of on-line documentation in the idas project. In: Applied Natural Language Processing, pp. 64–71 (1992)
283. Relf, P.A.: Achieving software quality through identifier names. In: Qualcon 2004 (2004)
284. Richards, D., Fure, A.B., Aguilera, O.: An approach to visualise and reconcile use case descriptions from multiple viewpoints. In: Proceedings of the 11th IEEE International Conference on Requirements Engineering, RE 2003, pp. 373–374. IEEE Computer Society (2003)
285. Rittgen, P.: Negotiating models. In: Krogstie, J., Opdahl, A.L., Sindre, G. (eds.) CAiSE 2007 and WES 2007. LNCS, vol. 4495, pp. 561–573. Springer, Heidelberg (2007)
286. Rittgen, P.: Success factors of e-collaboration in business process modeling. In: Pernici, B. (ed.) CAiSE 2010. LNCS, vol. 6051, pp. 24–37. Springer, Heidelberg (2010)
287. Rolland, C., Souveyet, C., Achour, C.: Guiding goal modeling using scenarios. IEEE Transactions on Software Engineering 24(12), 1055–1071 (1998)
288. Rosch, E.: Cognitive representations of semantic categories. Journal of Experimental Psychology: General 104(3), 192–233 (1975)
289. Rosemann, M.: Potential Pitfalls of Process Modeling: Part A. Business Process Management Journal 12(2), 249–254 (2006)
290. Russell, B.: Descriptions and incomplete Symbols. In: Logic and Knowledge: Essays 1901-1950. Allen and Unwin, London (1956)
291. Sagot, B., Fišer, D.: Building a free french wordnet from multilingual resources. In: Ontolex 2008, Marrakech, Maroc (2008)
292. Sapir, E.: Language an Introduction to the Study of Speech. Kessinger Publishing (2010)
293. Saussure, F.D.: Cours de linguistique générale. Bayot, Paris (1916)
294. Scheer, A.: EDV-orientierte Betriebswirtschaftslehre. Heidelberger Taschenbücher, vol. 236. Springer, Berlin (1984)
295. Scheer, A.: Aris: Business Process Modeling. Springer (2000)
296. Schober, D., Kusnirczyk, W., Lewis, S.E., Lomax, J., Members, P., Mungall, C., Rocca-Serra, P., Smith, B., Sansone, S.A.: Towards naming conventions for use in controlled vocabulary and ontology engineering (2007)
297. Schuette, R., Rotthowe, T.: The guidelines of modeling - an approach to enhance the quality in information models. In: Proceedings of the 17th International Conference on Conceptual Modeling, pp. 240–254. Springer, London (1998)
298. Schuler, K.K.: Verbnet: a broad-coverage, comprehensive verb lexicon. Ph.D. thesis, Philadelphia, PA, USA (2005)
299. Sewing, J.H., Rosemann, M., Dumas, M.: Process-oriented assessment of web services. International Journal of E-Business Research 2(1), 19–44 (2006)
300. Shanks, G., Tansley, E., Weber, R.: Using ontology to validate conceptual models. Communications of the ACM 46(10), 85–89 (2003)
301. Sharp, A., McDermott, P.: Workflow Modeling: Tools for Process Improvement and Application Development. Artech House Publishers (2001)
302. Shoup, K., Loberger, G.: Webster's New World English Grammar Handbook. Wiley (2009)
303. Sidorova, N., Stahl, C., Trcka, N.: Soundness Verification for Conceptual Workflow Nets with Data: Early Detection of Errors with the Most Precision Possible. Information Systems 36(7), 1026–1043 (2011)
304. Silver, B.: BPMN Method and Style, with BPMN Implementer's Guide, 2nd edn. Cody-Cassidy Press (2011)

305. Sinha, A., Paradkar, A.: Use Cases to Process Specifications in Business Process Modeling Notation. In: Proceedings of the IEEE International Conference on Web Services, pp. 473–480. IEEE (2010)
306. Smets, M., Gamon, M., Corston-Oliver, S., Ringger, E.: The adaptation of a machine-learned sentence realization system to french. In: Proceedings of the 10th Conference on European Chapter of the Association for Computational Linguistics, EACL 2003, pp. 323–330. Association for Computational Linguistics, Stroudsburg (2003)
307. Smirnov, S., Weidlich, M., Mendling, J.: Business process model abstraction based on synthesis from consistent behavioural profiles. International Journal of Cooperative Information Systems 21 (2012)
308. Smirnov, S., Weidlich, M., Mendling, J., Weske, M.: Action patterns in business process model repositories. Computers in Industry 63 (2012)
309. Sneed, H.: Integrating legacy software into a service oriented architecture. In: Proceedings of the 10th European Conference on Software Maintenance and Reengineering, pp. 11–14 (2006)
310. Stachowiak, H.: Allgemeine Modelltheorie. Springer, Wien, New York (1973)
311. Stede, M.: Lexical choice criteria in language generation. In: Proceedings of the 6th Conference on European Chapter of the Association for Computational Linguistics, EACL 1993, pp. 454–459. Association for Computational Linguistics, Stroudsburg (1993)
312. Stede, M.: Lexicalization in natural language generation: A survey. Artificial Intelligence Review 8, 309–336 (1994)
313. Strembeck, M., Mendling, J.: Modeling Process-related RBAC Models with Extended UML Activity Models. Information and Software Technology 53(5), 456–483 (2011)
314. Subirats, C., Ortega, M.: Corpus del español actual (2012)
315. Sun, S., Zhao, J., Nunamaker, J., Liu Sheng, O.: Formulating the Data-Flow Perspective for Business Process Management. Information Systems Research 17(4), 374–391 (2006)
316. Taylor, F.: The principles of scientific management (1911)
317. Thalheim, B.: Syntax, semantics and pragmatics of conceptual modelling. In: Bouma, G., Ittoo, A., Métais, E., Wortmann, H. (eds.) NLDB 2012. LNCS, vol. 7337, pp. 1–10. Springer, Heidelberg (2012)
318. Thomas, K.: Matters of (Meta-)Modeling. Software and Systems Modeling 5(4), 369–385 (2006)
319. Toutanova, K., Manning, C.D.: Enriching the knowledge sources used in a maximum entropy part-of-speech tagger. In: Joint SIGDAT Conference on Empirical Methods in Natural Language Processing and Very Large Corpora, pp. 63–70 (2000)
320. Tseng, F.S., Chen, A.L., Yang, W.P.: On mapping natural language constructs into relational algebra through e-r representation. Data & Knowledge Engineering 9(1), 97–118 (1992)
321. Tseng, F.S., Chen, C.L.: Extending the uml concepts to transform natural language queries with fuzzy semantics into sql. Information and Software Technology 48(9), 901–914 (2006)
322. Vanhatalo, J., Völzer, H., Koehler, J.: The refined process structure tree. Data & Knowledge Engineering 68(9), 793–818 (2009)
323. Verheijen, G., Bekkum, J.V.: NIAM, an information analysis method. In: Proceedings of the Conference on Comparative Review of Information System Methodologies. North-Holland (1982)
324. van der Vos, B., Gulla, J.A., van de Riet, R.: Verification of conceptual models based on linguistic knowledge. Data & Knowledge Engineering 21(2), 147–163 (1997)

325. Vossen, P. (ed.): EuroWordNet: a multilingual database with lexical semantic networks. Kluwer Academic Publishers, Norwell (1998)
326. Voutilainen, A.: A syntax-based part-of-speech analyser. In: Proceedings of the EACL, pp. 157–164 (1995)
327. Wahlster, W., Andre, E., Finkler, W., Profitlich, H.J., Rist, T.: Plan-based integration of natural language and graphics generation. Artificial Intelligence 63, 387–427 (1993)
328. Wand, Y., Weber, R.: On the deep structure of information systems. Information Systems Journal 5(3), 203–223 (1995)
329. Wand, Y., Weber, R.: Research commentary: Information systems and conceptual modeling–a research agenda. Information Systems Research 13(4), 363–376 (2002)
330. Weber, B., Reichert, M., Mendling, J., Reijers, H.: Refactoring large process model repositories. Computers in Industry 62(5), 467–486 (2011)
331. Weber, B., Reichert, M., Mendling, J., Reijers, H.A.: Refactoring large process model repositories. Computers in Industry 62(5), 467–486 (2011)
332. Weber, I., Hoffmann, J., Mendling, J.: Beyond Soundness: on the Verification of Semantic Business Process Models. Distributed and Parallel Databases 27(3), 271–343 (2010)
333. Weidlich, M., Dijkman, R.M., Mendling, J.: The iCoP framework: Identification of correspondences between process models. In: Pernici, B. (ed.) CAiSE 2010. LNCS, vol. 6051, pp. 483–498. Springer, Heidelberg (2010)
334. Weidlich, M., Mendling, J., Weske, M.: Efficient consistency measurement based on behavioral profiles of process models. IEEE Trans. Software Eng. 37(3), 410–429 (2011)
335. Weske, M.: Business Process Management: Concepts, Languages, Architectures, 2nd edn. Springer (2012)
336. White, S., Miers, D.: BPMN Modeling and Reference Guide: Understanding and Using BPMN. Future Strategies Incorporated (2008)
337. Wittgenstein, L.: Philosophical Investigations, The German Text with an English Translation, 4th edn. Basil Blackwell, Oxford (2009)
338. Wohed, P., van der Aalst, W.M.P., Dumas, M., ter Hofstede, A.H.M., Russell, N.: Pattern-based analysis of BPMN – an extensive evaluation of the control-flow, the data and the resource perspectives (revised version). Tech. Rep. BPM-06-17. BPMcenter.org (2006)
339. Yousef, R., Odeh, M., Coward, D., Sharieh, A.: Bpaontosoa: A generic framework to derive software service oriented models from business process architectures. In: Proceedings of the 2nd International Conference on the Applications of Digital Information and Web Technologies, pp. 50–55 (2009)
340. Yule, G.: The Study of Language. Cambridge University Press (2010)
341. Yun, Z., Huayou, S., Yulin, N., Hengnian, Q.: A service-oriented analysis and design approach based on data flow diagram. In: International Conference on Computational Intelligence and Software Engineering, pp. 1–5. IEEE (2009)
342. Zhang, Z., Liu, R., Yang, H.: Service identification and packaging in service oriented reengineering. In: Proceedings of the 7th International Conference on Software Engineering and Knowledge Engineering, pp. 241–249 (2005)
343. Zhang, Z., Yang, H.: Incubating services in legacy systems for architectural migration. In: Proeedings of the 11th Software Engineering Conference, pp. 196–203 (2004)
344. Zimmermann, O., Krogdahl, P., Gee, C.: Elements of service-oriented analysis and design. IBM developerworks (2004)